Post-War Homelessness Policy in the UK

Jamie Harding

Post-War Homelessness Policy in the UK

Making and Implementation

palgrave
macmillan

Jamie Harding
Northumbria University
Newcastle upon Tyne, UK

ISBN 978-3-030-22116-4   ISBN 978-3-030-22117-1 (eBook)
https://doi.org/10.1007/978-3-030-22117-1

This Palgrave Macmillan imprint is published by the registered company Springer Nature Switzerland AG
The registered company address is: Gewerbestrasse 11, 6330 Cham, Switzerland

This book is dedicated to my parents, Sally and Jim, who have always loved and supported me, especially on several occasions when I wanted to give up studying.

Preface

“I didn’t come to study this; I came to find out about people living in cardboard boxes.” I remember the words of one of my fellow undergraduate students who was not impressed by being required to study Policy Making and Implementation as part of his Social Policy degree. One of several substantial debts that I owe to the lecturer that day, Professor Michael Hill, is that he demonstrated to me the importance of the policy process—policies that can improve the situation of the most disadvantaged people, particularly those who are homeless, are more likely to be made and implemented by those who understand the process.

The voice of homeless people themselves is rarely heard directly in this book, but I hope that they may benefit indirectly from a better understanding of the forces that have shaped policy in the post-war period. Criticism (ideally polite and constructive) of the arguments set out here is welcomed: debate is good and will help to shape the ideas to be included in a second edition, should I be fortunate enough to have the opportunity to write one. By then, I hope that fewer people will be experiencing homelessness and that the period for which they are homeless will be shorter and less uncomfortable.

Newcastle upon Tyne, UK — Jamie Harding

Acknowledgements

Many thanks are due to the people who were interviewed for this book for giving up their time—and in some cases, quite substantial amounts of it—to provide invaluable insights. Also to Professor Nicholas Crowson, Dr Mary Laing, Dr Leona Skelton, Dr Avram Taylor, Dr Rachael Chapman, Dr Siobhan Daly, Dr Adele Irving, Jane Brough, Professor Michael Rowe and Professor Keith Shaw for their advice and support. The group of professionals who recently studied an Understanding Homeless module with me have been very helpful in providing insights as to what policies look like when working directly with homeless people. The patience of Jemima Warren and Oliver Foster at Palgrave Macmillan is greatly appreciated. Finally, huge thanks to my wife Allison for her constant support and particularly for the key conversation when she advised me not to be afraid to develop my own analytical framework for the book.

Contents

Abbreviations

ALMO	Arm's Length Management Organisation
ASBO	Anti-social Behaviour Order
CHAR	Campaign for the Homeless and Rootless (later the Housing Campaign for Single People)
DCLG	Department for Communities and Local Government
DETR	Department of the Environment, Transport and the Regions
DHSS	Department of Health and Social Security
DoE	Department of the Environment
DWP	Department of Work and Pensions
HMII	Homeless Mentally Ill Initiative
JCG	Joint Charities Group
LHA	Local Housing Allowance
MHCLG	Ministry of Housing Communities and Local Government
NAB	National Assistance Board
NAO	National Audit Office
RSI	Rough Sleepers' Initiative
RSU	Rough Sleepers' Initiative
YTS	Youth Training Scheme

CHAPTER 1

Introduction: Definitions, Neglected Issues and Pre-War Position

Introduction

This chapter provides the background information that is needed to read and understand the remainder of the book, particularly for those who are less familiar with the area of homelessness. It covers key definitions, an outline of some methodological issues that arise in the historical study of homelessness, a discussion of the key developments that shaped the situation at the end of World War II and an explanation of why some issues are (perhaps surprisingly) referred to infrequently in discussions of homelessness.

Definitions

There is no single definition of the word 'homeless'. Clearly, someone living alone in a property that they own would not be considered homeless, while someone who was sleeping on the streets would. However, there are a number of other housing situations—particularly when someone is staying in accommodation that is only meant to be temporary, sharing accommodation unwillingly with another household or at risk of violence—where opinions would differ as to whether they should be defined as homeless. Judgments as to what constitutes acceptable living arrangements are, of course, relative: to take an extreme example, at the time of writing, fighting had recently ended in the cities of Aleppo in Syria and Mosul in Libya. With so much of the housing in these cities having been destroyed or

J. Harding, *Post-War Homelessness Policy in the UK*,
https://doi.org/10.1007/978-3-030-22117-1_1

made uninhabitable, and so many civilians having fled, the concept of homelessness appears to have little value in this context.

Bramley (1988, p. 26) has identified seven housing situations in the United Kingdom that could be identified as homelessness, with people literally roofless at one end of the spectrum, while at the other end are individuals or groups who are living with another household but who would like their own accommodation. The homeless charity Shelter adopted from its conception a broad definition of homelessness, including anyone living in conditions which were incompatible with 'normal family life'. This definition covered those living in overcrowded or unsatisfactory conditions, as well as people who were roofless (Raynsford, 1986, p. 52). In contrast, the Conservative governments of 1979–1997 sought to promote a definition of homelessness which was closer to the absolute term of 'rooflessness' (Lund, 1996, pp. 88–89).

Internationally, Niemi and Ahola (2017, p. 40) argue that there is now less discussion around definitions, with agreement having been reached that a number of groups should be considered homeless: those who sleep on the streets, who live in emergency accommodation, who live in accommodation set aside for homeless people, who stay longer than necessary in institutions because there is no accommodation available to them, who live in non-conventional dwellings (such as mobile or abandoned homes) and who stay temporarily with family or friends. It is this definition that will be adopted in the material that follows. It is also helpful to understand definitions of key terms that are used when discussing homelessness in the United Kingdom:

Statutorily homeless—this is the term widely used to describe households to whom local authorities have a duty to secure an offer of accommodation under the criteria established by the 1977 Housing (Homeless Persons) Act, that is, households that are unintentionally homeless, have a connection with the local authority that they are applying to and are in a priority need group (usually because they have dependent children).

Non-statutorily homeless—this term refers to households who could be considered to be homeless but to whom the local authority has no obligation to secure an offer of accommodation. The lack of obligation arises because the household is deemed to be intentionally homeless or not in priority need.

Single homelessness—the households covered by this term overlap substantially with those considered to be non-statutorily homeless and include people without dependent children, even when they are part of a couple. The term does not cover lone parents with dependent children.

Hidden homelessness—this term tends to refer to people who do not appear in official homelessness statistics. While those who stay in temporary accommodation are not visible to the public—and even those who sleep rough are likely to find places to bed down that are out of sight—the term usually refers to two other groups of people: those who stay with friends or family temporarily, in squats or other situations where they have no legal right to be; or those who remain in unsatisfactory or violent relationships because they have nowhere else to go.

Hostels—this is a broad term, usually taken to refer to temporary accommodation in which residents may or may not have their own bedroom but will usually have to share a bathroom and other facilities.

Supported housing projects—these have many similarities with hostels but have the distinctive feature of being run by non-profit organisations, usually in the voluntary sector, and providing services that are intended to promote resettlement.

Temporary accommodation—this term tends to refer to accommodation organised on a short-term basis by local authorities for homeless people. It can include hostels, supported housing projects, properties let by the local authority on a short-term lease and bed-and-breakfast hotels. It is not so widely used for short-term accommodation that people arrange for themselves, for example, by booking into a bed-and-breakfast hotel because they have nowhere else to go, even though the number in this situation is substantially higher than those who are placed into bed-and-breakfast accommodation by the local authority (Rose, Maciver, & Davies, 2016, p. 5).

Defining Social Rented Housing

Social rented housing is a broad term used to describe rented housing where the landlord does not make a profit. Local authorities were the main providers of social rented housing in the immediate post-war period. From the 1980s onwards, governments encouraged the transfer of the management and/or ownership of local authority stock to other bodies such as housing associations, which had previously been a small part of the not-for-profit sector, but were to gradually grow to become the majority.

At the time of writing, approximately 17% of housing stock in England is owned by social landlords, 10% by housing associations and 7% by local authorities (Fitzpatrick & Watts, 2017, p. 1022). Local authorities, housing associations and smaller bodies such as housing co-operatives are often referred to as 'social landlords'.

In addition to being not for profit, there are two distinctive characteristics of the social rented sector. The first is that rents are not set at market levels. There was a post-war consensus that houses needed to be provided at rents that tenants could afford, subsidised by central and local government (Young & Rao, 1997, p. 54). Subsequent changes to housing finance meant that social housing ceased to attract substantial direct cash support from government but continued to be let at below market rents (Fitzpatrick & Watts, 2017, p. 1025). Raynsford (2016, pp. 48–49) noted that social rented housing continued to be let at considerably lower rents than properties in the private rented sector. Despite this difference, social housing tenants were more likely to be receiving Housing Benefit (the means tested benefit paid to provide help with rental costs)—68% of housing association tenants were paid this benefit in 2015, compared to 29% of private tenants.

The key reason for tenants in the social rented sector being more likely to receive Housing Benefit, and the second departure from market principles, is that properties are not allocated according to ability to pay. Fitzpatrick and Stephens (1999, pp. 415–416) argue that the two bases of allocation of social rented housing are 'housing need' and 'desert', with desert having been historically determined by length of time spent on a waiting list, together with more judgmental criteria such as housekeeping standards.

Over time, there has been a shift towards more allocation systems making need the key criteria, but systems tend to include elements of both need and desert (Fitzpatrick & Stephens, 1999, p. 416). A survey of all local authorities and housing associations in 2000 showed that 85% were allocating properties according to points systems (with points awarded for various indicators of housing need), 9% operated date order systems, 7% operated 'merit' systems and 4% operated systems that placed tenants into bands according to their circumstance (Brown, Hunt, & Yates, 2000, p. 17). However, in the subsequent decade, the Labour government's concern to increase 'choice' in public services, together with a growing body of evidence that point-based systems were leading to geographical concentrations of the most vulnerable households, led to choice-based lettings schemes being widely introduced. These schemes seek to combine an assessment of needs/deserts with greater opportunity for applicants to specify the area and type of property that they wish to live in (Brown & Yates, 2005). Later, Conservative and Conservative-led administrations encouraged social landlords to return to giving more weighting to 'desert'—specifically by prioritising former armed service personnel and applicants who were judged to be contributing to the community (Fitzpatrick & Watts, 2017, p. 1023).

The role of social rented housing is particularly important in the history of homelessness because, after the passing of the 1977 Housing (Homeless Persons) Act, local authorities tended to discharge their duties to statutorily homeless households by securing an offer of accommodation in the social rented sector. It was not until the passing of the 2011 Localism Act that local authorities in England were able to discharge their duties with an offer in the private rented sector, regardless of whether this was what the homeless household wanted—a similar change was brought about in Wales through the 2014 Housing (Wales) Act.

Difficulties in Quantifying Homelessness

A group that is difficult to define is inevitably also difficult to count. The number of different situations that can be considered to represent homelessness, and the number of these situations that are out of public view, mean that it is very difficult to arrive at an accurate figure for the number of people who are homeless. Much of the data collected historically has reflected the legal responsibilities and practices of organisations. Under the 1948 National Assistance Act, it was not mandatory for local authorities to provide the Ministry of Health with statistics and many failed to do so. When statistics were completed, they were limited in nature, consisting of the number of people in the local authority's temporary accommodation on the last day of June and September each year, and a record of whether homelessness had come about through evictions or 'other reasons'. In the 1960s, a requirement was added to record the number of homeless applications received (Richards, 1981, p. 12). The length of the local authority waiting list gave some indication of housing need in general but not homelessness in particular (Morris Committee, 1975).

After the passing of the 1977 Housing (Homeless Persons) Act, figures were collected for the number of people who were assessed by local authorities to determine what (if any) their statutory responsibilities were.

This gave a fuller picture than previously because it included some non-statutorily homeless people. However, the figures could not count those who considered themselves homeless but did not make an application because they believed they would receive no help.

Counting the number of single homeless people has always presented particular difficulties. The first attempt to reach any figure beyond the numbers using government run Reception Centres did not take place until 1966, when National Assistance Board officers were asked to count people using a number of other forms of shelter: lodging-houses run by local authorities, voluntary organisations and the private sectors; crypts and shelters run by voluntary organisations, church groups and others; and non-statutory hostels for specific groups such as alcoholics and former prisoners. However, even then, there were forms of accommodation that were surprisingly excluded, that is, some industrial hostels, YMCA hostels and establishments providing fewer than six beds "because at that point the establishment tends to become less of a lodging-house and more a place catering for a few lodgers" (National Assistance Board, 1966, p. 7).

The difficulties of counting the 'hidden homeless' in particular continued into the 1970s, with voluntary organisations responding to the lack of data by developing their own counting strategies (Hilton, McKay, Crowson, & Mouhot, 2013). One method of seeking to produce more comprehensive data—agencies adding together the number of people who approach them as homeless—is criticised by Shaw, Bloor, Cormack, and Williamson (1996, pp. 69–70) on the grounds that two opposite difficulties arise: some people will appear on the lists of more than one agency and others will not appear on any list. Although more sophisticated methods, such as using dates of birth (rather than names, to protect confidentiality), can now reduce the risk of double counting, there remains a difficulty in seeking to quantify the size of a group who may not approach any agency.

Rough sleepers are also very difficult to count. Census enumerators have failed in the past to identify this group, with agencies pointing scornfully to the nil figure for rough sleepers recorded in Birmingham and Cardiff in 1991 (Hutson & Liddiard, 1994, p. 31). The Labour governments of 1997–2010 required local authorities which believed that they had a rough sleeping problem to compile statistics and more sophisticated methods of counting were developed, often involving visiting known sites for rough sleeping very early in the morning. The Combined Housing and Information Network (CHAIN), a multi-agency database, was commissioned and funded by the Mayor of London to record detailed information about individuals who were sleeping rough in the capital. Although this information was primarily used to ensure that appropriate services were provided to rough sleepers, at a strategic level, it was also used to identify broad trends in numbers (https://data.london.gov.uk/dataset/chain-reports).

Despite the progress made on recording, attempts to quantify homelessness were still assessed as flawed by the UK Statistics Authority (2015, section 1.5). Their report argued that, subject to certain improvements, the figures for statutory homelessness produced by the Department of Communities and Local Government (now the Ministry of Housing, Communities and Local Government) were of sufficiently high standard to be considered national statistics. However, the figures on rough sleeping were not judged to meet the required standards of trustworthiness, quality and value. Although the coalition government of 2010–2015 had changed the rules so that all local authorities had to provide rough sleeping figures, some were taking actual counts while others were using estimates and there were a number of factors affecting the accuracy of recording (UK Statistics Authority, 2015, section 1.1.2). Fitzpatrick et al. (2018, p. 49) asked local authority staff about the rough sleepers counts or estimates that they provided and found that less than half perceived their figures to be 'very reliable'. While praising the CHAIN database, Jeremy Swain was clear in interview that it remained difficult to measure the number of rough sleepers:

> And I think the rough sleepers snapshot street count that we do every year is limited in terms of trying to measure numbers and the data is not as strong or as useful as the CHAIN data for London. The fact that only 17% of the snapshot street counts are actual counts now and the rest are estimates I think illustrates the fact that those counts as a means of trying to get a grasp on the overall number of rough sleepers have to be treated with great care. As a way of measuring progress in trying to reduce rough sleeping, they have their place.

So, seeking to quantify the extent of homelessness in all its possible forms remains elusive, despite the improvements in the methods used.

Methodological Issues

There were a number of methodological difficulties that were encountered in seeking to provide a comprehensive view of post-war homelessness. Most obviously, there was a disparity in the types of sources that were available for studying more recent and more distant periods of time.

The development of the Internet, and the commitment of the Labour governments of 1997–2010 to making material available online, meant that there was substantially more documentary material available from the late 1990s onwards. Further information about more recent periods was provided by conducting interviews with key players who had been involved in homelessness policy and practice. Most of the interview respondents were willing to be named, although some preferred to be referred to by their roles. Those who were willing to be named were:

- Nick Raynsford, who was Director of Shelter Housing Aid Centre from 1976 to 1986. He was an MP from 1986 to 1987 and then from 1997 to 2015, holding ministerial posts between 1997 and 2005 where he had responsibility for London, housing, planning, construction and local government.
- Des Wilson, who was the first director of Shelter.
- Jeremy Swain, Chief Executive of Thames Reach, who has worked for over 30 years in the homelessness sector in London.
- Neil Munslow MBE, Service Manager: Active Inclusion with Newcastle City Council, who has worked in the area of homelessness with the council for 30 years.
- Steve Hilditch, whose experience in the voluntary sector and local authority sector in London dates back to the 1970s.
- Neil Morland, who worked in both the voluntary and local authority sectors before becoming a Communities and Local Government adviser from 2007 to 2010.

Interviews were also conducted with a former Conservative Minister and another respondent with substantial experience in the voluntary and local authority sectors.

The generosity of these respondents in giving up their time to be interviewed provided an invaluable and rich source of information but again highlighted disparities between different periods, as the earliest personal memories that could be provided were from 1966.

For the period before the 1960s, in addition to published academic literature and reports, the main source of information used was Hansard because it provided a record of most of the policies proposed and adopted by Parliament and many of the views expressed by MPs in relation to homelessness. However, in other areas, there was no such substantial record. In particular, it proved impossible to gain a clear overview of local authority practice prior to the 1970s. Indeed, Chap. 4 argues that the absence of comprehensive information on local authority practice was one of the factors that delayed the introduction of specific homelessness legislation until 1977. The growth of housing aid centres and Shelter's survey of local authorities entitled *The Grief Report* (Bailey & Ruddock, 1972) provided more systematic information; this information was one of the catalysts to eventual change. So, assessments of local authority policy and practice prior to the 1970s are made on the balance of the limited available evidence.

When considering the factors that have influenced homelessness policy, it is difficult to evaluate the role of public opinion and the media for two reasons. The first is the lack of systematic information, even in the most recent time periods. A YouGov survey conducted in 2013 (https://yougov.co.uk/news/2013/10/22/public-conflicted-homeless/) and one conducted for Crisis in 2017 (O'Neil, Gerstein Pineau, Kendall-Taylor, Volmert, & Stevens, 2017) were rare examples of systematic attempts to gain an overview of public opinion on homelessness. Similarly, discussion of the role of the media often concentrates on a small number of newspaper articles, with the type of broad systematic content analysis offered by Buck, Toro, and Ramos (2004) in relation to homelessness in the United States being relatively rare.

The second difficulty is that the relationship between the media, public opinion and policy has been shown to be a complex one (Ertas, 2015; Powlick & Katz, 1998).

Research has indicated that media coverage can have an influence both over the issues that are considered important by the public (e.g. Guo & Vu, 2018) and over the opinions that the public hold on a subject (e.g. Shanahan, McBeth, & Hathaway, 2011). Davis (2007, p. 186) found that most politicians could provide examples where a media campaign had had an influence on policy—legislation on gambling, hand guns and dangerous dogs were all cited as examples. However, studies in this area have suggested that although the media have some influence on the issues that reach the political agenda, they are not the most influential factor and their influence is often limited to very specific issues (Van Aelst & Walgrave, 2011, p. 296). Davis (2007, pp. 188–189) found that influence was often indirect: politicians in power considered how policies would be received by the media and those in opposition would sometimes seek to influence the media to add to the pressure to act on select committee findings, for example. There has been recent debate as to whether alternative sources of news have diminished the impact of the traditional media in agenda setting (e.g. Shehata & Stromback, 2013), but this is not an issue that is relevant to the majority of the time period discussed in this book.

In view of the complexity of the relationships, caution has been exercised in suggesting that public opinion and the media have influenced policy, except where this influence is explicit: for example, when the Housing Minister requested to watch the TV drama-documentary *Cathy Come Home* (Crisis, 2017, pp. 22–26).

Under-Discussed Issues in the Study of Homelessness

It is appropriate to identify some issues that the reader may be surprised to find little or no reference to in the following chapters. Asylum seekers and refugees are groups who frequently experience extreme housing difficulties; the reason for not discussing them in this book is that the 1999 Immigration and Asylum Act created a separate legal system to provide their accommodation. The Act stated that where accommodation was needed, it should be organised outside London and the South East (House of Commons Library, 2016). Initially, local authorities, and then private landlords, were contracted to provide accommodation in other regions on a 'no choice' basis. The provision of accommodation under this system has frequently been shown to be inadequate to meet even basic needs (e.g. Dwyer & Brown, 2008). In addition, the risk of homelessness that arises when an asylum seeker's case is decided—either positively or negatively—is a topic that is worthy of substantial study. However, space does not allow the consideration of such a separate system here.

Rural homelessness is an area that has been neglected in terms of both policy and academic discussion. It is recognised that there may be particularly acute difficulties in many rural areas related to the presence of second and holiday homes, travelling distance to services and the problems of trying to quantify homeless people who may be sleeping in widely spread locations such as barns, outhouses, tents and parked cars (Snelling, 2017, pp. 3–4). However, the greater numbers and visibility of homeless people in cities has meant that they have overwhelmingly been the focus of policy.

There is also a surprising absence from policy and academic debate of substantial, detailed discussion of the relationship between homelessness and some of the most commonly identified forms of inequality in the United Kingdom, such as those based on ethnicity, gender, sexuality and social class. The limited evidence available on these relationships, at the time of writing, is summarised here.

Studies have suggested that young people from minority ethnic backgrounds are particularly likely to become homeless, as are those who are gay or lesbian (Quilgars, Johnsen, & Pleace, 2008, p. 41). In addition, research has suggested that, across all age groups, being part of a minority ethnic group increases the risk of homelessness (e.g. London Housing Forum, 1988 and London Research Centre, 1991, both cited in Edwards, 1995, p. 65). Grimshaw (2008, p. 39) lists a number of factors that have been found to reduce the use of housing services among minority ethnic households, including those who are homeless: lack of knowledge of services and rights, language difficulties, negative images of public housing, fear of being housed in 'White only' areas or unsafe areas, and distrust of authority. However, compared to the body of theory that has arisen from other forms of ethnic difference in housing—for example, the under-representation of some minority ethnic groups in public sector accommodation in the second half of the twentieth century (e.g. Rex, 1971)—discussion of racial inequality in the area of homelessness is theoretically under-developed. Peters (2012, p. 322) notes that "there is still very little research on the varied experiences of different racialized or cultural groups" when homeless. There have also been few specific policy responses.

Class has a substantial bearing on housing, with some areas of cities being occupied primarily by working-class people and others primarily by middle-class people (see, e.g. Davidson & Wyly, 2012). Tenure is clearly one of the factors affecting this division: as will be shown in subsequent chapters, despite an end to the pre-World War II restriction that council housing should only be provided for the working classes, social rented housing has increasingly become the preserve of the poorest people in society, including those who are re-housed as homeless. However, the role of class—while clearly related to income—has largely been ignored, as poverty has been the focus of structural discussions of homelessness. The exception is some analysis in relation to youth homelessness—Jones (1995, pp. 146–147) argues that the policies of the Conservative Governments of the 1980s and 1990s failed to acknowledge the expectation of working class households that young people would leave home permanently and achieve financial independence immediately: "Policies have been based on an expectation that middle-class patterns of family support can operate in working-class families in two respects: the opportunity to return to the family home … and access to family economic support ….” Similarly, Fitzpatrick (2000, p. 5) argues that young people returning home is a middle-class tradition and suggests that where there is no opportunity to return, homelessness may be the result.

The extent of writing and analysis in relation to gender and homelessness is also acknowledged to be limited (e.g. Cramer, 2005, p. 737; Mayock, Sheridan, & Parker, 2015, p. 878). Research has demonstrated differences between men and women in terms of reasons for becoming homeless, survival methods and the types of support that are available (Cramer, 2005, p. 737). However, some widely accepted assumptions about gender differences in homelessness lack supporting evidence: for example, recent research has challenged long-held assumptions that single women are likely to be homeless for shorter periods of time, with less chance of homelessness being repeated, than is the case for single men (Mayock et al., 2015, p. 879).

While gender has rarely influenced policy directly, the homelessness legislation has played an important role in shaping the different experiences of men and women because of the priority given to households with children and the large number of lone parent households that are female headed. So, while the greater economic power of men gives them more access and choice in other areas of housing, more women have been able to access social housing via the homelessness legislation. The DCLG’s (Department for Communities and Local Government) live tables on homelessness (https://www.gov.uk/government/statistical-data-sets/live-tables-on-homelessness#statutory-homelessness-and-prevention-and-relief-live-tables) show that, for the second quarter of 2017 in England, 21% of the households accepted as homeless were couples with dependent children, 4% were male-lone-parent-headed households, 47% were female-lone-parent-headed households, 13% were male single applicants, 10% were female single applicants and 5% were other types of household.

A further factor contributing to the higher incidence of female headed households found to be statutorily homeless is women’s greater risk of experiencing domestic violence. Watson and Austerberry (1986, pp. 163–164) suggest that women remain in unsatisfactory relationships because their economic power does not allow them alternatives, which is a key reason for arguing that women’s homelessness is more likely to be hidden than men’s. However, research has consistently demonstrated that women are more likely than men to apply as homelessness due to domestic violence (Cramer, 2005, p. 743), mirroring the tendency for men to be perpetrators of this crime and women to be victims. From 2009 to 2016, violent relationship breakdown was the fourth most common reason for losing previous accommodation among household owed the main homelessness duty, after the end of an assured shorthold tenancy, parents being unable to accommodate and friends/relatives being unable to accommodate (DCLG, 2017).

So there is some evidence to suggest that the homelessness legislation has played a role in tackling gender inequalities in housing—although, as will be shown in later chapters, the offer of social rented housing has sometimes meant moving into a tenure seen as a last resort. The discussion of gender issues, although limited, represents a more developed argument than those relating to class, ethnicity or sexuality.

The Pre-1945 Position

In order to understand better the manner in which governments and other agencies sought to tackle homelessness in the post-war period, it is helpful to be aware of some of the key policies and debates prior to 1945. Humphreys (1999, p. 167) notes that throughout history, governments have tended to blame increases in homelessness on the individuals concerned and to ignore 'the factors which at that particular time were causing more of their citizens to wander around poverty-stricken'. This view was reflected in a range of punitive measures: for example, repeated vagrancy becoming punishable by death in 1535 (Chambliss, 1964, pp. 72–73) and the 1662 Law of Settlement and Removal allowed parishes to exclude from relief anyone who could not show that they had a local connection or some right to settle (Lowe, 1997, pp. 20–21). While the Victorian workhouse was a source of fear for all poor people (Rose, 1971, pp. 160–161), it held particular terrors for those who were homeless: the assistance provided to them was the provision of bare boards and a sparse diet of bread and gruel (Watchman & Robson, 1989, pp. 26–27). Despite these hardships, workhouses remained full because they were better than the alternative. Anyone sleeping in a public place would be relentlessly moved on by the police (Glastonbury, 1971, p. 30).

Towards the end of the nineteenth century, some voluntary efforts were directed to specific services for homeless people: the Salvation Army began to provide food and shelter from the 1880s (Watson & Austerberry,

1986, p. 36). However, the continuing view of homeless people as deviant was reflected in the Charity Organisation Society's 1894 report on the 'Homeless Poor of London', which recommended that some large night refuges should be converted to smaller units for the 'treatment' of homeless people, that is, to help them find 'better ways of living' (Watson & Austerberry, 1986, p. 37).

Powers were given to local authorities to build houses under the 1851 Labouring Classes' Lodging Houses Act, and treasury loans to local authorities became possible in 1866 (Lund, 1996, pp. 23–25). However, early twentieth century municipal housing projects were aimed at the more affluent workers who would be able to pay their way in an age in which there was no state support for meeting housing costs (Fraser, 1984, p. 125), so there were few homeless people who received any benefit from this development.

The need for state involvement in housing became apparent during and after World War I, as private landlordism had slumped during the early twentieth century and 9.7 million families were left occupying 8.8 million dwellings. The 1919 Housing and Town Planning Act offered central government subsidies to local authorities to build housing at existing rents plus a penny rate (Lund, 1996, p. 29). In the Inter-War period, from a total of 4 million new homes built, 1,330,000 were in the public sector. The incidence of unfit, overcrowded and slum properties reduced dramatically (Lund, 1996, pp. 36–37). However, there remained difficulties as to how to provide housing for those with little or no income so many authorities introduced differential rent schemes, meaning that tenants' rents were decided by their income rather than the size and cost of their house—those with income below a certain level paid no rent at all (Thane, 1982, p. 211).

During World War II, local authorities were given powers to requisition properties, and many used these powers to bring property back into use (Young & Rao, 1997, p. 35). The prospect of war led to some rudimentary arrangements being made for those who had to leave their homes due to bombing. In 1938, the Relief in Kind Committee, acting under the auspices of the Ministry of Health, set about organising the relief that was expected to be needed after bombing raids, but assumed that people would only require food and shelter for a few hours until they returned home, to family or friends, to billeted accommodation or into the country. However, once the war started and these arrangements proved to be inadequate, a range of new services were developed: advice and information centres were created, temporary shelters provided assistance payments, 'half way houses' were created for households who were difficult to rehouse and local authorities were encouraged to give homeless households priority in the allocation of accommodation (Glastonbury, 1971, p. 38). Many of these measures were to re-appear, in various forms, during the post-war period.

As the outcome of the war became increasingly clear, attention began to be paid to the population's anticipated needs after the conflict. The publication of the Beveridge Report in 1942, often regarded as the blueprint for the welfare state, represented a key development. The Ministry of Health acknowledged in March 1944 that: "Our primary task must be to meet the needs of those who have no homes of their own" (quoted in Young & Rao, 1997, p. 35).

The Ministry argued that need could not be met by the provision of permanent housing alone and that prefabricated temporary homes would play a role. The 1944 Housing (Temporary Accommodation) Act created the legal basis for the provision of such homes (Young & Rao, 1997, pp. 35–36). More significantly in the longer term, local authority housing at cheap rents was acknowledged as a key part of the reconstruction process in Ministry of Health documents from 1943 (Young & Rao, 1997, p. 37). A White Paper issued by the war time coalition government in March 1945 argued that local authorities should, at least in the short term, play a central role in providing new housing (Young & Rao, 1997, p. 53).

The growth of local authority housing in the inter-war years, the acknowledgement that it should play an important part in the post-war housing programme and the provision of immediate systems of relief for those made homeless by bombing were all important factors when considering how services for homeless people were to develop in the post-war period. However, perhaps the most important historical factor to note is the prevalence of the belief through several centuries that some or all homeless people were deviant. The continuing importance of this view in the post-war period will be demonstrated in subsequent chapters.

References

Bailey, R., & Ruddock, J. (1972). *The grief report*. London, UK: Shelter.

Bramley, G. (1988). The definition and measurement of homelessness. In G. Bramley, K. Doogan, P. Leather, A. Murie, & E. Watson (Eds.), *Homelessness*

and the London housing market (pp. 24–43). Bristol, UK: School of Advanced, Urban Studies, University of Bristol.
Brown, T., Hunt, R., & Yates, N. (2000). *Lettings: A question of choice.* Coventry, UK: Chartered Institute of Housing.
Brown, T., & Yates, N. (2005). Allocations and lettings—Taking customer choice forward in England? *European Journal of Housing Policy, 5*(3), 343–357.
Buck, P. O., Toro, P. A., & Ramos, M. A. (2004). Media and professional interest in homelessness over 30 years (1974–2003). *Analyses of Social Issues and Public Policy, 4*(1), 151–171.
Chambliss, W. J. (1964). A sociological analysis of the laws of vagrancy. *Social Problems, 12*(1), 67–77.
Cramer, H. (2005). Informal and gendered practices in a Homeless Persons Unit. *Housing Studies, 20*(5), 737–751.
Crisis. (2017). *Not yet home: A history of Britain's attempts to tackle homelessness.* London, UK: Crisis.
Davidson, M., & Wyly, E. (2012). Class-ifying London. *City: Analysis of Urban Trends, Culture, Theory, Policy, Action, 16*(4), 395–421.
Davis, A. (2007). Investigating journalist influences on political agendas at Westminster. *Political Communication, 24*(2), 181–199.
Department for Communities and Local Government. (2017). *Statutory homelessness prevention and relief, October to December 2016: England.* London, UK: Department for Communities and Local Government.
Dwyer, P., & Brown, D. (2008). Accommodating 'others'? Housing dispersed, forced migrants in the UK. *Journal of Social Welfare and Family Law, 30*(3), 203–218.
Edwards, R. (1995). Making temporary accommodation permanent: The cost for homeless families. *Critical Social Policy, 15*(1), 60–75.
Ertas, N. (2015). Narrative policy framework: The influence of policy narratives on public opinion. *Politics and Policy, 43*(3), 426–451.
Fitzpatrick, S. (2000). *Young homeless people.* Basingstoke, UK: Palgrave Macmillan.
Fitzpatrick, S., Pawson, H., Bramley, G., Wilcox, S., Watts, B., & Wood, J. (2018). *The homelessness monitor: England 2018.* London, UK: Crisis and the Joseph Rowntree Foundation.
Fitzpatrick, S., & Stephens, M. (1999). Homelessness, need and desert in the allocation of council housing. *Housing Studies, 14*(4), 413–441.
Fitzpatrick, S., & Watts, B. (2017). Competing visions: Security of tenure and the welfarisation of English social housing. *Housing Studies, 32*(8), 1021–1038.
Fraser, D. (1984). *The evolution of the British welfare state* (2nd ed.). Basingstoke, UK: Macmillan.
Glastonbury, B. (1971). *Homeless near a thousand homes.* London, UK: George Allen & Unwin.
Grimshaw, J. M. (2008). *Family homelessness: Causes, consequences and the policy response in England.* London, UK: The British Library.

Guo, L., & Vu, H. T. (2018). Media vs. Reality. *The Agenda Setting Journal. Theory, Practice Critique, 2*(1), 3–24.

Hilton, M., McKay, J., Crowson, N., & Mouhot, J. (2013). *The politics of expertise: How NGOs shaped modern Britain.* Oxford, UK: Oxford University Press.

House of Commons Library. (2016). *Policy on the dispersal of asylum seekers.* London, UK: House of Commons. Retrieved October 31, 2017, from http://researchbriefings.parliament.uk/ResearchBriefing/Summary/CDP-2016-0095

Humphreys, R. (1999). *No fixed abode.* Basingstoke, UK: Macmillan.

Hutson, S., & Liddiard, M. (1994). *Youth homelessness.* Basingstoke, UK: Macmillan.

Jones, G. (1995). *Leaving home.* Buckingham, UK: Open University Press.

Lowe, S. (1997). Homelessness and the law. In R. Burrows, N. Pleace, & D. Quilgars (Eds.), *Homelessness and social policy* (pp. 19–34). London, UK: Routledge.

Lund, B. (1996). *Housing problems and housing policy.* Harlow, UK: Longman.

Mayock, P., Sheridan, S., & Parker, S. (2015). 'It's just like we're going around in circles and going back to the same thing ...' The dynamics of women's unresolved homelessness. *Housing Studies, 30*(6), 877–900.

Morris Committee. (1975). *Housing and social work a joint approach.* Edinburgh, Scotland: Scottish Development Department, Her Majesty's Stationery Office.

National Assistance Board. (1966). *Homeless single persons.* London, UK: HMSO.

Niemi, V., & Ahola, E. (2017). Pathways between housing and homelessness of young income support recipients in Helsinki, Finland. *European Journal of Homelessness, 11*(2), 39–61.

O'Neil, M., Gerstein Pineau, M., Kendall-Taylor, N., Volmert, D., & Stevens, A. (2017). *Finding a better frame: How to create more effective messages on homelessness in the United Kingdom.* Retrieved from https://www.crisis.org.uk/about-us/latest-news/report-reveals-public-attitudes-to-homelessness-and-role-of-sector-in-shaping-them/

Peters, E. (2012). 'I like to let them have their time.' Hidden homeless First Nation people in the city and their management of household relationships. *Social and Cultural Geography, 13*(4), 321–338.

Powlick, P. J., & Katz, A. Z. (1998). Defining the American public opinion/foreign policy nexus. *The International Studies Review, 42*(1), 29–61.

Quilgars, D., Johnsen, S., & Pleace, N. (2008). *Youth homelessness in the UK: A decade of progress?* York, UK: Joseph Rowntree Foundation.

Raynsford, N. (1986). The 1977 Housing (Homeless) Persons Act. In N. Deakin (Ed.), *Policy change in government* (pp. 33–62). London, UK: Royal Institute of Public Administration.

Raynsford, N. (2016). *Substance not spin: An insider's view of success and failure in government.* Bristol, UK: Policy Press.

Rex, J. (1971). The concept of housing class and the sociology of race relations. *The Sociological Review, 12*(3), 293–301.
Richards, J. (1981). The Housing (Homeless Persons) Act 1977: A study in policy making. *Working Paper 22*, School of Advanced Urban Studies, University of Bristol, Bristol, UK.
Rose, A., Maciver, C., & Davies, B. (2016). *Nowhere fast: The journey in and out of unsupported temporary accommodation*. Manchester, UK: Institute of Public Policy Research North.
Rose, M. E. (1971). *English poor law 1780–1930*. Newton Abbott, UK: David and Charles Publishers.
Shanahan, E. A., McBeth, M. K., & Hathaway, P. L. (2011). Narrative policy framework: The influence of media policy narratives on public opinion. *Politics and Policy, 39*(3), 373–400.
Shaw, I., Bloor, M., Cormack, R., & Williamson, H. (1996). Estimating the prevalence of hard-to-reach populations: The illustration of mark-recapture methods in the study of homelessness. *Social Policy and Administration, 30*(1), 69–85.
Shehata, A., & Stromback, J. (2013). Not (yet) a new era of minimal effects: A study of agenda setting at the aggregate and individual levels. *International Journal of Press/Politics, 18*(2), 234–255.
Snelling, C. (2017). *Right to home? Rethinking homelessness in rural communities*. London, UK: Institute for Public Policy Research.
Thane, P. (1982). *The foundations of the welfare state*. Harlow, UK: Longman.
UK Statistics Authority. (2015). *Statistics on homelessness and rough sleeping in England*. London, UK: UK Statistics Authority.
Van Aelst, P., & Walgrave, S. (2011). Minimal or massive? The political agenda-setting power of the mass media according to different methods. *The International Journal of Press/Politics, 16*(3), 295–313.
Watchman, P. Q., & Robson, P. (1989). *Homelessness and the law in Britain*. Glasgow: The Planning Exchange.
Watson, S., & Austerberry, H. (1986). *Housing and homelessness: A Feminist perspective*. London, UK: Routledge and Kegan Paul.
Young, K., & Rao, N. (1997). *Local government since 1945*. Oxford, UK: Blackwell Publishing.

CHAPTER 2

Key Themes in Post-War Homelessness

Introduction

Homelessness is sometimes described as a 'wicked' problem, of which there is no definite understanding and where the full consequences of policy initiatives can never fully be known (McConnell, 2018, pp. 165–167). The complexity of the problem, and of the range of policies that have been devised to tackle it, is reflected in the absence of a single conceptual framework which can provide a substantial understanding of responses to homelessness. Instead, policy is best understood by considering the influence of five key factors.

The first of these factors is the explanation of homelessness that is favoured. Academics and others have engaged in near constant debate about the causes of homelessness, with this debate developing from a simple individual/structural distinction to incorporate a more complex set of explanations. While policy makers have not necessarily followed all the nuances of these debates, it is noticeable that governments since 1997 have acknowledged a wide range of causes of homelessness in their policy documents.

The second factor is the manner in which homeless people are categorised and the characteristics that are associated with different categories. From the implementation of the 1948 National Assistance Act, there has been a clear assumption in policy that households with dependent children should receive the most significant protection from homelessness, with 'single homeless people' treated as a lesser priority. However, single

J. Harding, *Post-War Homelessness Policy in the UK*,
https://doi.org/10.1007/978-3-030-22117-1_2

homeless people have often been assumed to have a greater range of needs than families. Further distinctions are often made between single people whose homelessness is hidden and those who sleep rough, with a growing recognition by policy makers that many rough sleepers have particularly complex needs, requiring a holistic response.

Third, there is the level of demand for housing, particularly social rented housing. Where the level of demand is high, homeless people are often perceived to be in competition for social housing with waiting-list applicants, leading to restrictive policies and assumptions that homeless people are less deserving. In addition to the overall balance between demand and supply of accommodation, the extent to which social rented housing is perceived as a desirable tenure is important here.

The fourth factor affecting the services received by a homeless person is their location. Much homelessness legislation has consisted of central government creating powers and duties to be implemented by local authorities, but there has been limited control exercised over the manner in which these powers and duties have been interpreted, leading to substantial geographical variation in services. The delegation of housing powers to Scotland, Wales and Northern Ireland has further widened the gap between different areas of the United Kingdom.

Finally, there is the question of whether policy makers focus on primary, secondary or tertiary prevention of homelessness. Primary prevention involves the provision of universal services that benefit all (particularly the poorer parts of the population), secondary prevention targets those individuals and groups at greatest risk and tertiary prevention concentrates on those who are already homeless. The complex nature of homelessness is reflected in the wide range of policies of all of these types that have been introduced by governments in the post-war period.

These five factors are, of course, inter-related. For example, the local authorities that are most generous to homeless households tend to be those with the lowest level of demand for social rented housing. Housing pressures also appear to affect to affect beliefs about the causes of homelessness, with homeless people being most frequently blamed for their own situation in the 1950s, when accommodation shortages and demand for public sector housing were at their highest level.

The remainder of this chapter will be devoted to discussion of the thinking of academics, policy makers and others in relation to each of these factors. This will set the scene for subsequent chapters in which the impact of these factors on policy in different time periods is explored.

Explanations of Homelessness

Somerville (2013, p. 388) argues that different explanations of homelessness have dominated discussion at different stages of the post-war period. He suggests that, until the 1960s, discussion continued to be based on pre-1945 assumptions of deviance (or 'sin talk'), where homeless people were regarded as culpable for their own situation. From the 1960s to the 1980s, 'system talk' began to be heard, with homelessness being blamed on structural factors. From the 1980s, there was more discussion of 'sick talk', with the homeless person being seen as 'vulnerable' and likely to be experiencing a number of major difficulties. While other explanations will be added to this list, these seem an appropriate starting point for discussion.

Deviance-based Explanations ('Sin Talk')

The belief that homeless and other severely disadvantaged people are to blame for their own circumstances, because they adopt a different set of values to other members of society, is a very popular and longstanding one. It is a belief that is often linked, either implicitly or explicitly, to the concept of the underclass, whose most influential advocate is Charles Murray (MacDonald (1997, p. 7).

Murray (1990, p. 23) argues that a distinction can be made between the deserving poor, who are simply those of low income, and the undeserving poor, who indicate through various forms of anti-social behaviour that they are part of an underclass which has rejected the values held by the majority of society. An increase in three indicators shows that an underclass is developing—illegitimacy, violent crime and unemployment among healthy, working age people (Murray, 1990, p. 23). People living in this underclass are 'raising their children to live in it' (Murray, 1990, p. 26).

Murray's focus on wrong values, and the fear that these might be transmitted between generations, is consistent with concerns expressed both before and since by some British politicians. For example, in the 1970s, Secretary of State for Health and Social Security Sir Keith Joseph claimed to have identified a 'cycle of deprivation'—a process whereby multiple deprivation and social disadvantage were transmitted inter-generationally (Macnicol, 1987, pp. 293–295).

In discussing the growth of the underclass in the United States, Murray (1990, p. 24) specifically identifies homeless people as being among its members. Those politicians who have drawn on the ideas of Murray have tended to see homelessness either as a deviant choice made by individuals or as a consequence of other deviant choices. Parsell and Parsell (2012, pp. 422–424) note that there have been a number of international leaders who have portrayed homeless people as having exercised their 'personal freedom' in order to choose a particular 'lifestyle'. Jones (1997, pp. 99–100) argues that the political right in Britain have sought to portray young homeless people in particular as deviant.

Individual-based explanations of social problems in general, and homelessness in particular, have been widely attacked. Walker (1990, p. 66) claims that Murray's discussion has no scientific basis, but arises from "innuendoes, assertions and anecdotes". Indeed, when reading Murray's work, the shortage of empirical evidence is quite noticeable, and his use of statistics has been criticised (Brown, 1990 in the case of illegitimacy and Deacon, 1990, in the case of violent crime). His condemnation of illegitimacy now seems dated, but his view that its growth is linked to the 1977 Housing (Homeless Persons) Act (Murray, 1990, pp. 47–48) has been echoed by some Conservative politicians, as will be seen in Chap. 5. Large fluctuations in the level of violent crime, and more particularly unemployment, seem difficult to reconcile with Murray's belief in an ever-growing underclass.

One piece of evidence that could be used to support deviancy-based explanations of homelessness is the high incidence of criminal records among homeless people shown by numerous studies (e.g. Harding, Irving, & Whowell, 2011). Somerville (2013, p. 392) notes that crime commonly pre-dates first homelessness, suggesting that it is more commonly a cause than a consequence. However, suggestions that homelessness is a deviant choice, reflecting different values to those of the rest of society, have been criticised by both academics and those working with homeless people. Parsell and Parsell (2012, p. 43) question the idea that homelessness could be an attractive option for some people, saying: "We are yet to see any empirical or theoretical work that demonstrates the pleasurable or beneficial dimensions of homelessness." They argue that, where homeless people exercise any choice at all, it is to choose homelessness over undesirable hostel accommodation (Parsell & Parsell, 2012, p. 425). Reeve's (2013, p. 837) study of sex workers who were both homeless and drug users showed that many remained attached to conventional social norms and felt shame that their actions departed from such norms.

If poverty and homelessness are the result of inappropriate values on the part of the individual, this raises the question of what action should be taken to remedy these social problems. Murray (1990, p. 40), discussing the UK situation, suggests that, no matter how extensive the support provided to those sleeping rough, they would very soon return to the same situation. In addition to the 1977 Housing (Homeless Persons) Act, he also blames an over-generous benefit system for the growth of illegitimacy (Murray, 1990, pp. 47–48). Other thinkers on the political right such as Marsland (1996, p. 129) and Green (1998, p. viii) have similarly suggested that too much welfare provision can encourage individuals to concentrate on qualifying for benefits rather than seeking work. Solutions to social problems, therefore, lie in providing less rather than more for people in some forms of need. Such thinking appears to be linked to the actions of a number of local authorities that have taken steps to discourage the public from giving money to people who beg (a group not identical to homeless people, but with a high degree of overlap) and to give instead to charities seeking more sustainable methods of meeting needs (Johnsen & Fitzpatrick, 2010).

One solution advocated by Murray to the perceived problem of a group with different values to the majority of society is to allow them self-government. The area in which they live could adopt their alternative values, while other areas could maintain the values held by the rest of society and people could have freedom to move between the two (Murray, 1990, p. 52). The practicalities of such a system are not made clear by Murray and have been compared to apartheid (Deacon, 1990, p. 79). However, the principle of seeking to separate homeless people from at least some parts of society has been reflected in policies and practices adopted by a number of cities, in the United States and elsewhere, which are designed to remove homeless people from urban centres. Such policies can take the form of discouragement through defensive architecture (e.g. public benches with arm rests in the centre to prevent anyone sleeping on them), displacement (e.g. the possessions of homeless people being hosed down, supposedly on the grounds of hygiene and public health) and deterrence (e.g. fines for people who store possessions in public places) (see, e.g. Johnsen & Fitzpatrick, 2010, p. 1704). De Verteuil, May, and von Mahs (2009) argue that such policies have often been part of a programme seeking to attract businesses, tourists and high-income residents into city centres, although they should not be seen in isolation from more supportive measures for rough sleepers.

Structural Explanations ('System Talk')

Structural explanations see homelessness as being the product of an unequal society; Marxism and Fabian Socialism are among the ideologies that may underpin such explanations. Marxist theory sees individuals within society as acting in a self-interested manner. So people who own capital and run businesses (the ruling class in general or landlords in particular) will seek to maximise their own profits, whatever the costs to the workers in terms of poverty, poor health and so on (Rubington & Weinberg, 1995, pp. 234–235). Arguments that homeless people are being removed from city centres in the interests of business and tourism fit well with this type of thinking. Marxists often view social policies as helping to make capitalism more productive (e.g. by providing trained workers) and/or preventing disorder by giving the impression that all are benefiting from capitalism (Mishra, 1984, p. 67). So, subsidised housing may be necessary for low paid workers, but there is no need to provide for those homeless people who are unlikely ever to work, unless their situation makes the failings of the social and economic system too obvious and visible.

In contrast to Marxism, Mishra (1984, pp. 124–125) argues that post-war social democratic politics have always lacked a strong intellectual basis: the Centre Left has instead concerned itself with incremental steps to tackle social problems. Fabian Socialists have traditionally advocated the use of social expenditure to redistribute resources to the poor (Mishra, 1984, p. 133) and much writing about structural causes of homelessness had suggested that the unequal distribution of resources is the key reason for the problem. In particular, unjust policies in specific policy areas—most often housing and/or social security—have been argued to create, re-enforce or fail to alleviate inequalities which have contributed to homelessness.

One simple structural explanation of homelessness—which seemed self-evident in the immediate post-war period and was advanced strongly by Shelter in the late 1960s—is that there are insufficient dwellings for the number of households, so some people will inevitably go without a home. Evaluation of such claims rests on a complex set of calculations about housing supply and demand (such as those of Holmans, 1995) and a number of value judgements (Barnett & Lowe, 1990). The arguments have become more complicated as the United Kingdom has moved from a position of net emigration to one of net immigration. However, the need for housing is not just a matter of comparing the population size with the number of properties: calculations must take into account the historical tendency for people to live in smaller units. The overall population of England and Wales increased by only 0.5% between 1971 and 1981, but there was an estimated increase of over 10% in the number of households in this period (Brynin, 1987, p. 26 cited in Hutson & Liddiard, 1994, p. 57). This trend has continued with the Department for Communities and Local Government (2016) predicting that the average household size would fall from 2.35 in 2014 to 2.21 in 2039 and that single person households would increase by 68,000 per year, making up one third (33%) of the total household growth in the same period.

However, arguments that homelessness is solely a result of an insufficient number of dwellings became more difficult to support in some northern cities in the 1990s, where households continued to become homelessness despite property being demolished because of low demand (Keenan, Lowe, & Spencer, 1999, p. 704). A more nuanced approach is to consider the match between properties and those who are seeking housing, in terms of factors such as property type, geographical area and ease of access. On this last point, there have been numerous historical arguments that allocations policies of social landlords are hostile to single people in general (Anderson & Morgan, 1997; Venn, 1985) and young, single people in particular (e.g. Darke, Conway, & Holman, 1993, pp. 33–35). Private landlords have frequently been shown to be reluctant to let property to people who are homeless and/or on low incomes (e.g. Bevan, Kemp, & Rhodes, 1995; Reeve et al., 2016).

A key reason for this reluctance on the part of private landlords has been concern over whether tenants have the resources to pay the rent. In the periods of Conservative (or Conservative led) governments that began in 1979 and 2010, specific change to benefits were often argued to have made access to housing for low-income people more difficult and so to have increased homelessness. However, findings evidence to clearly support these arguments was often difficult, as subsequent chapters will show. Taking a much broader view, the analysis of Bramley and Fitzpatrick (2018) supports that of previous studies by indicating that poverty is the factor most closely associated with homelessness, with experience of childhood poverty substantially increasing the risk of homelessness in later life.

An alternative source of evidence for structural explanations is taken from international comparisons. While noting the difficulties created by limited comparable data on homelessness, Stephens and Fitzpatrick (2007, pp. 208–209) suggest that the available evidence indicates that the level of homelessness in a country is affected by the supply of housing—both in broad terms and specifically the number of lettings of social rented housing. Welfare regimes that produce high levels of poverty and inequality are also linked to high levels of homelessness because of the lack of purchasing power of the poorest people and because poverty is linked to relationship breakdown, mental health problems and substance misuse. Although both the United States and the United Kingdom have welfare regimes that produce high levels of inequality and poverty, lower levels of homelessness in the United Kingdom may be attributable to a larger social rented sector and more generous housing allowances for those on the lowest incomes.

The solutions that have been suggested by advocates of structural explanations of homelessness have tended to concentrate on making more housing available and/or reducing the gap between its costs and the financial resources available to the poorest parts of the population. So, for example, Rowe and Wagstaff (2017, pp. 12–15) recommend the removal of the powers of social landlords to exclude people in need from their waiting lists and the introduction of measures to increase the supply of properties that single homeless people can afford. Recommendations have also frequently been made to reverse social security measures such as the ending of entitlement to means tested benefits for 16–17 year olds (e.g. Harding & Kirk, 1996; Killeen, 1988).

At a local level, there have been a number of initiatives taken by local authorities and voluntary organisations to seek to redress the perceived structural disadvantages of homeless people and others. Local authorities in the 1980s introduced a number of generic initiatives to tackle increasing poverty in their area, including the provision of free or low-cost services, welfare rights work (Balloch & Jones, 1990, pp. 40–54) and the letting of part furnished accommodation to low-income households (Harding & Keenan, 1998).

Explanations Based on Vulnerability ('Sick Talk')

Bramley and Fitzpatrick (2018, p. 97) suggest that one reason for the preference for structural explanations of homelessness among academic commentators is that explanations that focus on the individual have connotations of 'blameworthiness'—connotations that are clearly made specific in the deviance-based explanations discussed above. However, there are some factors linked to homelessness that cannot reasonably be held to be the fault of the individual, most obviously mental health problems. The increasingly used term vulnerability is clearly not synonymous with sickness, but has been widely applied to people with mental health problems and/or addictions: Sherwood-Johnson (2013, p. 910) argues that the concept of vulnerability has been extended beyond those who lack mental capacity to incorporate those whose present decisions are thought to threaten their autonomy in the long term.

Indeed, vulnerability has become prevalent in discussions of many areas of social policy, including children's services, anti-social behaviour and family policy, education policy, drugs policy, youth offending, public health and social care (Brown, 2015, p. 57). Brown (2015, pp. 64–65) argues that in a policy context where access to services is discretionary, and definitions of vulnerability are vague, classing someone as vulnerable may go alongside considering them deserving of assistance. This rationing function of the term was demonstrated by the 1977 Housing (Homeless Persons) Act specifying that a household should be classed as being in priority need (and therefore owed the main homelessness duty) if it included dependent children, someone who was pregnant or someone who was vulnerable for another reason.

There is strong evidence to suggest that homeless people are particularly likely to have physical and mental health problems—and so be vulnerable according to many definitions. Bines (1994) found that rough sleepers were more likely than the general population to suffer from physical conditions such as chronic chest or breathing problems, wounds, skin ulcers and other skin complaints, and musculoskeletal problems. More recently, Homeless Link (2014) found that homeless people were also particularly likely to suffer from illnesses less obviously connected to their situation, that is, stomach and urinary problems.

In the case of mental health problems, Bines (1994) found that, compared to the general population, mental health problems were 8 times more likely among hostel and bed-and-breakfast residents and 11 times more likely among rough sleepers. Similarly, Homeless Link (2014), comparing their own survey of people experiencing homelessness to the General Lifestyle Survey, found that homeless people were more likely to experience personality disorder (7% compared to 3–5%), bipolar disorder (6% compared to 1–3%) and depression (a large difference of 36% compared to 3%). The differences between the homeless population and the general population have been found to be greater in other studies, some of which have estimated that as many as 70% of homeless people have personality disorders (Somerville, 2013, p. 393). Studies of homeless people have also suggested that a high percentage have experienced traumatic events, that is, events that they have witnessed or experienced where their reaction has been intense fear, helplessness or horror (Somerville, 2013, p. 392).

The impact of mental health problems is complicated by the tendency for such problems to occur alongside problems of addiction (see, e.g. Kim, Ford, Howard, & Bradford, 2010). Although there is no clear definition of dual diagnosis it has, in recent years, been used largely to refer to individuals with a substance misuse problem and a coexisting psychiatric disorder (Rassool, 2006, p. 3). A high percentage of people with substance misuse problems have been found also to have psychiatric disorders and vice versa and the incidence of dual diagnosis is particularly high among homeless people (Rassool, 2006, p. 5). Cleary, Hunt, Matheson, and Walter (2008, p. 239) suggest that, among those with mental health problems, using substances even in mild doses increases the risk of a number of negative consequences, including homelessness. Homeless Link (2014) found that 41% of all respondents to their survey reported using drugs or alcohol to cope with mental health issues.

To confirm the links between homelessness, mental health problems and substance misuse, studies from a range of countries (e.g. Johnson & Chamberlain, 2008 in Australia; Neale, 2001 in the United Kingdom), have found an over-representation of addiction problems among homeless people. Kemp, Neale, and Robertson (2006, p. 320) note that the risk factors for drug misuse are very similar to those for homelessness.

Two difficulties arise in attributing homelessness to mental health problems and/or addictions—one practical and one more conceptual. The practical problem is in establishing the pattern of cause and effect between the three factors. Research has often produced conflicting reports as to whether homelessness is more likely to lead to drug misuse or vice versa (e.g. Johnson & Chamberlain, 2008; McNaughton, 2008, pp. 181–182). The Department of Health's (2002) *Dual Diagnosis Good Practice Guide* noted that psychiatric illness could lead to, or aggravate, a substance misuse problem, but the opposite relationship could also occur (Rassool, 2006, p. 4). So, there is no clear picture as to which of the three difficulties is most likely to occur first in a person's life.

At a more conceptual level, being classified as 'vulnerable' may have negative implications: some commentators have suggested that the term is used to stigmatise or control some groups (Brown, 2015, pp. 62–67) or to evoke images of weakness and passivity (Wiles, 2011, p. 579). Longstanding debates as to whether rough sleepers in particular should be coerced into accepting housing options that are not their preference fit with these concerns.

A number of measures have sought to address very specifically the needs of homeless people with mental health problems: most notably the 1990 Homelessness Mentally Ill Initiative (which is discussed in Chap. 5) and Pathways Housing First (which is considered in Chap. 7).

Explanations Specific to Young People

Discussions of homelessness among young people often involve putting the above three explanations into a more specific context. For example, explanations that blame cuts to benefits have often focused on young people, who have tended to bear the brunt of these cuts. Chapter 5 will demonstrate that there was a disagreement in Mrs Thatcher's government as to whether restoring benefits to young people would tackle youth homelessness or would encourage more to make the deviant choice of leaving their parents' home unnecessarily.

The tendency to see young people as 'vulnerable' or 'at risk' is demonstrated by the names of some of the schemes that have sought to prevent youth homelessness, such as Safe in the City and Safe Moves (Quilgars, Johnsen, & Pleace, 2008, p. 1). This terminology has been argued to have various connotations: Abel and Wahab (2017, p. 1392) claim that concerns to protect young people 'at risk' have reduced efforts to meet their needs and welfare, Philip (2000, p. 1) suggests that there is a tension between seeing young people as 'at risk' from society and as presenting a risk to themselves and others, and Bancroft and Wilson (2007), p. 312) argue that as children grow older they progress from being seen as vulnerable to presenting a risk of problematic behaviour.

The child model of youth homelessness is one of a number developed by Brandon, Wells, Francis, and Ramsay (1980, p. 74) to categorise the explanations of agency workers as to why young newcomers to London became homeless. According to this model, the young people were impulsive, typically drawn to the capital by a desire to find the bright lights or to escape from home. Young homeless people were thought to seek illusions rather than reality and to be deceived by adults who exploited them. In this model, there was a need for young people to be rescued from their destructive environment.

Concerns over young people travelling to London with no home and no job reduced after the time when Brandon et al. were writing. However, assumptions that young people became homeless because they were not ready for adult responsibilities remained and found some support in Harding's (2004, pp. 108–109) study of 16–17-year-olds who were re-housed as homeless by Newcastle City Council. Young people were more likely to succeed in a tenancy, meaning that they did not become homeless again in the short term, if they were cautious as to how they spent their money and had realistic expectations at the start of their tenancy, acknowledging that living independently would be difficult.

The role of families is often emphasised in discussions of youth homelessness. While many studies have noted the high incidence of childhood trauma among homeless people of all ages, discussions of family problems tend to gain particular prominence when considering young people. Arguments often centre on whether the decision to leave the family home has been an immature one, based on a desire for independence that the young person is not yet ready for, or a rational response to unacceptable or abusive home circumstances.

Jones and Stephens' (1994) analysis of the Scottish Young People's Survey (a nationally representative sample of 19-year-olds) suggested that those who had left home at a younger age were more likely to become homeless. However, a simplistic assumption that homeless could simply be attributed to an immature decision to leave was challenged by further analysis of the same dataset by Jones (1995). This analysis showed that the age of leaving home interacted with whether the young person had left for a 'traditional' or 'problem' reason. 'Problem' reasons were defined as moving to another location because there were no jobs in the area or leaving because of family conflict (Jones, 1995, p. 42). In contrast, 'traditional' reasons were leaving to marry or set up a partnership, to enter higher education or to take a job. Only 2% of the traditional leavers had been homeless since leaving home, compared to 23% of those who had left for problem reasons. The increased risk of homelessness among those leaving home at a young age only applied when the reason for leaving home was one that fell into the 'problem' category (Jones, 1995, p. 45).

More recent research has further demonstrated the impact of problematic family relationships: a number of studies have indicated that the risk of homelessness is increased for young people who have difficulty getting on with their parents, witness or experience violence within the family home, live in a family where there are financial difficulties, run away from home or spend time in the care of the local authority (Quilgars et al., 2008, pp. 38–39). Analysis of data from Scottish local authorities in 2006–2007 suggested that the majority of 16–17-year-olds who approached them as homeless did so because their parents were no longer willing or able to accommodate them (Quilgars et al., 2008, p. 44). However, research has also identified a number of factors not directly related to family circumstances that increase young people's risk of subsequent homelessness, that is, suspension or exclusion from school, having 'missed a lot of school' and being involved in crime or anti-social behaviour (Quilgars et al., 2008, p. 39).

If youth homelessness is seen to arise from an immature decision to leave the family home unnecessarily, then it follows that the solutions lie in seeking to dissuade young people from making this choice and/or encouraging them to return once they have left. In the first category can be placed measures such as the introduction of adolescent support teams (see Biehal, Clayden, & Byford, 2000) and the provision of leaving home education. School-based prevention services are often peer education programme that seek, among other aims, to dispel myths about the availability of social housing and increase young people's awareness of the 'harsh realities' of homelessness (Quilgars et al., 2008, p. 68). Governments have advocated such programmes for a number of decades; the Department of the Environment's (1991) Code of Guidance on Part 3 of the 1985 Housing Act identified education as: ".... crucial to help young people with independent living, and to ensure that they are aware of the risks of homelessness" (quoted in Gholam, 1993, p. 2).

Among the measures facilitating returning home is Nightstop, which provides very short-term accommodation for young people who have left the family home suddenly, to give them space to consider their options. In addition, the provision of mediation services for families, which can provide services at the point before or after young people leave home, increased as the Labour governments of 1997 to 2010 moved the focus of homelessness services towards prevention (Quilgars et al., 2008, p. 62).

However, the Labour governments of 1997 to 2010 also acknowledged that there were some young people who could not return to the family home: the 2002 Homelessness (Priority Need for Accommodation) (England) Order placed all unintentionally homeless 16–17-year-olds into the priority need category of the homelessness legislation. The Department for Communities and Local Government (2008, p. 10) found that 70% of statutorily homeless 16–17-year-olds were homeless because of a relationship breakdown (almost always with parents or step-parents) and in 41% of these cases violence had been involved.

Young people who must leave the family home before the age of 16, and so go into the care of the local authority, have been a particular concern for recent governments, as will be shown in subsequent chapters. The experience of those in care, who tend to move to independence in their teens, has become more sharply contrasted with that of other young people as the average age of leaving home has increased: Hill and Hirsch (2019, p. 2) found that, in 2016–2017, approximately two thirds of single people in their 20s were living with one or both parents.

More Complex Explanations

More recent academic explanations of homelessness have tended to acknowledge the value of multiple perspectives and argue that structural inequalities are likely to have most impact on vulnerable individuals with high support needs. Such explanations acknowledge that poverty and mental health problems cannot be seen as the sole causes of homeless because most poor people, and most of those with mental health problems, do not become homeless (Bramley & Fitzpatrick, 2018, pp. 97–98).

Bramley and Fitzpatrick (2018, pp. 98–100) argue that a critical realist perspective can help to understand the very different causal routes that lead individual to homelessness. They suggest that it is important not just to acknowledge that both individual and structural factors have a role but also to understand the nature of the interactions between them.

Bramley and Fitzpatrick's (2018, pp. 112–113) critical realist analysis of several datasets suggested that childhood poverty was central to the risk of subsequent homelessness, but also important were several health and support needs and behavioural issues, particularly when they arose in the teenage years. Having a partner and being able to live in the family home as an adult child were protective factors, and risk was affected to a smaller extent by the housing market and economic conditions of an area. Bramley and Fitzpatrick (2018, p. 113) concluded that: "Overall, therefore, this paper lends support to a predominantly structural analysis of homelessness, without discounting the possibility of a wholly individualistic causation in specific cases, whilst also still recognizing the potential positive impact of strong social support networks."

The development of academic thinking with regard to more complex explanations has been reflected to some extent at a policy level, although with a limited level of analysis. For example, in the Ministerial forward to the 2011 policy document *No Second Night Out*, Minister for Housing and Local Government Grant Shapps wrote: "Homelessness is not just a problem of scale. It's a problem of complexity—no two people lose their home for the same reason" (DCLG, 2011, p. 5).

The *No Second Night Out* document then discussed wide-ranging recommendations to tackle homelessness with commitments under six headings—helping people off the streets, helping people into healthcare, helping people into work, reducing bureaucratic burdens, increasing local control over investment in services and devolving responsibility for tackling homelessness (DCLG, 2011, pp. 9–11). The effectiveness of this approach will be considered in Chap. 7.

Categories of Homeless People

There has been a longstanding distinction, both in policy terms and public perception, between homeless households with dependent children and 'single homeless people'. The 1948 National Assistance Act was assumed to place obligations onto local authorities only in the case of households with children and the 1977 Housing (Homeless Persons) Act also privileged this group over households without children in most cases (although this position was to change substantially in Scotland). Evans (1999, p. 133) argues that the awarding of 'priority need' status to households with dependent children under the 1977 Act reflected a need to ration services, but Somerville (1999, pp. 34–35) suggests that it was a method of defining those who were deserving of state assistance.

Raynsford (2016, p. 27) argues that negative stereotypes have determined perceptions of single homeless people historically: "The pejorative view of the homeless as separate and problematic derived in large measure from stereotypes of single homeless people as vagrants prone to alcoholism or common lodging houses, immortalised in George Orwell's *Down and Out in Paris and London.*"

Watson and Austerberry (1986, pp. 76–77) suggest that single homeless people are assumed to require 'special needs' housing, a point that is developed further in Chap. 5. The debate outlined above as to whether mental health problems are a cause or a consequence of homelessness has tended to concentrate on single homeless people (Pleace, 1998, p. 50). This contrasts with discussions of health and homelessness among families with children, which have been clearly focused on physical and mental health problems as a consequence of homelessness, often the result of living in poor quality temporary accommodation (Grimshaw, 2008, pp. 76–77). Resettlement programmes have tended to be focused on single homeless people: these programmes were initially intended to teach independent living skills that were assumed to be lacking but in some cases developed into much broader programmes incorporating care, social development and inclusion in society (Pleace, 1998, p. 51). In contrast, Pleace, Fitzpatrick, Johnsen, Quilgars, and Sanderson (2008, p. 7) found that 63% of homeless adults in families had received 'practical' support, but only 16% had received 'personal' support.

Further distinctions are made between different groups of single homeless people. Many are believed to fall into the particularly difficult to quantify hidden homeless category, that is, those who are not visible because they are staying with friends, remaining in unsatisfactory relationships due to lack of alternative accommodation, squatting and so on. Fitzpatrick et al. (2017, p. 72) estimated that, in 2016, there were 2.27 million households in England which included single adults who intended to move out or had a preference to do so. However, as Peters (2012, p. 322) notes, the experience of hidden homelessness is one that has received little attention in research and the same can be said of policy.

In contrast, the relatively small number of single homeless people who sleep rough have been a focus of policy almost continually since 1990. This focus has, on occasions, narrowed to a sub-group of rough sleepers who are difficult to resettle and are believed to have particularly complex needs. Reflecting similar distinctions that have been made in the United States (see, e.g. Benjaminsen & Andrade, 2015, p. 859), May (2000, pp. 622–633) identifies three broad categories of single homeless people in the United Kingdom. The first is the long-term homeless who have multiple vulnerabilities and for who homelessness had become, effectively, a permanent condition. Second, there are the episodically homeless who became homeless for short periods of time on numerous occasions. These people tend to live in insecure accommodation between periods of homelessness; their housing situation is linked to a disadvantaged position in the labour market. The final group is the first time homeless—who might, of course, progress to be long-term or episodically homeless—but may also be experiencing their only period of homelessness. This is the most diverse group; homelessness could arise from a period of unemployment or from a number of vulnerabilities.

In recent years, those who have complex needs and whose homelessness is long term have been described as experiencing multiple exclusion homelessness. Multiply excluded homeless people are sometimes defined as those who experience a large number of difficulties, routinely fail to receive the services that they need and tend to have chaotic lives that are costly both to themselves and society (Dwyer & Somerville, 2011, p. 496). Fitzpatrick, Johnsen, and White (2011, pp. 504–505) suggest that this group tends to have four characteristics: a wide range of experiences of homelessness (staying with friends, staying in a hostel, sleeping rough, applying to the council as homeless, etc.), experience of institutional care (local authority care as a child, prison, young offenders institution and/or hospital as a result of a mental health issue), experience of some form of substance misuse (illegal drugs, solvents, gas, glue or alcohol to excess) and involvement in street cultural activities (begging, street drinking and/or shoplifting). This group are also likely to be highly visible, particularly in city centres, which is an important factor affecting the policy response to them.

It may not seem a particularly nuanced approach to distinguish homeless people with dependent children from those without, and to sub-divide the single homeless group between those who are multiply excluded (often sleeping rough) and those who are not (usually in more hidden forms of homelessness). However, it is these divisions that have been most widely acknowledged in policy, as will be shown in subsequent chapters.

Levels of Demand for Public Sector Housing

The explanations for homelessness that have been favoured by policy makers and the public often appear to have been influenced by the level of demand for social rented housing—and the extent to which there is perceived to be competition for it between groups. The time of greatest hostility towards homeless people appeared to be the late 1940s and the 1950s when the housing crisis was most acute and social rented housing was much sought after. As will be argued in Chap. 4, one factor leading to the passing of the 1977 Housing (Homeless Persons) Act was a softening of public attitudes to homeless households, which appeared to be linked to an easing of demand for social rented housing. By the time the Act was passed, social rented housing was already been seen as an unfavourable option—a process that was to gather pace in the 1980s (see, e.g. Jones & Murie, 1998).

The 1977 Act did not end debates about the extent to which homeless people should have access to social rented housing, with Conservative governments in particular seeing such housing as a public resource that should be carefully rationed. Both the 1996 Housing Act and the 2011 Localism Act sought to redress a perceived advantage that applicants who were accepted as homeless had over those who applied for social rented housing through the waiting list (or housing register). In contrast, one criticism of the Scottish Government's extension of the main homelessness duty to more households is that it resulted in the majority of public sector housing allocations in some areas being made to people who were accepted as homeless (McKee & Philips, 2012).

The picture is complicated by the different ideas that policy makers and others have about the social rented sector. The Chartered Institute of Housing (2018, p. 5) notes that three broad views can be taken of the sector. The first, firmly held by Aneurin Bevan (the first post-war Housing Minister) is that it should provide affordable housing for a wide range of groups, competing with the private sector and so driving up standards and driving down rents. The second is of a 'safety net' for homeless people and other groups that cannot afford market housing—a view held by the Labour governments of 1997 to 2010. The third is of a service providing mainly short-term housing for those whose income and other circumstances leaves them in need of temporary support; a view made explicit in the policies of the governments led by David Cameron.

Differences Between Geographical Areas

The demand for social rented housing is clearly substantially influenced by the nature of the local housing market—and local housing markets vary significantly. Wilcox, Perry, and Williams (2015, p. 9) suggest that differences in house prices between London and the United Kingdom are cyclical, widening in economic upturns and narrowing in downturns. In 2015, house prices in London were 85 % above the UK average—a post-war high. Affordability in the private sector clearly affects the level of demand for public sector housing and appears to also impact upon the attitudes to homelessness among local policy makers. Studies of local authority practice (e.g. Evans & Duncan, 1988) have frequently shown more restrictive interpretations of the homelessness legislation in areas with higher demand for social housing. In addition, Johnsen and Teixeira (2012, p. 195) note that homeless people are more likely to be regarded as needing to 'earn' an offer of housing in areas where demand substantially exceeds supply.

The devolution of homelessness responsibilities to Scotland, Wales and Northern Ireland has created legal differences between the individual nations of the United Kingdom but, even in contexts where the law is the same, studies have frequently shown substantial differences in local authority interpretation. There is disagreement about the extent to which local authorities have autonomy in the United Kingdom. Leach and Percy-Smith (2001, pp. 211–212) outline the legal limits to the powers of local authorities:

> The United Kingdom is, as the name suggests, at least in theory, a unitary rather than a federal state. Supreme power or sovereignty is not divided, as it is in the federal system, but concentrated in the hands of the central government ... It follows that the rights and very existence of local government are conditional rather than absolute. Local government can only do what it is explicitly permitted to do by Parliament—other activities are ultra vires or beyond their powers. The role of local government is thus strictly subordinate and its relationship with central government very unequal.

However, a different perspective is presented by Gray (1994, p. 87), who focuses on the practical difficulties involved in central government enforcing its powers:

> [T]he only real, direct control that the centre has over SNG [*sub-national government, usually local authorities*] is the legislative one, and this is such a dubious one—in terms of the time and effort involved in using it—that the centre is forced back on informal mechanisms of control.

Since the 1980s, local government has become increasingly dependent on central government for its finance and regularly re-shaped in terms of responsibilities, powers and functions. However, there is no consensus as to how far these changes have altered the relationship between central and local government (Griggs & Sullivan, 2012, p. 496).

Exworthy, Berney, and Powell (2002, p. 83) note that the policy intentions of central government are not always fulfilled at local level. The relative autonomy of local agencies and practitioners may be used to undermine the intentions of policy makers, thus creating an 'implementation gap'. While discussion of this issue has sometimes used the term 'deficit', and assumed that differences between the intentions and outcomes of policy are negative, others have suggested that policies can be enhanced by those at the ground level making their own interpretations as they put them into practice (Hill & Hupe, 2003, p. 472).

Leach and Percy-Smith (2001), pp. 212–213) argue that some commentators have failed to acknowledge the role of organisations beyond local authorities in the implementation of policy. The post-war trend to increase the role of local authorities, particularly through developments such as the 1948 National Assistance Act and local government reorganisation in 1972, were reversed from the 1980s, with authorities having progressively fewer responsibilities for the direct provision of services (Kelly, 2006, p. 607). Moves towards privatisation and the contracting out of services increased the number of non-government agencies involved in the delivery of policies (Bache, 2003, p. 301). This has been particularly evident in housing policy since the 1980s, as will be shown in subsequent chapters.

There are difficulties for central government in seeking to maintain its influence when services are delivered by complex networks of organisations, some of which fall outside state control (Moseley & James, 2008, p. 117). One perspective is that the range of agencies involved in policy delivery, and the number of non-government actors involved, has led to the 'hollowing out of the state' and a reduction in central power. The role of government is sometimes referred to as 'governance' as it seeks to co-ordinate and steer networks rather than manage in a hierarchical fashion (Bache, 2003, pp. 301–302). A linked but contrasting concept is that of meta-governance. This is sometimes defined as the 'governance of governance' which suggests that central government can maintain more control over local networks than the 'hollow state' phrase suggests (Moseley & James, 2008, pp. 118–119). This concept will be explored further when discussing the Labour governments of 1997 to 2010.

Looking beyond the level of the organisation, the approach of an individual staff member can also have an impact on the services that are received by the homeless person. Studies of the policy process often draw on the model of Lipsky (1980), where the term 'street level bureaucrat' is used to refer to practitioners whose interpretation of laws and policies influence the types of services that are received by service users. Niner (1989, p. 151) found that most of the decisions made by officers to determine whether an applicant was statutorily homeless were not formally controlled or monitored. Alden (2015, pp. 70–74) noted that many homelessness officers described themselves as either 'harsh' or 'soft' decision makers and characterised their colleagues in a similar manner. Personal judgements could often be the key to whether a person was classified as being statutorily homeless, although organisational objectives and the influence of managers could also be important factors. Pressures to interpret the law in a more restrictive manner were strongest in areas where there were fewer housing options, again demonstrating the influence of housing demand.

In discussions of the stakeholders who have affected policy, homeless people themselves have been largely absent, with exceptions arising from some direct action by homeless families in the 1960s (discussed in Chap. 4). Greene (2014, p. 136) notes that there are a range of factors that make it difficult for homeless people to take collective action, namely their mobility, lack of resources, lack of social ties and concerns with meeting basic needs. He suggests that, although such difficulties have sometimes been overcome by homeless people in North America, the method of managing poverty in the United Kingdom has contributed to the lack of collective action (Greene, 2014, p. 316).

Favoured Forms of Prevention

A clear distinction can be made between policies and services that are developed for the households who have become homeless and those that seek to prevent homelessness from occurring. Johnson, Scutella, Tseng, and Wood (2015) urge policy makers to think about entries and exits into homelessness separately and argue that: "Getting the right balance between prevention and reactive services that assist homeless people to exit more rapidly is, however, a significant and ongoing challenge facing policy-makers."

However, other analyses see measures taken for those who are already homeless as part of a broad spectrum of prevention. For example, Jones and Pleace (2010, p. 46) make a distinction between three types of homelessness prevention. Primary prevention activities seek to reduce the risk of homelessness among the entire population, or significant parts of it: the major programme of council housebuilding that took place after World War II can be placed in this category. Secondary prevention focuses on people who are in crisis or at high risk of homelessness. Tertiary prevention methods are targeted on those who have already become homeless and seek to prevent further homelessness. Jones and Pleace (2010, p. 46) argue that measures to 'resettle' homeless people fall into the final category: the Scottish and Welsh governments have specifically recognised the importance of the prevention of repeat homelessness (Pawson & Davidson, 2008, p. 47).

Secondary prevention has been the subject of some academic debate; the logic of targeting prevention efforts on those most at risk of homelessness seems compelling, given the evidence provided by Bramley and Fitzpatrick (2018) that the risk of homelessness is not evenly distributed among the population. Stephens, Fitzpatrick, Marja, Van Steen, and Chzen (2010, p. 269) judge the United Kingdom and Germany to have more sophisticated interventions targeted on homelessness prevention than Hungary, the Netherlands, Portugal or Sweden. However, Shinn, Baumohl, and Hopper (2001, pp. 118–119) argue that efforts to target those at risk of homelessness in the United States have been largely unsuccessful and suggest that there are three fundamental difficulties with such an approach. First, data on the key causal factors need to be constantly modified to keep up with changes over time and between locations. Second, there is a difficulty with informing people of the reasons that they have been targeted. Finally, without the provision of more housing, prevention efforts run the risk of simply changing which people are homeless rather than reducing the overall volume of homelessness. This final point underlay much of the campaigning of Shelter in the late 1960s—as Des Wilson put it succinctly in interview:

> I used to say if you have a party and you invite 30 people and you've only got 10 chairs—whose fault is it? The 20 standing up?

Summary

The five factors discussed above are certainly not the only ones that have affected policy: each post-war time period has had its own unique set of influences, as will be demonstrated in later chapters. However, it is the contention of this book that these factors can substantially explain policy and practice in the area of homelessness in post-war Britain. The factors interact with each other, sometimes in a fairly straightforward manner and sometimes in a more complex one. For example, while primary prevention programmes are consistent with a structural view of homelessness, secondary prevention programmes could focus on structural factors (if a support worker assists someone in rent arrears to claim benefits that have been deliberately poorly advertised) or individual ones (if a support worker assists someone in rent arrears to improve their money management skills). The chapters that follow will map changes to these factors, the relative importance of each of them in different time periods, the complex relationships between them and the manner in which they have affected services.

References

Abel, G., & Wahab, S. (2017). 'Build a friendship with them': The discourse of 'at-risk' as a barrier to relationship building between young people who trade sex and social workers'. *Child and Family Social Work, 22*, 1391–1398.

Alden, S. (2015). On the frontline: The gatekeeper in statutory homelessness services. *Housing Studies, 30*(6), 924–941.

Anderson, I., & Morgan, J. (1997). *Single people's access to housing*. York, UK: Joseph Rowntree Foundation.

Bache, I. (2003). Governing through governance: Education policy control under New Labour. *Political Studies, 51*(2), 300–314.

Balloch, S., & Jones, B. (1990). *Poverty and anti-poverty strategy: The local government response*. London, UK: Association of Metropolitan Authorities.

Bancroft, A., & Wilson, S. (2007). The 'risk gradient' in policy on children of drug and alcohol users: Framing young people as risky. *Health, Risk and Society, 9*(3), 311–322.

Barnett, R., & Lowe, S. (1990). Measuring housing need and the provision of social housing. *Housing Studies, 5*(3), 184–194.

Benjaminsen, L., & Andrade, S. B. (2015). Testing a typology of homelessness across welfare regimes: Shelter use in Denmark and the USA. *Housing Studies, 30*(6), 858–876.

Bevan, M., Kemp, P. A., & Rhodes, D. (1995). *Private landlords and housing benefit*. York, UK: Centre for Housing Policy, University of York.

Biehal, N., Clayden, J., & Byford, S. (2000). *Preventative work with teenagers: Evaluation of an adolescent support team*. York, UK: Joseph Rowntree Foundation.

Bines, W. (1994). *The health of single homeless people*. York, UK: Centre for Housing Policy, University of York.

Bramley, G., & Fitzpatrick, S. (2018). Homelessness in the UK: Who is most at risk? *Housing Studies, 33*(1), 96–116.

Brandon, D., Wells, K., Francis, C., & Ramsay, E. (1980). *The survivors*. London, UK: Routledge and Kegan Paul.

Brown, J. C. (1990). The focus on single mothers. In R. Lister (Ed.), *Charles Murray and the underclass* (pp. 61–65). London, UK: Institute of Economic Affairs Health and Welfare Unit.

Brown, K. (2015). *Vulnerability and young people*. Bristol, UK: Policy Press.
Chartered Institute of Housing. (2018). *Rethinking social housing: Final report*. Coventry, UK: Chartered Institute of Housing.
Cleary, M., Hunt, G. E., Matheson, S., & Walter, G. (2008). Psychosocial treatment for people with co-occurring severe mental illness and substance misuse: Systematic review. *Journal of Advanced Nursing, 65*(2), 238–258.
Darke, J., Conway, J., & Holman, C. (1993). *Homes for our children*. London, UK: National Housing Forum.
De Verteuil, G., May, J., & von Mahs, J. (2009). Complexity not collapse: Recasting the geographies of homelessness in a 'punitive' age. *Progress in Human Geography, 33*, 646–666.
Deacon, N. (1990). Mr Murray's ark. In R. Lister (Ed.), *Charles Murray and the underclass* (pp. 75–80). London, UK: Institute of Economic Affairs Health and Welfare Unit.
Department for Communities and Local Government. (2008). *Statutory homelessness in England: The experience of families and 16–17 year olds* (Homelessness Research Summary Number 7). London, UK: Department for Communities and Local Government.
Department for Communities and Local Government. (2011). *Vision to end rough sleeping: No second night out nationwide*. London, UK: Department of Communities and Local Government.
Department for Communities and Local Government. (2016). *2014-based household projections: England, 2014–2039. Housing statistical release 12 July 2016*. London, UK: Department of Communities and Local Government.
Department of Health. (2002). *Dual diagnosis good practice guide*. London, UK: Department of Health.
Dwyer, P., & Somerville, P. (2011). Introduction: Themed section on multiple exclusion homelessness. *Social Policy and Society, 10*(4), 495–500.
Evans, A. (1999). Rationing device or passport to social housing? The operation of the homelessness legislation in Britain in the 1990s. In S. Hutson & D. Clapham (Eds.), *Homelessness: Public policies and private troubles* (pp. 133–154). London, UK: Cassell.
Evans, A., & Duncan, S. (1988). *Responding to homelessness, local authority policy and practice*. London, UK: Department of the Environment.
Exworthy, M., Berney, L., & Powell, M. (2002). How great expectations in Westminster may be dashed locally': The local implementation of national policy on health inequalities. *Policy and Politics, 30*(1), 79–96.
Fitzpatrick, S., Johnsen, S., & White, M. (2011). Multiple exclusion homelessness in the UK: Key patterns and intersections. *Social Policy and Society, 10*(4), 501–512.

Fitzpatrick, S., Pawson, H., Bramley, G., Wilcox, S., Watts, B., & Wood, J. (2017). *The homelessness monitor: England 2017*. London, UK: Crisis and the Joseph Rowntree Foundation.

Gholam, G. (1993). *Before you go*. London, UK: Centrepoint, Leaving Home Project.

Gray, C. (1994). *Government beyond the centre*. Basingstoke, UK: Macmillan.

Green, D. G. (1998). *Benefit dependency*. London, UK: Institute of Economic Affairs Health and Welfare Unit.

Greene, J. (2014). Managing poverty, managing dissent: Homeless politics and collective action in London. *Policy and Politics, 42*(3), 315–331.

Griggs, S., & Sullivan, H. (2012). Puzzling agency in centre-local relations: Regulatory governance and accounts of change under New Labour. *British Journal of Politics and International Relations, 16*(3), 495–514.

Grimshaw, J. M. (2008). *Family homelessness: Causes, consequences and the policy response in England*. London, UK: The British Library.

Harding, J. (2004). *Making it work—The keys to success for young people living independently*. Bristol, UK: Policy Press.

Harding, J., Irving, A., & Whowell, M. (2011). *Homelessness, pathways to exclusion and opportunities for intervention*. Newcastle, UK: Northumbria University Arts and Social Sciences Press.

Harding, J., & Keenan, P. (1998). The provision of furnished accommodation by local authorities. *Housing Studies, 13*(3), 377–390.

Harding, J., & Kirk, R. (1996). *No light at the end of the tunnel: A study of youth homelessness in areas of industrial decline*. London, UK: Crisis.

Hill, K., & Hirsch, D. (2019). *Family sharing—A minimum income standard for people in their 20s living with parents*. Loughborough, UK: Centre for Research in Social Policy, Loughborough University.

Hill, M., & Hupe, P. (2003). The multi-layer problem in implementation research. *Public Management Review, 5*(4), 471–490.

Holmans, A. (1995). *Housing demand and need in England 1991–2011*. York, UK: York Publishing Services Ltd.

Homeless Link. (2014). *The unhealthy state of homelessness: Health audit results 2014*. London, UK: Homeless Link.

Hutson, S., & Liddiard, M. (1994). *Youth homelessness*. Basingstoke, UK: Macmillan.

Johnsen, S., & Fitzpatrick, S. (2010). Revanchist sanitisation or coercive care? The use of enforcement to combat begging, street drinking and rough sleeping in England. *Urban Studies, 47*(8), 1703–1723.

Johnsen, S., & Teixeira, L. (2012). 'Doing it already?': Stakeholder perceptions of Housing First in the UK. *International Journal of Housing Policy, 12*(2), 183–203.

Johnson, G., & Chamberlain, C. (2008). Homelessness and substance abuse: Which comes first? *Australian Social Work, 61*(4), 342–356.

Johnson, G., Scutella, R., Tseng, Y., & Wood, G. (2015). *Entries and exits from homelessness: A dynamic analysis of the relationship between structural conditions and individual characteristics.* Melbourne, Australia: Australian Housing and Urban Research Institute.

Jones, A., & Pleace, N. (2010). *A review of single homelessness in the UK 2000–2010.* London, UK: Crisis and the University of York.

Jones, C., & Murie, A. (1998). *Reviewing the right to buy.* York, UK: Joseph Rowntree Foundation Findings.

Jones, G. (1995). *Leaving home.* Buckingham, UK: Open University Press.

Jones, G. (1997). Youth homelessness and the 'underclass'. In R. MacDonald (Ed.), *Youth, the 'underclass' and social exclusion* (pp. 96–112). London, UK: Routledge.

Jones, G., & Stephens, J. (1994). *Young people in and out of the housing market* (Housing Research Findings 108). York, UK: Joseph Rowntree Foundation.

Keenan, P., Lowe, S., & Spencer, S. (1999). Housing abandonment in inner cities—The politics of low demand for housing. *Housing Studies, 14*(5), 703–716.

Kelly, J. (2006). Central regulation of English local authorities: An example of meta-governance? *Public Administration, 84*(3), 603–621.

Kemp, P. A., Neale, J., & Robertson, M. (2006). Homelessness among problem drug users: Prevalence, risk factors and trigger events. *Health and Social Care in the Community, 14*(4), 319–328.

Killeen, D. (1988). *Estranged.* Edinburgh, Scotland: Shelter Scottish Campaign for the Homeless.

Kim, M. M., Ford, J. D., Howard, D. L., & Bradford, D. W. (2010). Assessing trauma, substance abuse and mental health in a sample of homeless men. *Health and Social Work, 35*(1), 39–48.

Leach, R., & Percy-Smith, J. (2001). *Local governance in Britain.* London, UK: Palgrave.

Lipsky, M. (1980). *Street-level bureaucracy: Dilemmas of the individual in public services.* New York: Russell Sage Foundation.

MacDonald, R. (1997). Dangerous youth and the dangerous class. In R. MacDonald (Ed.), *Youth, the 'underclass' and social exclusion* (pp. 96–112). London, UK: Routledge.

Macnicol, J. (1987). In pursuit of the underclass. *Journal of Social Policy, 16*(3), 293–318.

Marsland, D. (1996). *Welfare or welfare state?* Basingstoke, UK: Macmillan.

May, J. (2000). Housing histories and homeless careers: A biographical approach. *Housing Studies, 15*(4), 613–638.

McConnell, A. (2018). Rethinking wicked problems as political problems and policy problems. *Policy and Politics, 46*(1), 165–180.

McKee, K., & Philips, D. (2012). Social housing and homelessness policies. In G. Mooney & G. Scott (Eds.), *Social justice and social policy in Scotland* (pp. 223–228). Bristol, UK: Policy Press.

McNaughton, C. (2008). Transitions through homelessness, substance use, and the effects of material marginalisation and psychological trauma. *Drugs: Education, Prevention and Policy, 15*(2), 177–188.

Mishra, R. (1984). *The welfare state in crisis.* Brighton, UK: Wheatsheaf Books.

Moseley, A., & James, O. (2008). Central state steering of local collaboration: Assessing the impact of tools of meta-governance in homelessness services in England. *Public Organization Review, 8*, 117–136.

Murray, C. (1990). The emerging British underclass. In R. Lister (Ed.), *Charles Murray and the underclass* (pp. 23–53). London, UK: Institute of Economic Affairs Health and Welfare Unit.

Neale, J. (2001). Homelessness among drug users: A double jeopardy explored. *International Journal of Drug Policy, 12*, 353–369.

Niner, P. (1989). *Homelessness in nine local authorities: Case studies of policy and practice.* London, UK: Department of the Environment, Her Majesty's Stationery Office.

Parsell, C., & Parsell, M. (2012). Homelessness as a choice. *Housing, Theory and Society, 29*(4), 420–434.

Pawson, H., & Davidson, E. (2008). Radically divergent? Homelessness policy and practice in post-devolution Scotland. *International Journal of Housing Policy, 8*(1), 39–60.

Peters, E. (2012). 'I like to let them have their time.' Hidden homeless First Nation people in the city and their management of household relationships. *Social and Cultural Geography, 13*(4), 321–338.

Philip, K. (2000). Mentoring: Pitfalls and potential for young people? *Youth and Policy, 67*, 1–15.

Pleace, N. (1998). Single homelessness as social exclusion: The unique and the extreme. *Social Policy and Administration, 32*(1), 46–59.

Pleace, N., Fitzpatrick, S., Johnsen, S., Quilgars, D., & Sanderson, D. (2008). *Statutory homelessness in England: The experience of families and 16–17 year olds.* London, UK: Department for Communities and Local Government.

Quilgars, D., Johnsen, S., & Pleace, N. (2008). *Youth homelessness in the UK: A decade of progress?* York, UK: Joseph Rowntree Foundation.

Rassool, G. H. (2006). Understanding dual diagnosis: An overview. In G. H. Rassool (Ed.), *Dual diagnosis nursing* (pp. 3–15). Oxford: Blackwell Publishing.

Raynsford, N. (2016). *Substance not spin: An insider's view of success and failure in government.* Bristol: Policy Press.

Reeve, K. (2013). The morality of the 'immoral': The case of homeless, drug-using street prostitutes. *Deviant Behaviour, 34*(10), 824–840.

Reeve, K., Cole, I., Batty, E., Foden, M., Green, S., & Pattison, B. (2016). *Home. No less will do: Homeless people's access to the private rented sector*. London, UK: Crisis.

Rowe, S., & Wagstaff, T. (2017). *Moving on: Improving access to housing for single homeless people in England*. London, UK: Crisis.

Rubington, E., & Weinberg, M. S. (1995). *The study of social problems* (5th ed.). New York: Oxford University Press.

Sherwood-Johnson, F. (2013). Constructions of 'vulnerability' in comparative perspective: Scottish protection policies and the trouble with 'adults at risk. *Disability and Society, 28*(7), 908–921.

Shinn, M., Baumohl, J., & Hopper, K. (2001). The prevention of homelessness revisited. *Analyses of Social Issues and Public Policy, 1*(1), 95–127.

Somerville, P. (1999). The making and unmaking of homelessness legislation. In S. Hutson & D. Clapham (Eds.), *Homelessness: Public policies and private troubles* (pp. 29–57). London, UK: Cassell.

Somerville, P. (2013). Understanding homelessness. *Housing, Theory and Society, 30*(4), 384–415.

Stephens, M., & Fitzpatrick, S. (2007). Welfare regimes, housing systems and homelessness: How are they linked? *European Journal of Homelessness, 1*, 201–212.

Stephens, M., Fitzpatrick, S., Marja, E., Van Steen, G., & Chzen, Y. (2010). *Study on housing exclusion: Welfare policies, labour market and housing provision*. Edinburgh, Scotland: Heriot-Watt University.

Venn, S. (1985). *Singled out*. London, UK: CHAR (Campaign for Single Homeless People).

Walker, A. (1990). Blaming the victims. In R. Lister (Ed.), *Charles Murray and the underclass* (pp. 66–74). London, UK: Institute of Economic Affairs Health and Welfare Unit.

Watson, S., & Austerberry, H. (1986). *Housing and homelessness: A feminist perspective*. London, UK: Routledge and Kegan Paul.

Wilcox, S., Perry, J., & Williams, P. (2015). *UK housing review: 2015 briefing paper*. Coventry, UK: Chartered Institute of Housing.

Wiles, J. (2011). Reflections on being a recipient of care: Vexing the concept of vulnerability. *Social and Cultural Geography, 12*(6), 573–588.

CHAPTER 3

1945–1961: From Everybody's Problem to Problem Families

Introduction

The starting point for this chapter was an obvious one, but the choice of 1961 as the endpoint may seem a little strange. However, as Chap. 4 will show, it appeared to be a key turning point in the public's perception of homeless people.

To provide the political background to this chapter, the Labour Party won the 1945 general election with a large majority but returned to power in 1950 with a majority of just five. Internal divisions and financial pressures forced Prime Minister Clement Attlee to call a general election in 1951, which was won by the Conservative Party, to begin a period of 13 years in which they formed the government.

The Post-War Housing Crisis and the Housebuilding Response

Campbell (1987, p. 153) notes that housing was the greatest concern of the electorate at the 1945 general election, some way ahead of full employment. When the war with Japan ended, housing need was at an unprecedented level, with one poll suggesting that one third of all Britons were in need of accommodation. Of the nation's stock of 12.5 million houses, nearly three quarters of a million had been destroyed by bombing, were severely damaged or had become uninhabitable (Watson, 2016, p. 48). Only 160,000 homes had been built during the war (Young & Rao, 1997, p. 35) and

J. Harding, *Post-War Homelessness Policy in the UK*,
https://doi.org/10.1007/978-3-030-22117-1_3

much housing was in a poor condition, with nearly half of all households lacking the sole use of a bathroom (Glennester, 2000, p. 60). Fifty thousand people were living in former military camps, shared houses or a succession of local authority properties in 1946 (Crowson, 2013, p. 431).

The birth rate rose in 1945–1948 (Glennester, 2000, p. 60) which added further to housing pressures; many private landlords did not want children staying in their homes, and there were some areas where families with children could not find any accommodation at all. Women being evicted from lodgings because they were pregnant had been identified as a problem in parliament even before the end of the war (Watson, 2016, p. 48).

The government's primary response to the crisis was a programme of housebuilding. Labour's 1945 Manifesto stated that:

> Housing will be one of the greatest and one of the earliest tests of a Government's real determination to put the nation first. Labour's pledge is firm and direct—it will proceed with a housing programme with the maximum practical speed until every family in this island has a good standard of accommodation.

In other areas of social policy, the government was guided by the 1942 Beveridge Report, where the key recommendations were to create a system of social insurance, maintain full employment and provide a National Health Service. As part of a new consensus in favour of state intervention in social policy, both main parties promised to implement the plan at the 1945 general election (Hill, 1993, pp. 20–24), although there is disagreement as to the extent to which the Labour governments of 1945–1951 achieved this (Glennester, 2000, p. 36). However, despite squalor being identified by Beveridge as one of the five giant evils to be overcome, he provided no blueprint for housing, unlike other areas such as social insurance (Glennester, 2000, pp. 29–31). In addition, there was no specific mention of homelessness in the report.

Despite the limited guidance that was available, Housing Minister Aneurin Bevan had a very clear view as to how to meet housing need. He favoured provision of rented housing by local authorities because their activities could be more easily controlled by government and they could take a direct role in providing rented housing for low-income households. Bevan set a high standard for the quality of property to be built (Kemp, 1991, p. 51).

In addition to the building programme, the powers that had been used to requisition property during the war were extended for purposes that included providing residential accommodation for those who were homeless or inadequately housed (HC Deb 04 April 1946 vol 421 cc1509-1510). Bevan announced in parliament that local authorities could continue to requisition unoccupied property where "it is needed for the rehousing of persons rendered homeless by enemy action and if it would otherwise be under-occupied" (HC Deb 29 November 1945 vol 416 cc1738W). Local authorities were instructed to de-requisition properties which were being used for non-residential purposes but to requisition those that were unoccupied and could be used to accommodate people (Foot, 1973, p. 68). Further measures taken by the government included banning the conversion of homes to offices and restoring houses that had been damaged during the war—60,000 were repaired and brought back into use in 1945 (Foot, 1973, p. 68).

Before coming to office, Bevan had promised to build 5 million homes quickly, and some of his colleagues had also made very optimistic predictions (Campbell, 1987, pp. 153–154). Once in government, Labour set itself a more modest target of 240,000 homes per year and built 900,000 by 1951. This represented a considerable achievement in the face of shortages of both labour and materials but fell well short of the target (Burnett, 1986, p. 286). A further half million dwellings were provided through temporary prefabs, conversions and repair of war-damaged properties (Foot, 1973, p. 86).

Labour's record on housing was attacked by the Conservatives who suggested that Bevan (who was also the Health Minister) had been distracted by the creation of the National Health Service and had fallen short of housebuilding targets due to a failure to effectively co-ordinate housing policy. The slower-than-promised speed of housebuilding led to frustration among those who had hoped to see their accommodation needs met quickly. Outbreaks of squatting in the West End of London and in disused army camps were attributed to the slow start to the housebuilding programme (Lowe, 2005, p. 258). Squatters often had the support of local councillors or Communist Party members (Watson, 2016).

The Conservative government that came to power in 1951 set itself a target of providing 300,000 new homes per year and exceeded this target in 1953. Housing output remained exceptionally high through the 1950s as the government continued to seek to make good war time losses and complete ambitious slum clearance programmes (Raynsford, 2016, pp. 54–56). However, the tenure balance of new dwellings began to change as the Conservative Party moved away from the post-war consensus over the value of council housing and instead expressed a preference for owner occupation. In July 1952, Lord Woolton spoke of the need to "apply the principle of a property owning democracy … instead of persisting in the Socialist policy of herding people into heavily subsidised council houses" (quoted in Young & Rao, 1997, p. 62). Housing Minister Harold Macmillan supported this view and lifted restrictions on private building while reducing subsidies to local authorities (Young & Rao, 1997, pp. 62–63). Standards for council housebuilding fell with Bevan's minimum standard of 900 square feet for a three-bedroom council house changed to a maximum in 1951 (Boughton, 2018, p. 106).

Subsidies for general needs housebuilding by local authorities were stopped in 1956 and made available only for slum clearance and the provision of one-bedroom properties for older people. The amount of local authority stock was also affected by the 1955 Housing (Amendment) Act, which set 31 March 1960 as the date by which all requisitioned properties were to be returned to their owners. Between 1955 and 1960, 50,000 properties were released and 75,000 occupiers resettled (HC Deb 04 February 1960 vol 616 cc1232-1233).

It was assumed that the private sector—incentivised through measures such as the 1957 Rent Act (discussed further below)—would meet general needs, leaving local authorities to play only a residual role. However, while local authority building declined, the private rented sector did not revive as hoped. This led the government to re-introduce subsidies to local authorities for general needs housing through the 1961 Housing Act (Kemp, 1991, p. 53).

Despite all the efforts put into housebuilding, and the increase in the housing stock, housing shortages remained severe throughout this period. The difficulties for young people seeking to set up their own home were noted by Harvey (1960, p. 11):

> A young couple making their first home in one room in a relative's house, have no hope of a home of their own from the council until they have a baby (which scores extra points); and they have a better chance the more babies they have—up to a certain limit. Yet there is often no room even for one baby, unless it sleeps on top of a chest-of-drawers or in its parents' bed; and, on its arrival, the husband may be forced to leave and either go into lodgings or back to his own parents.

On a similar theme, concerns were expressed a number of times in Parliament about the risk of eviction faced by council tenants who overcrowded their council properties by allowing married adult children to live with them (see, e.g. *HC Deb 16 November 1954 vol 533 cc205-6*). In England and Wales, it was estimated that one and a half million households were on local authority waiting lists in 1959, of which half a million were judged to be in urgent need (HC Deb 18 June 1959 vol 607 cc657-658).

The 1948 National Assistance Act and Homeless Families

While governments struggled to provide enough general needs housing, further difficulties were experienced when creating a legal framework within which to deal with homelessness. The 1948 National Assistance Act abolished the Poor Law and created a new system for people in need, with many responsibilities passing to local authorities, including responsibilities for homelessness. Section 21 (b) obliged local authorities to provide: "[T]emporary accommodation for persons who are in urgent need thereof, being need arising in circumstances which could not reasonably have been foreseen or in such other circumstances as the authority may in any case determine" (Watchman & Robson, 1989, p. 27). Circular 87/48 which accompanied the 1948 Act emphasised that the duties should not be used to assist the inadequately housed (Evans & Duncan, 1988, p. 5).

Section 24 (2) of the Act further specified that "The local authority liable under this part of this Act to provide temporary accommodation for any person shall be the authority in whose area the person is" (Raynsford, 1986, p. 37).

While the Act represented a major landmark in provision for homeless people, it was to prove inadequate for a number of reasons, discussed in the following sections.

Failure to Anticipate Causes of Homelessness

Although the 1948 Act did not specify which factors could lead to a household facing urgent need, it was clear that the government did not anticipate the numbers who became homeless through evictions. This was evident from Bevan's opening speech in the debate on the second reading of the Bill that was to become the Act:

> There will be some who will not be eligible for unemployment benefit, and there will be persons who will be the subject of sudden affliction, like fires and floods and circumstances of that kind, who will need to have help from some special organisation. (HC Deb 24 November 1947 vol 444 cc1603-716 1604)

Bevan's focus on floods is unsurprising, given that the Bill made its way through the commons late in 1947. Earlier that year, floods in more than 40 areas had left 100,000 properties damaged (Wainwright, 2007) and the government had provided £1 million for flood relief (HC Deb 25 March 1947 vol 435 cc1076).

Although the Government sought to increase security of tenure for some classes of tenant through the Landlord and Tenant (Rent Control) Act 1949, it quickly became clear that the most likely cause of urgent need for households seeking assistance under Section 21(b) of the Act was eviction. The 1950 annual report of the Ministry of Health acknowledged that initial assumptions as to the reason why people would seek emergency accommodation had been flawed (Raynsford, 1986, p. 35). Hansard shows that, in 1950, there were 71 references to eviction in the Commons and Lords, compared to only 42 for homelessness; questions were asked about the evictions of people from service accommodation, tied accommodation and leasehold accommodation. There were no national figures for the number of households evicted, but Mr Shurmer, the Member of Parliament for Birmingham, Sparbrook, reported that there were "hundreds of evictions taking place every month" in his city (HC Deb 06 November 1950 vol 480 cc675).

As Raynsford (1986, p. 36) notes, had temporary accommodation catered mainly for those made homeless by fire or flood, it would have been expected that such households could return to their former home once the damage had been made good. However, for those who were evicted, there was no prospect of returning. In addition, the opportunities to find alternative accommodation were extremely limited.

Although very low by modern day standards, the numbers of people resident in temporary accommodation provided under the National Assistance Act grew from an estimated 5870 in early 1951 (HC Deb 08 February 1951 vol 483 c240W) to approximately 7800 by 1954 (HC Deb 14 December 1954 vol 535 c1561). These numbers were higher than had been anticipated at the time the legislation was passed.

Failure to Locate Responsibility with the Correct Department

The 1948 Act did not specify whether housing or welfare departments should take responsibility for providing (or arranging) temporary accommodation. However, Section 21 (2) indicated that, in exercising its duty to homeless households, the local authority "shall have regard to the welfare of all persons for whom accommodation is provided" (http://www.legislation.gov.uk/ukpga/Geo6/11-12/29/section/21/enacted).

The focus on the welfare of homeless households is also evident when considering the intentions of the Act as a whole. In introducing the debate on the second reading, Bevan announced that, alongside the creation of the National Health Service and new Child Welfare Services, the Act would bring about the abolition of the Poor Law. The former functions of the Poor Law were to be divided so that the National Assistance Board (NAB) was responsible for meeting the financial needs of uninsured persons while needs relating to welfare were to be met by local authorities (HC Deb 24 November 1947 vol 444 cc1603-1604).

Watchman and Robson (1989, p. 28) argue that assuming that responsibility should be given to welfare departments implied that homelessness was an individual failing, to be tackled by measures such as counselling. This fitted with the view that was widely taken of homeless households, as will be demonstrated below. However, at a practical level, it meant that the department providing the temporary accommodation differed from the one that was building the new council houses.

The Lack of Entitlement to Permanent Housing

With no legal entitlement to council housing, homeless households were unlikely to be given priority access to a scarce national resource. Central government had no powers to determine how local authorities allocated their housing and could only have acquired such powers through new legislation.

As a result, the government could only make limited and ineffective efforts to persuade local authorities to allocate permanent accommodation to those who were homeless. The government's Central Housing Advisory Committee recommended in 1945 that homeless families be given priority in the allocation of council houses and that residential qualifications be removed. The response to this exhortation among local authorities appears to have been very limited (Richards, 1981, p. 10).

This point is illustrated further by the response of William Deedes, Parliamentary Secretary to the Ministry of Housing and Local Government, to a question asked in 1955 about the operation of local authority waiting lists:

> My right hon. Friend has no powers beyond the statutory provisions of the various housing Acts ... My right hon. Friend can guide, advise, persuade and even recommend, but he cannot compel. I think that there is always a tendency for us all to believe in local government autonomy and in the independence of the local council until it does not do something which we wish it to do, and then the Minister is asked to intervene decisively. (HC Deb 21 June 1955 vol 542 cc1276)

Even if central government had had the power to significantly influence the allocation of dwellings, it is not clear that this power would have been exercised in favour of homeless households. Bevan in particular appeared to face a quandary with regard to the allocation of council housing. One of his justifications for making local authorities the focus of the building programme was that they would supply housing for those in need, rather than choosing who occupied it on other grounds (Foot, 1973, p. 73). However, households accommodated under the 1948 Act were one of several groups who had a strong claim to council housing. Lowe (2005, pp. 256–257) argues that Labour faced a dilemma as to whether the provision of new housing should focus on industrial workers (to promote labour mobility and economic growth), returning soldiers (to avoid the scorn heaped upon Lloyd George for his failure to provide 'homes fit for heroes') or those in the greatest need (the traditional Labour Party approach).

The issue of meeting the greatest need was further complicated by Bevan's vision of a council house sector that would cater for a wide range of social groups (Kemp, 1991, p. 51). Bevan removed the legal requirement for local authorities only to build housing for the working class (Lowe & Hughes, 1991, p. 179) and, in his first speech to the Commons, expressed a determination that areas of council housing should not become working class ghettos. Instead, property should be built in a range of sizes to suit every income, so avoiding stigma and encouraging a healthy social mix (Campbell, 1987, pp. 163–164). Bevan's difficulty was illustrated when he was asked in the Commons why flats requisitioned by the Ministry of Works, and subsequently offered to Kensington Borough Council, were not used specifically to re-house homeless households. He replied: "As I have already explained on a variety of occasions, London is a great capital City, and there is need for accommodation in London for all types of persons" (HC Deb 17 October 1946 vol 427 cc1043-41044).

Under little pressure from central government, many local authorities continued to apply residential qualifications, to allocate housing according to strict waiting list criteria and to assume that homeless households would make bad tenants (Richards, 1981, p. 16). Given the pressures on accommodation and the widespread perceptions of homeless people (see below), it is not surprising that, as Glastonbury (1971, p. 40) notes: "housing managers were often reluctant to take on unsatisfactory tenants, or give homeless families the degree of priority in relation to other prospective tenants which welfare agencies wanted".

The Assumption of Blame on the Part of Homeless Households

The evidence available in relation to this period strongly suggests that there was an increasingly hostile public view taken of homeless people, linked to intense competition for council housing. Prior to the passing of the 1948 National Assistance Act, it appears that homelessness was a term that was used widely and without connotations of blame. For example, in 1947, Sir David Robertson, the MP for Streatham, claimed that there were 10,000 homeless households living in his constituency and reminded the Commons that his was only one of 30 London boroughs (HC Deb 24 November 1947 vol 444 cc1603-716.) Foot's (1973, p. 62) observation of the post-war situation demonstrates the simple link that was being made between lack of housing and homelessness in this period:

> The housing shortage caused more anguish and frustration than any other of the nation's manifold post-war problems; all over the country the need was desperate and every M.P. and every local councillor was being besieged by the endless queue of the homeless.

However, the creation of specific (albeit limited) protection for homeless households by the 1948 Act, together with the numbers who sought its assistance as a result of eviction, was the trigger for a change to the way that homeless households were discussed. Specifically, an assumption began to be made that these households were 'problem families'.

When tracing the origins of this term, Welshman (2013) notes that, although 'problem families' was used before World War II, developments during the war gave it fresh impetus. One of these developments was the evacuation of children from major cities to rural areas. A report on the evacuation experience (*Our Towns*, published in 1943) suggested that it gave fresh hope to the children of problem families who were "on the edge of pauperism and crime, riddled with mental and physical defects, in and out of Courts for child neglect, a menace to the community..." (quoted in Welshman, 2013, p. 81).

Another relevant wartime development was that groups of pacifists formed themselves into support groups for families who they deemed to need assistance. These Pacifist Service Units developed into a national charity named Family Service Units in 1947 (Welshman, 2013, pp. 85–87). While practical support was provided, the tone of the organisation's discourse and publications was often critical, with phrases such as 'derelict families' used. Suggestions were sometimes made that the organisation should take over the parenting role of the families it was assisting (Welshman, 2013, p. 88).

The Eugenics Society—despite its association with Nazism—was active in the period after World War II, and supported investigations into the extent and characteristics of 'problem families'. In 1947, it formed a Problem Families Committee and persuaded the Medical Officers of Health in six areas (later reduced to five) to conduct investigations into families who placed heavy demands on statutory and voluntary services. The characteristics of these families were listed as "intractable ineducatability", "instability or infirmity of character", "the presentation by the family of multiple social problems" and a "squalid home" (quoted in Welshman, 2013, p. 83). The report on these investigations suggested that there were 379 problem families in the five areas. However, even those behind the report recognised weaknesses in its methodology and leading social policy academic Richard Titmuss, who had initially been eager to focus on the rehabilitation of the families, asked for his name to be removed (Welshman, 2013, pp. 84–85).

The language of the problem family began to be used by the Ministry of Health in the 1950s, with the phrase used in circulars in both 1950 and 1954 and also referred to in other documents (Welshman, 2013, p. 91). An indication that this label was being applied to homeless households was provided when the Minister of Health reported in 1956 that:

> The main burden of work by authorities and their officers under Part 3 of the National Assistance Act, 1948, lies, however, in the rehabilitation of problem families who have lost their homes, in order to help them achieve an acceptable standard preparatory to re-housing. (Quoted in Glastonbury, 1971, p. 42)

The high proportion of families who sought help under the 1948 Act as a result of eviction was an important factor when considering why the 'problem family' term was widely applied in discussions of homelessness. During the debate on the Queen's Speech of 1953, John Parker discussed families who could be found living in public parks during the summer:

> Usually it is found that these families have been evicted for non-payment of rent or unsocial behaviour, sometimes from a municipal housing estate and sometimes from private houses. In most cases the families have an income which would enable them to pay the rent, but they have not done so and eviction has followed. (HC Deb 03 November 1953 vol 520 cc133)

When William Deedes responded to a 1954 Commons question about households that spent more than two years in the temporary accommodation provided under the National Assistance Act, he argued that individualised services needed to be provided to "special problem families" (HC Deb 14 December 1954 vol 535 c1561). The families in London's temporary accommodation tended to be young and about one third were headed by a lone parent (Noble, 2009, p. 122), adding to the perception of them as undeserving. Harvey (1960, p. 27) notes that, in the 1959 Younghusband report into the role of social workers, "homeless and problem families are roughly grouped together, along with other 'social deviants"'.

Raynsford (1986, pp. 40–41) suggests that a distinction was often made between those who were evicted for rent arrears, and so were considered 'undeserving', and those who were evicted for other reasons, who were considered worthy of assistance. The Central Housing Advisory Committee (1955, p. 4) made a further sub-division of tenants who fell into rent arrears, suggesting that there were a deserving group who simply had insufficient income to pay the rent (and might be moved to cheaper accommodation), an underserving group whose income was sufficient to pay the rent but "cannot be induced to pay it with any regularity" and a third group who were "incompetent in managing their affairs".

Table 3.1 Number of mentions of homelessness in Hansard (1945–1960)

Year	*Number*
1945	78
1946	74
1947	55
1948	50
1949	67
1950	42
1951	26
1952	59
1953	39
1954	35
1955	35
1956	34
1957	31
1958	45
1959	31
1960	28

Watson and Austerberry (1986, p. 48) note that homelessness aroused little public or radical concern between World War II and the early 1960s. While it is acknowledged that the number of references to homelessness in Hansard each year is an imperfect measure of public or even political concern, and sometimes includes discussion of situations in other countries, the numbers and trend in Table 3.1 tell a clear story, particularly when compared to the three figure annual totals that were to be the norm in subsequent decades.

So, despite growing numbers of households living in temporary accommodation, they were frequently regarded as undeserving and not of great political concern. This lack of concern was often reflected in the local authority response to them.

The Local Authority Response

While there was no comprehensive review of local authority responses to homelessness in this period, commentators are unanimous in the view that a poor service was provided to most households who were provided with temporary accommodation under the 1948 Act. Schedule 6 of the Act specified that former workhouses were not to be used as temporary accommodation except as transitional provision, but their use was often much longer term in the absence of alternatives (Richards, 1981, p. 14). Lowe (1997, p. 22) argues that the Act abolished the Poor Law "only in name, for many of the practices of social exclusion, stigmatisation and outright punishment were less easily confined to the dustbins of history, none more so than in the treatment of homeless families". Similarly, Raynsford (1986, p. 36) argues that there was a reversion back to the Poor Law when considering how to manage hostels, and Glastonbury (1971, p. 40) suggests that "After a short honeymoon period during which the evicted family was accepted much as the bombed-out families had been, local authorities fell back on Poor Law practice."

Some local authorities sought to deter applications under the National Assistance Act by separating men from women and children in temporary accommodation (Glastonbury, 1971, p. 41), with men sometimes being refused assistance altogether and told to look for lodgings in Salvation Army hostels (Lund, 2016, p. 25). Other deterrent activities included the use of squalid temporary accommodation, consisting of communal dormitories or old caravans (Lund, 2016, p. 215), the employment of authoritarian wardens with experience in the armed services and the threat of having children taken into care (Glastonbury, 1971, p. 41). The majority of local authorities set time limits for the length of stay in temporary accommodation (Glastonbury, 1971, pp. 43–44). In Scotland, most temporary accommodation was provided in former poorhouses or sometimes families were admitted to bed-and-breakfast hotels where they had little privacy and were forced to spend much of the day outside (Watchman & Robson, 1989, p. 28).

Noble (2009, pp. 123–125) provides a detailed account of the manner in which London County Council put into practice the perceived distinction between the deserving and the undeserving when working with homeless people. Its welfare department categorised homeless households either as 'decent' families of wage-earning men who were homeless because of the housing shortage or as 'problem families' loosely defined by having disorderly domestic lives and a poor rent payment history. Problem families tended to stay longer in temporary accommodation because they were deemed unsuitable for permanent housing, but the housing shortage meant that even decent families could stay there for some time (Noble, 2009, p. 123).

Decent families tended to be accommodated in half way houses and rest centres, which offered a higher standard of accommodation, while problem families were placed in large, poor quality welfare homes. The welfare homes were old Poor Law institutions and were characterised by communal eating and sleeping (segregated by age and sex). They had already been overcrowded before homeless people began to be admitted. By the early 1950s, only women and children were being permitted to stay (Noble, 2009, p. 124).

An example of the hostility towards those who were considered problem families was provided by London County Council's Welfare Committee on Homeless Families, which expressed a desire to: "consider not only their present limited task of the temporary accommodation of a comparatively small section of problem families, but also what contribution they can make … towards the removal of this blot on the general community" (Report by the Chief Officer of the Welfare Department on Problem Families, June 30th 1950, quoted in Noble, 2009, p. 126).

In 1950–1951, the Welfare Department of London County Council began urging the Children's Department to take the children of families in welfare homes into care, ostensibly to encourage the parents to become independent in financial and housing terms, when their children could be returned to a more stable environment. In reality, the motivation was to facilitate the eviction of the mothers, so relieving the pressure on the accommodation. Resistance from the Children's Department meant that mothers began to be evicted with their children and provided with alternative accommodation in Newington Lodge, the worst quality accommodation of all, which residents were not allowed to occupy between nine o'clock and five o'clock. The outcome was often that mothers placed their children into care because they had nowhere to take them during the day, much to the anger of the Children's Department (Noble, 2009, pp. 133–135).

There were undoubtedly practical considerations that made it difficult for local authorities to provide a good service to homeless households. Local government was seeking to cope with huge change in the immediate post-war period, as it lost control of most elements of health services (while retaining its role in community and environmental health), but saw its role expand in housing, planning, education, environmental services, social services and leisure services (Leach & Percy-Smith, 2001, pp. 55–56). In addition, the legal responsibilities of authorities under the 1948 Act were not clearly defined (Lowe, 1997, p. 23) with no guidance even as to how to distinguish urgent from non-urgent need (Watchman & Robson, 1989, p. 29).

Welfare departments did not have sufficient or suitable temporary accommodation available to meet the needs of homeless households; local authorities had no money in their budgets for temporary accommodation (Lowe, 1997, p. 23). They were given powers to requisition large unoccupied houses and make adaptations, with reasonable costs being recoverable from the government (HC Deb 26 May 1949 vol 465 cc1435). In addition, they could use compulsory purchase powers, where appropriate, to provide accommodation for homeless households (HC Deb 29 July 1952 vol 504 cc113-4W).

However, Bevan acknowledged that it would take time to provide the temporary accommodation that was required by the Act and financial factors meant that building of new accommodation was even slower than had been expected. As a result, local authorities were often forced to use premises that had been available under the Poor Law, which were a sex-segregated form of provision and not easily converted into family units. Many of the units had to serve multiple purposes and sought to avoid friction by placing restrictions on both homeless households and the older people who they shared the premises with (Glastonbury, 1971, pp. 40–41).

In London, Halfway Houses were requisitioned by the Ministry of Health then transferred to the management of London County Council. The Ministry of Health set the rates charged. Halfway Houses could also be requisitioned by individual boroughs (Noble, 2009, p. 171). However, these measures could not tackle the shortage of move on accommodation: in 1956, London Council reduced the number of properties available to households housed by the Welfare Department from 450 to 50 per year in order to accelerate its slum clearance programme. The Welfare Department responded by further tightening its admissions policy and making conditions even more unpleasant (Noble, 2009, p. 134).

So, there were undoubtedly a number of reasons for local authorities tending to provide such a poor service to homeless households. However, the importance of the perception that some or all were 'problem families' should not be under-estimated.

The Narrow Focus of Central Government Action

Watchman and Robson (1989, pp. 27–28) write of the 1948 National Assistance Act:

> The provision, although well intentioned, was to falter partly because it was an inadequate response to the problem of homelessness and partly because of the misplaced belief that the solution to the housing problem was simply a question of building sufficient houses to meet general housing needs.

Indeed, government attempts to prevent homelessness were heavily focused on the provision of new dwellings, with limited energies devoted to initiatives that might relieve homelessness in the shorter term. The Labour government launched a 'share your house' appeal which was ridiculed by the press but appeared to have some impact (Foot, 1973, pp. 68–69). However, the limits to government support were clear from Bevan's answer to a parliamentary question suggesting that the government should provide bedding to those who took other households into their home:

> People who are invited to use spare rooms in an occupied house will ordinarily provide their own sheets and blankets unless the householder prefers to do so. The incoming lodgers will be in the same position for getting sheets and blankets as other members of the community similarly situated, and I do not think there is any need to ask for additions. (HC Deb 14 December 1945 vol 417 c883W)

Similarly, the Chancellor of the Exchequer, Hugh Dalton, refused to offer any encouragement to older people to take in homeless households in the form of a disregard of rent in the means test for the old age pension (HC Deb 28 March 1946 vol 421 c576).

Secondary prevention initiatives, focused on those who might become homeless in the future, were little discussed until 1959, when the Ministers of Health and Housing issued Circular 17/59. This urged local authorities to identify situations where a family was at risk of eviction and breaking up and to provide, or call in, services to prevent the eviction (HC Deb 16 December 1959 vol 615 cc1611-1618).

Issuing a circular advocating good practice was typical of the limited manner in which governments sought to influence local authorities in this period, despite having powers to take more forceful action. Section 36 (1) of the 1948 National Assistance Act gave the Secretary of State powers, where they believed that a local authority had failed to discharge its duties, to declare them in default, order them to take appropriate action or even take over their duties and provide services directly (Bailey &

Ruddock, 1972, pp. 124–125). In addition, Section 25 (1) of the Act gave powers to the NAB to require local authorities to provide temporary accommodation in accordance with their duties (Bailey & Ruddock, 1972, p. 124).

However, despite these powers being available, both Bevan and subsequent Conservative Ministers showed great reluctance to interfere in the manner in which authorities interpreted their responsibilities under the 1948 Act. In 1948, Bevan said that he 'deprecated' the separation of families in temporary accommodation, but that he had issued no direction on the matter (Glastonbury, 1971, p. 42). When replying to questions in the Commons about provision for households who had been evicted, he was non-committal saying that this was "a matter for consideration by the local authorities" (HC Deb 24 April 1950 vol 474 c71W).

Similarly, when Bevan's successor as Housing Minister, Harold Macmillan, was asked whether he would force local authorities to provide more temporary accommodation for "unfortunate people who are evicted", he replied only that he would do everything within his power to avoid hardship (HC Deb 28 October 1952 vol 505 c1709). The Minister of Health Harry Crookshank also took a cautious approach, as he demonstrated when asked a question about homeless households being moved to a hostel where men were not allowed to visit. Mr Crookshank replied only that that he was "asking the county council to reconsider the rule I understand they have made about visiting" (HC Deb 01 April 1952 vol 498 cc1411)

Government circulars and other documents were the main means by which attempts were made to influence local authority practice. When interpretations of the type of circumstances that should be considered to be 'unforeseen' proved problematic, circulars were issued, suggesting that the distinction that was being made between foreseeable and unforeseeable homeless was artificial. However, these circulars were widely ignored (Watchman & Robson, 1989, pp. 29–30). Further circulars encouraged housing departments to work with welfare departments in the re-housing of homeless families and the Minister of Health's annual report of 1958 was critical of the creation of time limits for temporary accommodation, but did no more than encourage change (Glastonbury, 1971, pp. 42–43).

In some cases, the government was reluctant even to issue advice. For example, in 1950 four local authority associations recommended that housing and welfare departments find ways of working together to avoid splitting up homeless families (HC Deb 23 February 1954 vol 524 cc18W). However, in 1954, the government declined to issue a circular to this effect, despite evidence that families continued to be separated in temporary accommodation (HC Deb 25 October 1954 vol 531 c240W). The recommendation of 1950 was finally advocated in a circular in 1959 (Richards, 1981, p. 17).

Despite many examples of hostile responses to homeless families (see, e.g. Watchman & Robson, 1989, pp. 28–32), there was no attempt made to gain an overview of local authority practice. In 1958 Minister of Housing and Local Government Henry Brooke refused to set up a departmental commission to consider accommodation for homeless families (HC Deb 11 February 1958 vol 582 cc187-8), In the same year, Harold Macmillan (now the Prime Minister) refused to set up a Departmental committee on this issue, saying:

> I have come to the conclusion that what is needed is an effort to improve existing arrangements rather than an inquiry by an inter-departmental committee ... There is the problem of people who are very difficult to look after in one way or another. I am informed and believe that still to be the case, but another Committee would not help us. (HC Deb 11 March 1958 vol 584 cc234-5)

So local authority practice went almost entirely unchallenged from the centre in this period, without even a parliamentary inquiry into the manner in which they responded to homelessness. Homeless households had no legal remedy to challenge local authorities through the courts—instead they had to present their case to the Secretary of State, who would then decide whether to take action (Bailey & Ruddock, 1972, pp. 124–125). With voluntary organisations concentrating on providing direct services to homeless people rather than campaigning, there was no realistic legal remedy available to homeless households who felt badly treated. Local authority powers to exercise their duties as they wished were largely unfettered.

Reception Centres for Those "Without a Settled Way of Living"

Local authorities had little involvement in the housing of single homeless people during this period, either through general needs housing or through the obligations created by the 1948 National Assistance Act. Council housing built in the inter-war years had consisted very largely of two- and three-bedroom family homes. Although post-war schemes began to provide some housing for single people, the large majority of the stock was for larger households (Boughton, 2018, p. 102). Section 21 of the 1948 Act did not specifically state that it was only families with children who should be provided with temporary accommodation, but this interpretation seems to have been universally applied (Lund, 2016, p. 214).

So, a separate form of provision was needed for visibly homeless single people (almost entirely men). In seeking to avoid the workhouse, the forms of accommodation to which this group had historically looked were common lodging houses, regulated by the 1875 Public Health Act (Stewart, 1975, p. 34), and the typically austere accommodation provided by organisations such as the Salvation Army (May, Cloke, & Johnsen, 2006, p. 713). In 1945, 68% of voluntary organisations projects providing accommodation for single homeless men were run by the Salvation Army, the YMCA or English Churches Housing Group (May et al., 2006, p. 717).

A 1946 government circular discussed the creation of reception and resettlement centres where 'rootless' men would be provided with accommodation, 'casework' and encouragement to develop work habits (Lund, 2016, p. 214). These ideas were embodied in Section 17(1) of the 1948 National Assistance Act, which placed a duty on the NAB "to make provision whereby persons without a settled way of living may be influenced to lead more settled lives" and to "provide and maintain centres to be known as reception centres for the temporary board and lodging of such persons" (NAB, 1952, p. 5). The phrase "without a settled way of living" sought to reduce the stigma of previous hostile language (Noble, 2009. p. 137). Bevan similarly avoided the harsh language of previous generations, while still making clear that personal failings were the reason for the situation of single homeless people, in his opening speech in the second reading debate on the National Assistance Bill:

> The Elizabethan Poor Law punished the homeless vagrant in the most savage manner .... We are a long way from that now, but we hope to take a step further still. Last year I sent a circular to the Poor Law authorities advising them that it is not the duty of the Poor Law authority now merely to pass the tramp on from one place to another, but to give him opportunities of rehabilitation towards a settled life. This system will be continued in the future on a larger scale. It will be the responsibility of the National Assistance Board to provide centres for training, education and reconditioning, and to make available to the applicants all the resources of the employment exchange. (HC Deb 24 November 1947 vol 444 cc1607)

However, the Act itself included clear echoes of the punitive approach of previous eras, with Section 18 stating that "people who persistently resort to reception centres when capable of maintaining themselves must do suitable work whilst there, or otherwise be liable to imprisonment" (Watson & Austerberry, 1986, p. 52).

Concerns about single homeless people choosing idleness were expressed in a Manchester Guardian article in 1950, under the headline, "Artful dodgers of the welfare state". This article complained that 'tramps' could access accommodation simply by arriving at a Reception Centre and feigning a willingness to look for work (Crisis, 2017, p. 14). There was a similarly critical tone to the NAB's (1952, p. 5) description of the people who used the Reception Centres in the early years:

> The nearest one can get to a comprehensive description of people who use reception centres, apart from the few real tramps, is to say that they belong to the fringes—the more disreputable or weaker or more irresponsible fringes—of the not inconsiderable sections of the community which has no home ties.

The same publication noted disappointments in seeking to persuade the users of Reception Centres to take up work but commented that:

> The attempt to persuade and help casuals to settle down and play a normal part in the community is worth pursuing with vigour, though it must be combined with the enforcement of a strict discipline, and other measures such as prosecution, to keep abuses in check. (NAB, 1952, p. 8)

A further example of the manner in which NAB reports of the time reinforced the view that users of Reception Centres were to blame for their own situation is provided by a discussion in its 1949 Annual Report of the reasons for homelessness. It reported that, when centre users were asked 'why they had abandoned a settled life', disagreements with their wife or their wife's parents were reported in 238 cases and disagreements with parents or step-parents in 54, while 59 said that they were orphans or had to leave a brother's or sister's home because there was no room for them. Fifty-three reported that they had been forced to leave home because of drunkenness or other misbehaviour, 122 said that they had had to leave because of incontinence or some other disability, 73 reported being unsettled by war service and "there were 114 Irishmen who had come to this country at one time or another to seek work". However, it is significant that all of these factors were listed before the report noted that 503 Reception Centre users said that they lived an unsettled life because they had been unable to find any accommodation (NAB, 1949, p. 3).

In practical terms, it was not possible in 1948 to build new buildings, employ new staff or set up new structures, so the old casual wards of the workhouse were used as Reception Centres and existing staff often continued to be employed. It was acknowledged that many Reception Centres were unsuitable to provide anything other than overnight accommodation, despite the legal requirement to undertake resettlement work (NAB, 1966, pp. 263–264). The NAB (1952, p. 15) noted concerns at the physical quality of some centres but argued that restraints on capital expenditure meant that no changes could be made. The largest centre was in Camberwell, London: an old workhouse with a particularly grim appearance, which could house approximately 600 men (Noble, 2009, pp. 138–139).

Numbers of Reception Centres and users fell steadily with time. Many of the casual wards had been little used in the last days of the Poor Law so, of the 290 in England and Wales, only 134 became Reception Centres, with the number falling to 91 by 1952. Similarly, in Scotland, 81 establishments for casual users in 1948 were reduced to 42 in 1952 (NAB, 1966, pp. 263–264). Censuses of the Reception Centres in 1950, 1955 and 1960 showed a steady fall in the number of users, with the very large majority continuing to be men (NAB, 1966, p. 265).

It appears that this was a period in which the distinctive qualities of homelessness among young adults began to be acknowledged: by 1959, the NAB was supporting three 'Re-establishment Centres' run by voluntary organisations for young people (NAB Annual Report, 1959, p. 30). However, a group for who no provision at all was made was single homeless people who were not judged to be 'unsettled' and who were refused assistance on these grounds. For this group, lodging houses and charitable organisations were the only options (Watson & Austerberry, 1986, pp. 51–52). Charitable provision remained haphazard and rudimentary in many cases: for example, Reverend Bertram E Peake became concerned at the number of ex-prisoners who asked him for money and so announced both in Sunday services and at his pitch at Speaker's Corner that offenders could find accommodation in the gallery of the church (Wallich-Clifford, 1962).

Summary

Apart from a brief period following the end of the war, in which homelessness was regarded as a problem affecting much of the population, the late 1940s and 1950s were characterised by widespread assumptions that homeless people were deviant and that their problems were of their own making. This assumption was applied to both those with dependent children and single homeless people. It was a key reason—together with numerous practical difficulties in providing services—that both groups received harsh treatment, albeit through quite different systems.

Hostility was linked to the desirability of council housing in an era where housing shortages were severe and living in with family in overcrowded conditions was a common experience. Governments were unwilling to intervene in the face of harsh local authority treatment of families who were homeless, except to attempt persuasion through circulars, which often produced very little response. Instead, the focus of government policy was almost entirely on the primary prevention method of building more houses—it was to take a series of events to change the policy focus towards those who had become homeless, as will be demonstrated in the next chapter.

References

Bailey, R., & Ruddock, J. (1972). *The grief report*. London, UK: Shelter.

Boughton, J. (2018). *Municipal dreams: The rise and fall of council housing*. London, UK: Verso Books.

Burnett, J. (1986). *A social history of housing 1815–1985* (2nd ed.). London, UK: Routledge.

Campbell, J. (1987). *Nye Bevan: A biography*. London, UK: Hodder and Stoughton Limited.

Central Housing Advisory Committee. (1955). *Unsatisfactory tenants, sixth report of the housing management sub-committee*. London, UK: Her Majesty's Stationery Office.

Crisis. (2017). *Not yet home: A history of Britain's attempts to tackle homelessness*. London, UK: Crisis.

Crowson, N. J. (2013). Revisiting the 1977 Housing (Homeless Persons) Act: Westminster, Whitehall and the homeless lobby. *Twentieth Century British History, 24*(3), 424–447.

Evans, A., & Duncan, S. (1988). *Responding to homelessness, local authority policy and practice*. London, UK: Department of the Environment, Her Majesty's Stationery Office.

Foot, M. (1973). *Aneurin Bevan: A biography, volume 2 1945–1960.* New York: Atheneum.
Glastonbury, B. (1971). *Homeless near a thousand homes.* London, UK: George Allen and Unwin.
Glennester, H. (2000). *British Social Policy since 1945* (2nd ed.). Oxford, UK: Blackwell Publishers Ltd.
Harvey, A. (1960). *Casualties of the Welfare State.* London, UK: Fabian Society.
Hill, M. (1993). *The Welfare State in Britain.* Aldershot, UK: Edward Elgar Publishing Limited.
Kemp, P. (1991). From solution to problem? In S. Lowe & D. Hughes (Eds.), *A new century of social housing* (pp. 44–58). Leicester, UK: Leicester University Press.
Leach, R., & Percy-Smith, J. (2001). *Local governance in Britain.* London, UK: Palgrave.
Lowe, R. (2005). *The Welfare State in Britain since 1945.* Basingstoke, UK: Palgrave Macmillan.
Lowe, S. (1997). Homelessness and the law. In R. Burrows, N. Pleace, & D. Quilgars (Eds.), *Homelessness and social policy* (pp. 19–34). London, UK: Routledge.
Lowe, S., & Hughes, D. (1991). Retrospect and prospect. In S. Lowe & D. Hughes (Eds.), *A new century of social housing* (pp. 175–190). Leicester, UK: Leicester University Press.
Lund, B. (2016). *Housing politics in the United Kingdom.* Bristol, UK: Policy Press.
May, J., Cloke, P., & Johnsen, S. (2006). Shelter at the margins: New Labour and the changing state of emergency accommodation for single homeless people in Britain. *Policy and Politics, 34*(4), 11–29.
National Assistance Board. (1949). *Report of the National Assistance Board for the year ended 31st December 1949.* London, UK: Her Majesty's Stationery Office.
National Assistance Board. (1952). *Reception Centres for people without a settled way of living.* London, UK: Her Majesty's Stationery Office.
National Assistance Board. (1959). *Report of the National Assistance Board for the year ended 31st December 1959.* London, UK: Her Majesty's Stationery Office.
National Assistance Board. (1966). *Homeless single persons.* London, UK: Her Majesty's Stationery Office.
Noble, V. A. (2009). *Inside the Welfare State: Foundations of policy and practice in Post-War Britain.* London, UK: Routledge.
Raynsford, N. (1986). The 1977 Housing (Homeless) Persons Act. In N. Deakin (Ed.), *Policy change in government* (pp. 33–62). London, UK: Royal Institute of Public Administration.
Raynsford, N. (2016). *Substance not spin: An insider's view of success and failure in government.* Bristol, UK: Policy Press.

Richards, J. (1981). The Housing (Homeless Persons) Act 1977: A study in policy making. *School of Advanced Urban Studies, Working Paper 22*, University of Bristol, Bristol, UK.

Stewart, J. (1975). *Of no fixed abode*. Manchester, UK: Manchester University Press.

Wainwright, M. (2007, July 25). The great floods of 1947. *The Guardian*. Retrieved from https://www.theguardian.com/world/2007/jul/25/weather.flooding1

Wallich-Clifford, A. (1962). *One man's answer ...: A survey of the work for homeless offenders undertaken at the Golborne Rehabilitation Centre 1957–1962*. Published by Anton Wallich-Clifford and available from the British Library archive.

Watchman, P. Q., & Robson, P. (1989). *Homelessness and the law in Britain*. Glasgow, Scotland: The Planning Exchange.

Watson, D. (2016). *Squatting in Britain 1945–1955: Housing, politics, and direct action*. Talgarth, Wales: Merlin Press Ltd.

Watson, S., & Austerberry, H. (1986). *Housing and homelessness: A Feminist perspective*. London, UK: Routledge and Kegan Paul.

Welshman, J. (2013). *Underclass*. London, UK: Bloomsbury Publishing plc.

Young, K., & Rao, N. (1997). *Local government since 1945*. Oxford, UK: Blackwell Publishing.

CHAPTER 4

1961–1979: The Long Road to Change

Introduction

The period from 1961 to the passing and implementation of the 1977 Housing (Homeless Persons) Act is one that saw a remarkable turnaround in the treatment of homeless households with dependent children. However, the process of change was a long drawn out and complex one, and, in order to chart it, the structure of this chapter is also complex. It begins by discussing the factors that appeared to bring about more sympathetic attitudes to homelessness in the 1960s, before highlighting the limited impact of these changes on policy and practice and suggesting possible reasons for this. It then considers the factors in the 1970s that made the case for change stronger, describes the long process which eventually brought about the 1977 Housing (Homeless Persons) Act and suggests reasons why there were so many changes of direction along the way. Finally, it discusses the treatment of single homeless people in this period, who were largely excluded from the main homeless duty under the 1977 legislation.

Changes in political control are relevant to an understanding of this period. Labour became the largest single party at the 1964 general election, although it fell short of an overall majority. However, in 1966, it achieved a comfortable majority. In 1970, the Conservatives unexpectedly returned to power, but Labour formed the government after the February 1974 general election, despite winning only 301 seats to the Conservatives

J. Harding, *Post-War Homelessness Policy in the UK*,
https://doi.org/10.1007/978-3-030-22117-1_4

297. Labour called a further general election in October 1974, improving its position by winning 319 seats, but still falling short of an overall majority—a factor that is important when considering the passage of the 1977 Housing (Homeless Persons) Act.

Factors Leading to a Change in Attitudes to Homeless Families

In 1962, hundreds of homeless people took part in a torch-lit parade, led by two Bishops, on one of the coldest nights of the year, in order to raise awareness of their situation (HC Deb 19 April 1962 vol 658 cc786; HC Deb 02 February 1962 vol 652 cc1506). Despite the difficulties inherent in seeking to measure public opinion, this event appeared to be reflective of growing public sympathy and a raised profile for homeless people in the 1960s, for which four key causes can be identified.

The Delayed Impact of the 1957 Rent Act

Although discussion of this Act might seem to properly belong in the previous chapter, it is considered here because its full impact was felt in the early 1960s. It was an attempt by the Conservative government to attract private investment into the rented housing sector. The key measure was to deregulate rents on unfurnished private rented properties; but in most cases, a higher rent could only be charged once the existing tenant moved out (Kemp, 1997, pp. 111–113). The incentive for landlords to find ways to evict existing tenants and let to new ones (who could be charged decontrolled rents) was obvious. However, various forms of transitional protection meant that the full impact of the Act was not felt until August 1961 (Montgomery, 1959, pp. 59–60).

In the late 1950s and early 1960s, stories began to emerge of landlords intimidating and evicting tenants, sometimes making them homeless, so that they could charge a decontrolled rent (Kemp, 1997, p. 114). However, it was the ending of transitional protection arrangements that heightened these concerns. Local authorities had powers to use compulsory purchase orders where exorbitant rents were being charged (HC Deb 13 November 1962 vol 667 cc21-2W), but these were acknowledged to be too slow to use to assist a household that was about to be evicted (HC Deb 30 July 1962 vol 664 cc320).

Somerville (1994, p. 164) suggests that attitudes to homeless households changed as it became obvious that some of those evicted were part of the 'mainstream'. Labour began to champion the case of homeless households, specifically blaming the 1957 Act. For example, Michael Stewart, the MP for Fulham, argued that the majority of homeless households were coming from furnished accommodation and explained this factor as follows:

> [T]he owner of furnished accommodation at present can be limited in what he charges by the Rent Tribunal. But, under the Rent Act, if he turns the tenant out of his furnished room and then lets it unfurnished, it becomes a new, uncontrolled tenancy and there is no tribunal or form of inquiry which can stop him from getting as much as the most eager and the most wealthy prospective tenant will afford. That is why people are being turned out of furnished accommodation. (HC Deb 06 November 1961 vol 648 cc641)

Joyce Butler, the MP for Wood Green, presented to Parliament an analysis of the 60 homelessness cases being considered by Tottenham Borough Council in December 1961, arguing that 16 of the households were homeless because of the Rent Act, in contrast to only four who were homeless because of rent arrears and two because of nuisance or annoyance (*HC Deb 27 November 1961 vol 650 cc199-200*). In the House of Lords, Lord Lathan linked the 1957 Rent Act not only to an increase in homeless but also to a change in public opinion:

> [T]he public conscience has recently been disturbed by the spectacle of the homeless—and well it might! This, of course, is one of the bitter fruits of the Tory Rent Act, which set the landlords free to oppress, and the people free to be evicted and to search for the houses which are not there. (HL Deb 07 February 1962 vol 237 cc179)

Greater political concern about homelessness was also evident in some of the language employed: Fenner Brockway, the MP for Eton and Slough, described homelessness as an 'epidemic' (HC Deb 12 December 1961 vol 651 cc201), while Michael Cliffe, the MP for Shoreditch and Finsbury, argued that it was "the most tragic problem with which we have to deal" (HC Deb 30 July 1962 vol 664 cc287). The Conservatives were forced onto the defensive, with the Minister for Housing and Local Government and Welsh Affairs, Dr Hill, regularly seeking to minimise the link between homelessness and the 1957 Act or to argue that local authorities had sufficient resources to meet any need that had arisen (e.g. HC Deb 24 January 1961 vol 633 cc18-9). He refused a suggestion that data be collected from local authorities about the number of people approaching them as a result of the 1957 Act on the grounds that "it would simply add to their burden of work which is already heavy enough" (HC Deb 12 December 1961 vol 651 cc201).

Although not mentioning homelessness specifically, Labour's 1964 general election manifesto emphasised the political advantage that it had gained from the Act:

> Under the Tories, the relentless pressure of decontrolled rents, Rachmanism [*see below*], high interest rates and soaring land prices have pushed housing and flats beyond the reach of many ordinary families and have condemned yet another generation to squalid and over-crowded housing.

Even the Conservatives seemed to implicitly acknowledge the negative perceptions of the Act—their 1964 manifesto promised "to take no further steps to remove rent control' and to provide additional safeguards for tenants "if shown to be necessary". After the 1964 election, Labour made good a key promise of its manifesto by reintroducing rent control through the 1965 Rent Act (Kemp, 1997, pp. 114–115).

Press Coverage

Homeless people began to receive some sympathetic press coverage in the 1960s. A number of reports were cited in the Commons, discussing the extent of homelessness, the circumstances of homeless people and the impact of the 1957 Rent Act. For example, in November 1961, the Birmingham Evening Despatch reported on an increase in homelessness in the city and attributed this to rising rents as a result of the Act. The same report noted that families were separated within the city's hostels (HC Deb 15 November 1961 vol 649 cc509-510).

Conditions in temporary accommodation became a regular feature of Commons discussion. One such discussion arose in 1961 from local and national press stories about Highgrove in Ruislip, West London. This establishment was used as temporary accommodation for homeless households by Middlesex County Council and was dubbed "Heartbreak House" by the press. A visit by the local Conservative MP Petre Crowder revealed one couple living in a room with nine children. Mr Crowder reported to the Commons that "children contracted dysentery because the passages were being used as lavatories, and nothing else" (HC Deb 18 May 1961 vol 640 cc1686). The outcry in the press and among politicians led to some level of improvement, with the number of households reduced from 20 to 15 and a resident warden employed (HC Deb 18 May 1961 vol 640 cc1683-1687).

In October 1961, the *Times* ran a sympathetic story about homelessness, arguing that most of the families involved were "ordinary decent people" on low incomes and endured conditions in temporary accommodation "that should have gone out with Oliver Twist" (quoted in Noble, 2009, p. 136). This view was reinforced by a report on homelessness in London, produced in 1962, which noted that noted that 50% of families living in welfare accommodation did not have access to a bathroom, but, in many cases, the situation still represented an improvement on their previous housing conditions (*HC Deb 28 November 1962 vol 668 cc512-513*).

Perceptions of homeless people may also have been indirectly changed by the Profumo scandal. Notorious West London private landlord Perec Rachman—whose attempts to remove existing tenants after the 1957 Rent Act had been particularly brutal—became posthumously embroiled in the scandal despite only having a tenuous link through the sex workers involved. However, this was sufficient for the press to carry stories about his harassment and eviction of tenants (Kemp, 1997, p. 114). Kemp (1997, p. 114) notes that: "The addition of slum landlordism to the already potent media cocktail of sex and national security allowed the press to inject new life into the Profumo affair."

So, the press narrative as to why people became homeless, and about the conditions that they endured when they did, appeared to be a sympathetic one in the early 1960s. While it is not possible to identify specific impacts on public opinion, the citing of such stories in the Commons suggests that the issue was rising on the political agenda.

Cathy Come Home

The showing of the drama-documentary *Cathy Come Home* in 1966 is seen as a hugely influential point in the history of homelessness, but it should be noted that its coming to air on the BBC was itself a product of changing social moods. Sandbrook (2006, pp. 566–567) argues that the popular image of the 1960s as being self-indulgent did not tell the whole story. Academics, politicians and commentators began to pay attention to issues of poverty and deprivation, which many had assumed to have been 'solved' by a period of full employment. The title of Geoffrey Moorhouse's book *The Other England* exemplified a growing concern for those who had been 'left behind', for example, poor people, older people and those with disabilities.

This concern was matched at an academic level by what is often referred to as the 're-discovery' of poverty in the mid-1960s. The report of Brian Abel-Smith and Peter Townsend, *The Poor and the Poorest*, was published just before Christmas in 1965 and demonstrated that the number of people living in poverty was far greater than had previously been assumed (Glennester, 2000, pp. 106–107). As Timmins (1995, quoted in Sandbrook, 2006, p. 567) notes: "the poor family, and the poor working family, were about to be re-born as a political issue".

It was in this environment that the BBC launched a series called The Wednesday Play, with the aim of presenting the difficulties experienced by ordinary people. *Cathy Come Home* was one such play. The writer, Jeremy Sandford, was curious when his neighbours disappeared without explanation and followed their story, which provided much of his material (Crisis, 2017, p. 22).

Cathy Come Home told the story of a young couple, Cathy and Reg, whose lives declined rapidly after an accident meant that Reg could no longer work: the family were forced into a series of insecure and unsatisfactory housing situations and then had no choice but to separate when placed in local authority temporary accommodation. In the final scene, Cathy's children were taken from her by unsympathetic social workers due to her homelessness (Sandbrook, 2006, pp. 563–564). Twelve million people watched the play on 16 November 1966 (Crisis, 2017, p. 21).

The BBC switchboard was jammed with calls after the showing of the play and the *Times* called it a "searing indictment of housing conditions" (Lund, 2016, p. 215). There were private showings for MPs and the Housing Minister requested to watch the programme a week after it was broadcast (Crisis, 2017, pp. 22–26).

In addition to changes to public and political opinion, the play brought some immediate benefits for homeless households. Children of homeless families began to be taken into care only if their safety was at risk (Crisis, 2017, p. 26). Some people in Birmingham were able to spot that a number of scenes had been filmed in the city, and, despite initial criticisms of the play, the Chair of the Housing Committee later announced that the segregation of families in temporary accommodation would be ended in the city within two years; this target was achieved ahead of schedule. In addition, the programme of housebuilding and slum clearance in the city accelerated (Chinn, 2015).

The Changing Role of the Voluntary Sector

Fundamental changes to the voluntary sector during this period added to the pressure for change. Hilton, McKay, Crowson, and Mouhot (2013, p. 112) argue that lobbying of parliament was in an embryonic form in the first two decades after 1945 and voluntary organisations had little involvement in such activities, concentrating instead on providing accommodation that was often very similar in character to Reception Centres. Jones and Pleace (2010, p. 56) argue that: "The charitably and church run night shelters were only intended to ensure people did not sleep on the street and were fed."

However, from the 1950s and particularly in the 1960s, some organisations—such as the Golborne Society, the Simon Community and the Cyrenians—began to question the basis of their provision and to seek to provide more therapeutic environments within the community (Hilton et al., 2013, p. 232). Other organisations such as the Catholic Housing Aid Society (CHAS) and the Salvation Army began to move beyond simply providing services and sought to understand better what led to the need for these services. The charities began to seek publicity for their cause, to point to the extent of hidden homelessness and to argue that adequate housing was the right of all. They tried to change the narrative from the 'problem' family to the 'homeless' family (Crowson, 2013, pp. 429–431).

In 1965–1966, the National Assistance Board (NAB) conducted a national survey of single homeless people. The survey was supported by an advisory board of voluntary groups dealing with homelessness (NAB, 1966, p. 2); their role in bringing about the survey was acknowledged in the report, albeit in language that continued to emphasise the personal characteristics of homeless people:

> In 1964 and 1965 a number of voluntary bodies expressed concern both to the Government and to Government Departments about what they regarded as the misfits and the drifters of society, particularly those who habitually live in lodging-houses and hostels or sleep rough. This concern was not in itself

> by any mean new, but it was clear that the problem was attracting increased public attention, and discussions were held among the Government Departments most concerned ... it emerged that there was little in the way of factual data about the problem of social misfits, other than among Reception Centre users, which one could use in considering what the problems were and how best they could be tackled. (NAB, 1966, p. 1)

The creation of the Child Poverty Action Group (CPAG) in 1965 in response to the 're-discovery of property' was to set a precedent for the creation of pressure groups working on behalf of those with specific needs, such as the Disablement Income Group and the mental health charity (Glennester, 2000, pp. 106–107). Shelter was one such group; by happy coincidence, its launch—long planned by five voluntary organisations—occurred two weeks after the broadcast of *Cathy Come Home*, meaning that it was able to take advantage of the public concern that the drama-documentary created.

Part of Shelter's early work involved raising money for housing associations to make property available to homeless households (Wilson, 1970, p. 148). However, Wilson (2011, p. 50) notes that, from the outset, the charity sought to bring about wider change through political campaigning: "We knew that for every family we could help, thousands would remain homeless; we would be letting the homeless down if we let the politicians off the hook."

The tone of its campaigning was deliberately controversial, with poster headlines such as "Christmas? You can stuff it for all we care" (Wilson, 2011, pp. 54–55). Shelter interpreted laws that charities should not become involved in 'political activity' as meaning that it should not be party political. Some MPs attacked its campaigns and the Charity Commissioners issued warnings about the nature of its activities (Wilson, 2011, pp. 51–52).

Following Shelter, further groups were created that were more professional and more interested in lobbying government than the traditional charity sector (Crowson, 2013, pp. 428–429). Crisis at Christmas (later Crisis) was formed in 1967, Centrepoint Soho in 1969 and the Campaign for the Homeless and Rootless (CHAR, later the Housing Campaign for Single People) in 1973 (Foord, Palmer, & Simpson, 1998, pp. 7–8). The origins of Crisis at Christmas in particular demonstrate how widespread concern over homelessness had become. It was formed when aspiring politician Bill Shearman was 'devastated' by a visit to homeless charity the

Simon Community in East London. He received cross-party support—including the Conservative Shadow Chancellor Iain Macleod—to form Crisis at Christmas in 1967. The organisation was chaired by young curate Nick Beacock, and raised its profile substantially when it held a 'reverse pilgrimage' from Canterbury to London in 1969, led by an Archbishop (Crisis, 2017, p. 28).

However, it was Shelter's campaign that was to gain the ear of the government in this period. Labour's Prime Minister Harold Wilson frequently shared platforms with Shelter's Director Des Wilson and on one occasion stated that:

> Shelter represents a healthy voice of protest, a voice which speaks always in the accents of urgency. Some would find it occasionally speaking in uncomfortably strident terms. But this housing problem is not going to be solved without idealism, the protest—but also the constructive approach—that Shelter provides. There is one thing I want of Shelter. That it is never satisfied. (Quoted in Wilson, 2011, p. 52).

The rapid development of Shelter further demonstrates the extent of public concern over homelessness. Wilson (2011, pp. 75–76) suggests that, in addition to raising over £3 million, establishing 350 local groups and helping to re-house 6000 families, Shelter "had made housing the major domestic political issue of the late Sixties". In interview, Wilson added some further indicators of public concern: Shelter had a mailing list of over 50,000, rose to ninth in the list of charities that the public were most aware of within two years of its formation and attracted crowds that exceeded those of either of the main party leaders during the 1970 election campaign.

Opinion Divided

Shelter's early years were focused on campaigning for more housing to be built—a campaign that achieved major success under the Labour government of 1966–1970, as will be shown in a later section. However, the voluntary sector brought forward no specific proposals to change the homelessness legislation in this period and there remained powerful forces that opposed more generous treatment of homeless people. For example, the *Daily Telegraph* was unimpressed with *Cathy Come Home*, arguing that many of the difficulties were caused by the movement of people to London for employment and could be solved by measures to move employment opportunities to other areas (Crisis, 2017, p. 26).

The case for change was hindered by apparent contradictions between two studies of homelessness which were commissioned by the Department of Health and Social Security (DHSS) and reported in 1971. Greve, Page, and Greve's (1971) study based in London suggested that the main causes of homelessness were a shortage of housing and inadequate resources for welfare departments. However, Glastonbury's (1971) study of South Wales and the West of England argued that the most likely causes were those associated with the breakdown of a family. Family disputes were linked most commonly to sexual misbehaviour, poor housing conditions and mental disorder. Marriage breakdowns were often the result of domestic violence, although there were also connections with drunkenness and overcrowding.

Raynsford (1986, p. 41) suggests that the conclusions of the two studies were not as different as they first appeared—both demonstrated that the immediate cause of homelessness should not be seen in isolation from the wider background of the family (including factors such as poverty, illness and family breakdown), both showed that homelessness was a greater problem than officially admitted and both highlighted the poor treatment received by those who were accommodated under the National Assistance Act. However, the perception that the two studies contradicted each other created difficulties at a political level, with the Department of Health and Social Security being unwilling initially to publish either of them (Crowson, 2013, p. 425).

Raynsford (1986, p. 43) argues that a delay in a political response to growing public concern over homelessness could also be attributed to a persisting assumption that homeless people were different from 'ordinary folk'. However, more important in his view was the perception that homeless households were competing with households on local authority waiting lists for the limited council stock that was available. Those on waiting lists were identified as 'locals' and usually had family and friends who would argue their case politically. A similar point was made by Greve et al. (1971, p. 127): "The more local authorities take responsibility for rehousing the most vulnerable families, the less popular they will be with the electorate still on the housing list."

However, it will be argued below that tensions over the allocation of local authority housing were to ease in the 1970s.

Local Authority Practice

When examining local authority responses to homelessness in the 1960s, there is the continuing difficulty of there being examples available of (mainly bad) practice, but no systematic overview. However, when moving into the 1970s, a more comprehensive picture emerges: Greve et al.'s (1971) study included substantial amount of information about the practices of London boroughs. In addition, Shelter conducted a national survey of all 174 local authorities in England and Wales to which 106 responded (Bailey & Ruddock, 1972, pp. 21–22). Their report, entitled *The Grief Report*, concentrated on bad practice and the consequences for families of receiving inadequate or no assistance—as befits a campaigning organisation—but also included an overview across a range of key areas.

The Context of Local Authority Practice

The context of local authority practice in this period was that many continued to face demand for services under the National Assistance Act that exceeded their ability to supply temporary accommodation. In 1962, it was noted in parliament that some local authorities, with their own temporary accommodation full, had to place homeless households some distance away (HC Deb 13 December 1962 vol 669 cc555-6). The number of households in temporary accommodation continued to grow through the late 1960s and 1970s (Bailey & Ruddock, 1972, p. 9). Greve et al. (1971, pp. 156–157) reported that, in the four weeks in which their study was conducted, one third of London Boroughs had to refuse admission to temporary accommodation because there was none available.

In considering how to respond to this level of demand, local authorities continued to experience little pressure from central government. For example, in 1961, Dr Hill urged authorities to give priority to re-housing homeless households on the grounds that "the circumstances of people in this category are, by the definition of homelessness, the worst that are conceivable". However, he made clear that central government would not interfere in the decisions made by local authorities in this area (HC Deb 06 November 1961 vol 648 cc661).

Labour's return to power resulted in more central government activity with Ministry of Housing and Health Joint Circular 20/66, issued in October 1966, attempting to lay down minimum standards for hostels for homeless households. Local authorities were required to review homelessness provision in their area and to report to the Minister their plans for dealing with the issue by March 1967 (Richards, 1981, pp. 25–26). This circular was a key reason for the government deciding that it would be inappropriate to take immediate action over local authority practice when *Cathy Come Home* was shown the following month (Richards, 1981, p. 27). However, only half of authorities responded with a review and plan, meaning that the government had a partial picture of practice (Richards, 1981, p. 29). So, the only immediate tangible response to *Cathy Come Home* was the issue of a further circular urging local authorities to make greater use of short life properties (Lund, 2016, p. 216).

As Des Wilson confirmed when interviewed, Shelter's focus in its early years was on the supply of housing rather than the manner in which local authorities implemented the 1948 Act. However, there were some examples of pressure being placed on local authorities by more direct action. In 1965–1966 a bitter battle occurred at King Hill Hostel in West Malling, Kent, over Kent County Council's exclusion of fathers of homeless families from hostels. A group of fathers, supported by the Homeless Hotels Campaign, moved into the hostel and refused to leave (Lowe, 1986, p. 141). Following the campaign, Kent County Council changed its rules to allow husbands into temporary accommodation, and lifted its three month time limit for families to stay there (Bailey & Ruddock, 1972, p. 127). The government issued two circulars urging other local authorities to take similar steps (Radford, 2004). Similarly, in 1966, Essex County Council was forced to close down its dormitory accommodation and convert it into family units following a battle with homeless residents (Bailey & Ruddock, 1972, p. 127).

Squatting was another form of direct action that was used to challenge local authority policies. The London Squatting Campaign was formed in 1968 and sought to re-housed families from slums or hostels by means of squatting (Lowe, 1986, p. 141). The People's Association in Notting Hill campaigned for low-income people in their area by fighting against evictions and introducing squatters into properties that were standing vacant (O'Malley, 1977, p. 107). Bailey and Ruddock (1972, p. 127) argue that the squatting campaigns was another factor that influenced the government circular urging local authorities to make use of short-life houses for homeless or badly housed families. However, these were relatively rare examples of direct action; for the most part, local authorities faced little pressure over their interpretation of their duties under the 1948 Act.

Punitive Practices in Temporary Accommodation

As the above examples show, the splitting of families was one particularly punitive practice that was adopted in temporary accommodation. A government circular of September 1967 noted that many local authorities still refused to admit men and boys to such accommodation, had communal arrangements as the norm and placed arbitrary time limits on the length of stay (Richards, 1981, p. 29). The 1968 Seebohm Committee on local authorities and allied services again urged authorities not to separate families (Clapham, Kemp, & Smith, 1990, pp. 118–119).

Bailey and Ruddock's (1972) national study and Greve et al.'s (1971) research in London demonstrated two further difficulties for homeless families: the quality of temporary accommodation was still often poor, and many families were refused assistance altogether. More than half of the authorities responding to Bailey and Ruddock's study said that they had formal or informal arrangements with voluntary organisations to provide accommodation, but some of the accommodation provided under such arrangements bore the marks of traditional hostels, such as families living in one room and a requirement to leave the premises during the day (Bailey & Ruddock, 1972, pp. 80–84). Brent's Director of Social Services said of the bed-and-breakfast hotels and guesthouses where the authority placed some homeless households: "We all know it's inadequate but it's better than leaving a family on the streets" (Bailey & Ruddock, 1972, p. 85). Southampton did not even arrange bed-and-breakfast accommodation itself, but gave families a list of providers (Bailey & Ruddock, 1972, p. 88). There were examples of old workhouses, old police stations, old army camps, public houses, transport cafes, holiday chalets and caravans being used as temporary accommodation. The use of caravan sites would, on occasions, breach public health legislation (Bailey & Ruddock, 1972, pp. 89–102).

Greve et al. (1971, p. 139) argued that, in London, the major guiding principle in the provision of temporary accommodation was a fear of being over-generous and encouraging abuse of the system. Direct rehousing into permanent accommodation was an option that was usually only sought for those households who were considered blameless for their circumstances (Greve et al., 1971, p. 144). Similarly, 'promotion' to better forms of temporary accommodation was usually on the basis of the perceived merit of the family concerned (Greve et al., 1971, p. 147). Greve et al. (1971, p. 147) quoted some of the comments that were made in social workers reports about homeless families such as: "Both are debauched and degraded; far from being a good family". While acknowledging that such comments were not typical, they suggested that "they were not so rare that they could be ignored".

Elsewhere, Bailey (1973, pp. 9–11) described the experience of visiting 150 hostels used under the 1948 National Assistance Act between 1964 and 1970; poor practice observed included hostile responses to complaints, families with two or three children occupying one room, the separation of families with the threat of imprisonment for men who visited and evictions for breaking rules. Bailey's (1973, p. 7) overall view was:

> if these places were not the end of the world for the occupants, they were certainly the end of the road. They were the end of normal life, the end of consideration as a human being, the end of hope, the beginning of life outside society.

Some families were denied access to temporary accommodation altogether. Bailey and Ruddock (1972, p. 51) found examples of welfare authorities only admitting families if the housing authority could guarantee re-housing within a specified time period. Despite the clear statement in the 1948 Act that the local authority where the homeless household was should take responsibility for them, some authorities went to considerable lengths to force families to look for help in another area (Bailey & Ruddock, 1972, pp. 69–78). In London, Greve et al. (1971), pp. 135–140) found that practices persisted such as refusing all families assistance in the first instance. Most boroughs put into practice a definition of homelessness that covered only those who would otherwise have no roof over their head; the admission to temporary accommodation was usually delayed until a Possession Order had been enforced by the bailiffs.

Bailey and Ruddock (1972, p. 21) noted the discrepancy between the 24,691 families who applied for temporary accommodation in 1971 and the 5630 who were admitted. Many authorities explained the difference by saying that people made their own arrangements with family and friends, but such arrangements often came about because the local authority's temporary accommodation was full and the fear of having children taken into care meant that parents would stay anywhere rather than remain homeless (Bailey & Ruddock, 1972, p. 37). Following some families who were refused access to temporary accommodation revealed examples of sleeping in cars, in an illegally parked caravan where the water supply was a nearby stream, in a church hall, in illegal squats and in a railway station (Bailey & Ruddock, 1972, pp. 57–59).

Taking Children into Care

The previous chapter noted the conflict between welfare departments and children's departments over the most punitive response of all to homeless families—taking children into care. The problem persisted into the 1960s: Mrs Joyce Butler noted in the Commons that, in a 22-week period in 1961, 302 families approached Middlesex County Council as homeless and 168 of these were told that the Council could do nothing for them. From these families, 137 children were taken into care because there was nowhere else for them to go. Mrs Butler commented:

> These were children of ordinary, decent, hard-working parents, not problem parents, who were forced to take this action simply because of the lack of accommodation in Middlesex. No one can estimate, I suggest, what the effect of this separation will be on those children. It is a problem for the future. (HC Deb 27 November 1961 vol 650 cc198)

The closing credits of *Cathy Come Home* stated that 4000 children per year were taken into care because their parents were homeless, although, as noted above, the showing of the play was a key factor in reducing this practice.

Examples of Improving Practice

Despite the examples of continuing poor practice discussed above, it is clear that there was movement towards providing better services to homeless households during this period, as argued by Donnison and Ungerson (1982, pp. 267–273). In 1962, it was noted that Camberwell Council were buying properties to house those who were evicted (HC Deb 30 July 1962 vol 664 cc257-258). The same year London County Council was commended for taking measures to meet the needs of homeless people such as extending hostel accommodation, modernising old buildings to bring them back into use as housing, purchasing empty properties and encouraging people who were living in properties that were larger than they needed to transfer (HC Deb 19 April 1962 vol 658 cc790).

Somerville (1994, pp. 30–31) argues that temporary accommodation was repeatedly extended in the early 1960s, as a result of both increasing needs and increasing public sympathy for homeless households. Bailey and Ruddock (1972, pp. 25–26) noted that the number of authorities enforcing time limits for stays in temporary accommodation appeared to be reducing. By the time of Greve et al.'s (1971, pp. 148–150) study, less than half the London boroughs required a minimum period of stay in temporary accommodation before making an offer of a permanent tenancy, and most gave priority to homeless households in the allocation of housing, although rent arrears or perceived anti-social tendencies could prevent or delay re-housing.

Greve et al. (1971, p. 126) also found that many boroughs had accepted the need to avoid communal living and splitting up families; they had created 'family' units for homeless households, consisting of property that would not be offered on a permanent basis. Indeed, by 1969, only 2% of temporary accommodation in London was shared with other households, and this was mainly reserved for emergency admission and short-term reception (Greve et al., 1971, p. 152). Only 4% of the total temporary accommodation provided in London was in ex-Poor Law accommodation, compared to a majority in the 1950s (Greve et al., 1971, p. 153). Some of the local authorities in Bailey and Ruddock's (1972, p. 26) study that were continuing to use hostel accommodation had plans to replace it.

In further evidence of change, Greve et al. (1971, pp. 82–84) showed that there was a general agreement among the London boroughs that housing shortage was a major factor contributing to homelessness in London. Although there was a tendency to divide homeless households into those homeless 'through no fault of their own' and those whose homelessness arose from personal failure, most boroughs regarded the latter group as a minority.

Finally, there was evidence of the beginnings of secondary prevention work by local authorities in this period. Greve et al. (1971, p. 142) noted that some welfare departments undertook negotiations with landlords to try to avoid eviction. Almost all local authorities responding to Bailey and Ruddock's (1972, pp. 22–24) survey discussed preventative work in some form—most often close working with housing authorities, but also offering to guarantee rent arrears and taking action in the case of harassment by landlords.

So, while there were continuing examples of poor practice, it seems clear that, by the early 1970s, the trend was towards more supportive services.

Welfare and Housing Departments

Difficulties continued to be created by welfare departments being assumed to have responsibility for the provision of temporary accommodation, while housing departments provided permanent tenancies. The difficulties were particularly acute in areas where county councils remained responsible for welfare, while local authorities were responsible for housing (Richards, 1981, p. 25). Bailey and Ruddock (1972, p. 122) demonstrated the difficulties that could be caused by the division of responsibility between different departments and layers of government:

> A family registered on Esher's housing list and becoming homeless in Esher becomes the responsibility of Surrey County Council. If Surrey provide the family with temporary accommodation in Weybridge, the Esher U.D.C. [*Urban District Council*] no longer regards that registration as valid because they have moved out of the area. Walton and Weybridge U.D.C. on the other hand will not permit registration on their list, as a stay in temporary accommodation does not qualify as a residential claim in the area.

The difficulties were eased in the capital in 1965, when London County Council was dissolved and its welfare responsibilities passed to London boroughs, meaning that the boroughs had responsibility for both housing and welfare (Noble, 2009, p. 170). Greve et al. (1971, p. 127) found that only one London borough had transferred responsibility for homelessness completely to the housing department, but elsewhere housing departments were playing an increasing role—by re-housing homeless families from welfare department accommodation or by providing and managing the temporary accommodation.

The 1968 Seebohm Committee recommended that responsibilities in the area of homelessness be transferred to housing departments, a recommendation that was echoed by the Cullingworth Committee of 1969 on council housing (Clapham et al., 1990, pp. 118–119). The 1970 Local Authority Social Services Act implemented most of the recommendations of the Seebohm Committee but stated that the provision of temporary accommodation was a welfare function (Richards, 1981, p. 30).

The Factors that Led to Change

So, despite a change in public and political attitudes to homelessness, there remained substantial difficulties at the start of the 1970s. There were no plans for new legislation, the provision of temporary accommodation remained largely the responsibility of welfare departments and, despite improvements in many areas, there were continuing examples of practice that was very damaging to homeless households. However, several key developments in this decade were to give impetus to demands for change and to lead eventually to the passing of the 1977 Housing (Homeless Persons) Act.

Changes to Demand for Social Rented Housing

Somerville (1994, pp. 165–166) suggests that several structural factors created the context for new legislation—among them the easing of housing shortages and a reduction in the popularity of council housing. While neither of these trends began in the 1970s, they appeared to reach a point in this decade where the provision of easier access for homeless people into the council sector became less politically hazardous.

To chart first the easing of housing shortages, in 1963, it was estimated that there were several million more households than dwellings (Barton, 1963, cited in Foot, 1973, p. 85). The Conservative government of the time—in the person of Dr Hill—argued that a combination of population growth, older housing and slums meant that 6 million new dwellings would be needed in the next 20 years (HC Deb 06 November 1961 vol 648 cc650-651). The Labour government's (1965) White Paper on housing used a different method of measurement but similarly identified a substantial need for new housing: "In Britain some three million families still live either in slums, near slums or in grossly overcrowded conditions" (quoted in Wilson, 1970, p. 36).

The 1965 White Paper was to prove an important turning point: in 1966, Labour pledged to build 500,000 homes by 1969–1970 (Boughton, 2018, p. 127) and council housebuilding expanded to a level not seen since the mid-1950s (Kemp, 1991, pp. 53–54). In 1968, completions by private enterprise, housing associations and local authorities reached their post-war peak at 352,540 (DCLG, 2017, p. 2).

Although housebuilding was to fall back again as a result of cuts to public expenditure, a crude housing surplus—more dwellings than households—had been achieved by 1971. This figure did not represent the full story because the surplus turned into a deficit when considering factors such as properties undergoing repairs and second homes. Nonetheless, the scale of housing shortage in the 1970s was not at the same level as it had been in the 1950s. Labour's 1977 Housing Policy Review Green Paper suggested that there was no longer a national housing shortage but a number of local ones (Kemp, 1991, p. 55).

This view was echoed by Steve Hilditch:

> I went to work for Camden in 1977. People talked about the end of the housing crisis being in sight and that housing supply was adequate to meet needs. I don't think that was quite true in places like Camden, but people were foreseeing it.

The decline in popularity of council housing is more difficult to chart, but there were some key landmarks. It was noted in the previous chapter that, from the early 1950s, the Conservatives had expressed a preference for owner occupation. Labour's 1965 White Paper presented a very different view to that of Aneurin Bevan when it argued that council housebuilding was a short-term measure designed to overcome housing shortage in the period after the war, but that need would be met in the longer term though owner occupation (Kemp, 1991, pp. 53–54). The preference for owner occupation over all forms of renting among the main political parties was reflected in the mood of the public. The late 1960s and early 1970s saw a reduction in demand for council housing (Holmans, 1987, cited in Kemp, 1991, p. 55).

The reputation of local authority housing suffered from its association with high rise developments. In the 1950s and 1960s, authorities looked for methods of building that were cheap and used less land, with high-rise developments seeming to offer a solution; 25.7% of approved tenders in 1966 were for dwellings of five stories or more and the following year 42.6% of approvals were for system-built dwellings (Darke, 1991, p. 166). However, high-rise housing came to be associated with crime and anti-social behaviour (Boughton, 2018, p. 122) and, in 1968, a gas explosion at Ronan Point in Newham led to a corner of the tower block collapsing like a deck of cards (Boughton, 2018, p. 136). Four people were killed and 17 injured at Ronan Point; Boughton (2018, p. 136) notes that the "collapse and the shocking defects it revealed are conventionally held to mark the death knell of system-built high-rise".

Evidence of Poor Local Authority Practice Compiled

While the studies of Bailey and Ruddock (1972) and Greve et al. (1971) had highlighted some poor local authority practice, the growth of the housing aid movement ensured that such practice continued to be highlighted and challenged. The Catholic Housing Aid Society (CHAS) was created in 1956 and one of its directors, Father Eammon Casey, was to become an influential member of Shelter's board. Shelter announced the creation of its first Housing Aid Centre in 1970 (Wilson, 1970, p. 70) and rapid growth followed, with 51 centres having opened by 1972 (Dean, Goodlad, & Rosengard, 2000, p. 234).

Some local authorities created their own housing aid centres which McDonnell (1982, p. 67)—while acknowledging a degree of oversimplification—describes as "little more than the public relations arm of the housing department. Their task is to say no in a more friendly manner." However, Shelter became the biggest provider of housing aid (Dean et al., 2000, p. 234) and independent advice centres played a very different role, often coming into conflict with local authorities in seeking to enforce moral rights to housing (Dean et al., 2000, pp. 239–240).

In addition to challenges to local authorities, the network of housing aid centres could provide more systematic evidence of poor practice than had been available previously. The type of overview and individual example that could be provided was demonstrated in an interview with a Housing Aid Centre worker from outside London. They suggested that, in the mid-1970s, one third of the local authorities they worked with did not acknowledge their responsibilities under the 1948 Act, while others met the requirements of the law in a manner that provided little hope for homeless families:

> I've got a strong memory of the Nissen hut with metal framed beds and something like a wardrobe and a chair and almost nothing else in the room … people had to share the whole room with their family, the whole family, and there was a shared kitchen … And sometimes because there wasn't an obligation to house them people were offered temporary accommodation and then there wasn't really anything after that.

Raynsford (2016, p. 26) notes that, by the time of a Labour government consultation over possible homelessness legislation in 1974, there was a substantial body of evidence about local authority practice that could be put to civil servants in the Department of the Environment (DoE):

> [A] great deal of effort went into documenting, for the benefit of the DoE, the wide variations in practice on the ground and the continuation of outdated and inappropriate responses. Not only did this present a forceful case for new legislation, but it also gave the civil servants access to much more information about what was happening then they could glean from local authority statistical returns.

Changes to the Law

The limited protection available to homeless households under the 1948 National Assistance Act was further weakened by two developments in the early 1970s. The first was a Court of Appeal Ruling. As was noted in Chap. 3, local authority decisions under the 1948 Act could not be legally challenged as there was the power for the Secretary of State to overrule them. However, one case where local authority interpretation of the Act was tested indirectly concerned a Possession Order that was obtained against squatters of an empty property by Southwark council. The squatters appealed to the Court of Appeal on the grounds that the local authority had a responsibility to them under the 1948 National Assistance Act. The response of Lord Justice Edmund Davies represented an extremely narrow interpretation of Section 21(1)(b) of the Act: "[T]he whole structure and wording of the sub-section seems to me to deal with an emergency [such as] cases of dispossession or deprivation of accommodation by sudden events such as fire, flood, or something of that kind" (Southwark London Borough Council v Williams and Another [1971] Ch 734, quoted in Watchman & Robson, 1989, p. 30).

Worse was to follow. In opposition, Conservative leader Edward Heath had promised to give "high priority to the problems of the homeless" (quoted in Wilson, 1970, p. 88). The 1970 Conservative Manifesto had been the first of either of the main parties to mention homelessness specifically—it identified one of the Conservatives' key objectives as "to house the homeless". However, once in power, the Conservatives opted not to publish the report of Greve et al. (so Greve published it privately) and to set up joint working parties in the areas where Greve and Glastonbury conducted their studies, further delaying the prospect of action (Raynsford, 1986, p. 43).

In addition, the 1972 Local Government Act brought about a change to the law for which the motivation remains a mystery. The Act reorganised local authorities into larger units that were able to take on more housing responsibilities. Schedule 23 reduced the responsibilities of local authorities to homeless households under the 1948 Act to discretionary powers—they were no longer 'liable' but 'empowered' to provide temporary accommodation. Somerville (1994, p. 167) notes that the change was introduced by the DoE "without any real debate or significant opposition". The Bill was guillotined in the Commons and analysis of the limited debate that occurred in the Commons and the Lords suggests that the change to homeless responsibilities was an aspect of it that went unnoticed by both houses.

Shelter drew attention to the change in the Grief Report. Once its implications were appreciated, this became the factor that moved the voluntary sector into more concerted political action, as Nick Raynsford explained in interview:

> If it was going to become ultimately an entirely discretionary power rather than a duty, we thought this would make it virtually impossible to continue to do what we were doing—putting pressure on authorities to accept responsibility. So, that was what triggered the campaign and it was only after a period of time that it became a campaign for new legislation. Initially, we were simply campaigning to restore the duty that existed before the 1972 Local Government Act.

The Political Process Leading to the 1977 Act

The process that began with the passing of the 1972 Local Government Act and ended with the passing of the 1977 Housing (Homeless Persons) Act is an extremely complex one. Events are presented here largely in chronological order, before analysis is provided of why, in particular, the Labour government changed its position so often.

The Creation of the Joint Charities Group

The response of the voluntary sector to the 1972 Act was for five charities—the Campaign for the Homeless and Rootless (CHAR), the Catholic Housing Aid Society (CHAS), the Child Poverty Action Group (CPAG), the London Housing Aid Centre (SHAC) and Shelter—to form a Joint Charities Group (JCG), seeking to restore the duties created by the 1948 National Assistance Act. The creation of a group enabled the charities to sidestep laws prohibiting them from undertaking political campaigning

(Hilton et al., 2013, p. 120). The group was to gain the ear of government and replace the Salvation Army as its favoured consultation partner (Crowson, 2013, pp. 437–440).

Conservative Change of Direction

The first campaign of the JCG was for the introduction of amendments to the 1974 Local Government Act to restore the 1948 duties, but imposed this time on housing departments. Although the Conservatives refused to introduce such amendments to the Act (which was passed just before it fell from office), Raynsford (2016, p. 24) argues that they were 'rattled' by suggestions that they were unconcerned about homelessness and so issued two circulars. The first, DHSS Circular 13/74, re-stated the 1948 duties by indicating that social services authorities should provide temporary accommodation under section 21 (1) (b) (Richards, 1981, pp. 40–41).

The second circular, DoE/DHSS circular (18/74), advised local authorities to transfer primary responsibility for providing temporary accommodation from social services to housing departments. However, it stressed that social services departments should continue to use their resources to prevent homelessness (Clapham et al., 1990, p. 117). The circular identified priority groups who should be accommodated, discouraged the more punitive practices of some local authorities and encouraged early warning and preventative practice (Raynsford, 1986, p. 45).

There is some disagreement as to the force that such circulars had. Somerville (1994, p. 167) argues that Circular 13/74 effectively restored the 1948 duties. However, Raynsford (1986, p. 46) argues of Circular 18/74:

> The only problem with the circular, which in many ways was exemplary of its commendation of good practice and forward looking policy, was that it lacked teeth. It was not accompanied by legislation, nor was its implementation pursued vigorously by the DoE or DHSS.

The limited impact of Circular 18/74 was demonstrated by 60% of local authorities in England and Wales transferring responsibility for the temporary housing of homeless households from welfare to housing departments prior to the passing of the 1977 Act (Watchman & Robson, 1989, p. 28). Other authorities resisted further exhortations to take this step from the Finer Committee (1974) on lone parent families and the

Morris Committee (1975) on the relationship between housing and social work in Scotland (Clapham et al., 1990, p. 118).

Labour's Uncertainty

Neither of Labour's manifestos in 1974 mentioned homelessness, despite a substantial part of the October manifesto being devoted to housing issues. However, Secretary of State for the Environment Anthony Crossland had given a pledge in opposition to restore the 1948 obligations if Labour were elected (Raynsford, 1986, p. 48). Once Labour were in power, Crossland appeared to go further by announcing to the Commons a review that would consider the need for entirely new legislation (Raynsford, 1986, pp. 48–49).

However, the review—which would, in any case, have delayed decision making—appeared to be pursued with little enthusiasm by Crossland (Raynsford, 1986, pp. 48–50). It concluded with a Consultation Paper in April 1975 giving the government's view that new legislation was unnecessary and that there were insufficient resources available to introduce a duty to provide accommodation, but that the final decision would depend on responses to the consultation (Richards, 1981, pp. 42–44).

The consultation was extensive and brought about a change of view. Crossland announced in November 1975 that the government intended to legislate. However, it became clear to the JCG in 1976 that the position had altered again and that homelessness legislation was not going to be included in the Queen's Speech; the JCG embarrassed the government by leaking this news to the London Evening Standard (Crowson, 2013, pp. 442–443). There then appeared to be a further change when the government suggested that it was only lack of time that had prevented the Bill from being introduced (Raynsford, 1986, p. 54). Reg Freeson, the Minister for Housing and Construction, let it be known that the Bill that had been drafted by the DoE would be available to any backbencher who wished to adopt it as a Private Member's Bill (Gibson, 1979, p. 37).

By the time of the ballot for Private Members' Bills, the JCG had received assurances from 40 MPs that they would introduce a bill on homelessness if they had the opportunity. One of these MPs—the Liberal Stephen Ross—came fourth in the ballot and was tracked down by the JCG within half an hour of the announcement of the result, to be reminded of his assurance (Crowson, 2013, pp. 442–443). Ross agreed to put forward a homelessness bill.

Although the JCG had drafted their own bill, all parties were happy for Ross to adopt the DoE Bill which eventually became the 1977 Act (Donnison & Ungerson, 1982, p. 274). As Hilton et al. (2013, p. 126) note, private members' bills have little chance of passing into law unless the government of the day is willing to give support and parliamentary time to them. Both the Bill and the Labour government, which was struggling to remain in power with no overall majority, were given a boost by a parliamentary arrangement between the Labour and Liberal parties, which came to be known as the Lib-Lab pact. The agreement that underpinned this pact consisted of seven points, one of which was the provision of parliamentary time to allow the passing of the Housing (Homeless Persons) Bill (Dorey, 2011, pp. 389–390).

The Bill originally applied to England and Wales only, as a voluntary code was being developed in Scotland. On 9 November 1976, the Secretary of State for Scotland, Bruce Millan, announced that primary responsibility for homeless households should pass from social work to housing departments but that this could be better achieved by 'voluntary agreement' than legislation (Gibson, 1979, p. 39). However, Shelter (Scotland) and other voluntary organisations campaigned for Scotland's inclusion and Ross manoeuvred skilfully to bring this about, despite the opposition of the Scottish Office. The Lib-Lab pact confirmed Scotland's inclusion in the legislation (Gibson, 1979, pp. 40–41).

As the Bill moved into committee stage, uncertainty about whether it would run out of time or the government would fall meant that concessions had to be made to the opposition: delays in committee or the House of Lords could have prevented it from reaching the statute book. Hugh Rossi, the Conservative spokesperson, did not seek to prevent the Bill's passage but to restrict and weaken the duties imposed on local authorities. The Association of District Councils was opposed to the Bill; it prepared briefings and proposed amendments, while the JCG continued to advocate and negotiate in its favour. The outcome was that local authorities were given more discretion than had been originally intended and lost many of their proposed responsibilities to those whose homelessness was considered 'intentional' (Raynsford, 1986, pp. 56–57).

However, DoE officials reassured the JCG that the Code of Guidance that was to accompany the legislation would favour their interpretation (Crowson, 2013, pp. 443–444). When the code was published, Rossi declared that it reinstated all that had been taken out of the Bill in parliament (Crowson, 2013, pp. 443–444; Lund, 2016, p. 217). For example, the Code of Guidance interpreted the duty to secure accommodation for a statutorily homeless household as meaning that a local authority or housing association tenancy should be provided (Lund, 2016, p. 217).

Reasons for the Changes in Direction

While there is not space here to examine the reasons for each of the changes of direction of the Labour government, it is clear that there was a delicate balance of forces for and against legislation, which could easily be tipped in either direction. Among the factors that prevented decisive action was the question of priorities—any proposed new piece of legislation must compete with others and lack of parliamentary time may genuinely have been part of the reason for not including a bill in the 1976 Queen's Speech.

A second factor was local authority resistance to the government's proposal for new legislation (Somerville, 1994, p. 170) and hostility to the influence of voluntary organisations. The April 1975 Consultation Paper expressed concern at the cost implications for local authorities of a new duty (Raynsford, 1986, pp. 49–50) and, as noted above, the Association of District Councils was one of the key opponents of the Bill when it passed through parliament (Raynsford, 1986, p. 56). Local authorities were so concerned by the role of voluntary agencies that the government was forced to consult with the two groups separately in the spring of 1976 (Raynsford, 1986, p. 52); the Director of Social Services in South Tyneside and other local authority figures were highly critical of the role of Shelter (Crowson, 2013, pp. 437–440).

Third, there was opposition within the Labour Party to new legislation. As Nick Raynsford put it in interview: "… not all government members were sympathetic. Some of them had quite reactionary views about the homeless".

Elsewhere, Raynsford (2016, p. 28) argues that a key reason for the legislation not appearing in the 1976 Queen's Speech was that Crossland was moved from the DoE and replaced by Peter Shore, who was less committed to legislation. Shore represented Tower Hamlets, an area of high housing pressure, where 82% of the population were living in council housing in 1981 (Boughton, 2018, p. 231). Allocations of social rented housing were to remain an area of controversy in the area for many years to come (Young, Gavron, & Dench, 2006): the council re-introduced a 'sons and daughters' policy in 1987, which was found to discriminate on racial grounds (Boughton, 2018, p. 215).

A fourth factor was differences between departments as the multifaceted nature of homelessness began to be recognised. The Department of Health and Social Security (DHSS) commissioned a working party on young people's homelessness, the Home Office undertook a review of the law on vagrancy and street homelessness and CHAR complained to the Home Office about police treatment of rough sleepers in London—although with little success. The DoE and the DHSS were more enthusiastic about new legislation than the Treasury or the Home Office (Crowson, 2013, pp. 435–437).

That the 1977 Act was eventually passed despite these difficulties appears to partly reflect the range of forces that were aligned to support it. Somerville (1994, p. 166) suggests that there was support for change among civil servants, backbench MPs and public opinion expressed through the media. Raynsford (2016, p. 27) argues that: "The importance of the civil service's input both in the decision to legislate and in securing the passage of the Housing (Homeless Persons) Act cannot be over-emphasised." The support was illustrated by the manner in which the civil service put together the Code of Guidance.

The pressure from backbenchers was demonstrated by Mr Canvan, Labour MP for Stirlingshire West, who asked during the debate on the 1976 Queen's Speech:

> In view of the extreme anger caused by the Government's failure so far to honour their promise to introduce new legislation to make adequate provision for the homeless, will my hon. Friend state clearly whether there is or is not the slightest chance of any new legislation to this effect being introduced this Session? If not, will he say that the Government will support a Private Member's Bill to make provision for homeless families and the single homeless, who include many young people?

Mr Ernest Armstong, a Junior Minister in the DoE replied:

> I understand the concern of many hon. Members that the homelessness Bill was not included in the Gracious Speech. However, we are committed to it and we will honour that commitment. In the meantime, if a Private Member comes forward with a Bill the Government will give it careful and detailed consideration. (HC Deb 08 December 1976 vol 922 cc447-8)

The support of backbench MPs was cultivated by the JCG, first by asking for resolutions to the Labour Party Conference calling for government action and then by seeking support for a Private Member's Bill. Somerville (1994, p. 168), although critical of the importance attached by other commentators to the role of the JCG in general, acknowledges that it exerted "a real influence on the legislative process" through its relationship with backbench MPs.

The growing evidence of poor local authority practice in some areas was another factor that appeared to have some influence; Crossland declared at the end of the 1976 review that three quarters of local authorities were interpreting their responsibilities in a limited manner (Crowson, 2013, pp. 442–443). Reg Freeson reported in the Commons that the DoE's own survey of local authorities showed that some still split up families in temporary accommodation on occasions, and a small number split them up all of the time (Raynsford, 1986, p. 51).

Once the Bill was before Parliament, its eventual success was partly due to the Lib-Lab pact and a piece of skilful political manoeuvring by James Callaghan, who had taken over as Prime Minister from Harold Wilson. The decision to make parliamentary time available for the Bill was promoted by the Liberals as one of their policy achievements brought about by the pact (Kirkup, 2016, p. 71); a view that seemed entirely consistent with the political position of Liberal leader David Steel, who had once played a major role in Shelter (Scotland) (Bartram, 1981, pp. 98–100). However, support for the Bill was not included in the Liberals' original communications with the Labour Party over the pact (Kirkup, 2016, p. 71). In fact, the government had already decided to make time available for the Bill (Michie & Hoggart, 1978, p. 50), but Callaghan judged that the inclusion of this point in the agreement would be favourably received by the Liberals (Kirkup, 2016, p. 71).

The Provisions of the Act and Early Issues with Implementation

The 1977 Housing (Homeless Persons) Act received royal assent in July 1977 and gave certain groups a right to permanent housing for the first time (Somerville, 1994, p. 165). Its key provision was that a local authority must secure suitable accommodation to an applicant who was homeless (or would be homeless within 28 days), was not intentionally homeless, had a local connection and was in priority need for one of four reasons: having dependent children, being pregnant, becoming homeless as a result of a disaster (e.g. fire or flood) or being vulnerable for some other special reason. In addition, the Act laid a legal duty on local authorities to provide advice and assistance to those who were homeless (or threatened with homelessness) and were either not in priority need or were intentionally homeless. Local authorities also had duties to those in priority need and unintentionally threatened with homelessness, to try to prevent homelessness and ensure that accommodation did not cease to be available to them. Where an applicant did not have a local connection, they were to be referred to an authority where such a connection existed (Grimshaw, 2008, pp. 15–16).

The implementation of the Act raised a number of difficult questions. Many local authorities were concerned that they would not have the resources to meet the new legal requirements (Lund, 2016, p. 217), particularly as the government made clear that there would be no new money, but instead re-allocation between social services and housing departments (Raynsford, 1986, p. 57).

In addition, there was uncertainty over the status of the Code of Guidance. It was mandatory for authorities to have regard to its contents but not necessary for them to adopt the recommended practice. The DoE, in its introduction to the Code, stated that it was "confident that authorities will do their utmost to implement the Code" (quoted in Richards, 1981, p. 83) and Nick Raynsford expressed the view in interview that it had a stronger influence on policy than previous circulars:

> The key thinking was that it made it stronger than just a circular. A circular is just advisory. We'd made the point that the earlier circular (18/74) had been ignored and that was one of our strong arguments to the Civil Service that if it was to work they had to give it more teeth. So, the requirement that 'local authorities shall have regard to…' was the Civil Service answer. We quoted it a lot during the implementation phase. I think it did have an impact because it made the point that the Code wasn't just advisory. Local authorities did not necessarily have to follow it but they couldn't just ignore it.

However, another voluntary sector worker complained in interview that the Code had little impact in legal cases: "… there were a lot of court cases in the early days where there was no progress made because it was the Code of Guidance you were relying on".

A 1980 Court of Appeal judgement held that the Code of Guidance was advisory only. However, Section 71 of the 1985 Housing Act made clear again that authorities were to "have regard" to its guidance (Clapham et al., 1990, p. 123).

The lack of remedies available to those aggrieved by their treatment under the 1948 National Assistance Act was discussed in Chap. 3. In contrast, the operation of the 1977 legislation could be challenged by judicial review. Watchman and Robson (1989, p. 48) note that the courts expressed grave concern as to whether this was the appropriate mechanism by which to challenge local authority decisions, but point out that the Act provided no alternative. Between 1977 and 1996, there were almost 750 applications to the court in relation to the Act, a considerably higher rate than in other areas of social welfare law (Greene, 2014, p. 321). In the case of intentional homelessness, Watchman and Robson (1989, p. 45) argue that the Act laid down a straightforward test of causality which was complicated by the courts to such an extent that it became difficult to state with confidence when an authority would not be justified in refusing accommodation to someone who has worsened their own housing conditions at some point in the past.

However, despite these difficulties, the 1977 Act came to be looked upon with envy by homelessness activists around the world (Fitzpatrick & Pleace, 2012, p. 233).

Single Homeless People: A Group of Lesser Concern

For single homeless people, the 1977 legislation meant something quite different.

Although at the time of the introduction of the Act, CHAR felt confident to declare that at least one third of single people would meet the definition of statutory homelessness (Crowson, 2013, pp. 443–444), the reality was that a large majority were excluded from the main protection of the Act because they could not demonstrate that they were vulnerable for some other special reason. This was symptomatic of a period in which single homeless people were of limited interest to policy makers.

The voices speaking for single homeless people were less powerful than those advocating for families; Des Wilson agreed in interview that the focus of Shelter in its early years was very much on families with children:

> No one consciously made a distinction, but I think it is fair to say there was a distinction in the sense that Shelter was very much about families. Our whole concept was, a decent home was the basis of family life and our society was based on the concept of the family, but we were not providing the fundamental necessity for family life which was a decent home .... Most of our advertisements showed children. We made a very big emphasis on children going to school from slum conditions and that kind of thing .... There were organisations like St Mungo's and others that were tackling the problem of the single homeless, so it wasn't as though we thought that no one was doing it.

The only issue associated with single homelessness that was to create substantial public debate during this period was the number of rough sleepers. In February 1962, the *Times* reported that increasing numbers of men were sleeping in London's railway terminals (Noble, 2009, p. 140). Later the same year, it reported a survey conducted by the Voluntary Housing Conference (a group concerned with the shortage of affordable lodgings for low income people) that suggested that over 1000 people slept rough in London every night. However, the Salvation Army conducted its own survey on the night of 21 December 1962 and found only 69 people sleeping out, while the Welfare Department of London County Council found 114 people in November 1963. Both these figures were used by the NAB to argue that the extent of the problem had been exaggerated, although it acknowledged that the 1963 survey had ignored private property and abandoned buildings (Noble, 2009, pp. 140–141).

The more substantial piece of research that the NAB undertook in 1965–1966 after pressure from the voluntary sector presented a different picture to the one that the Board had advocated previously. The research showed that between 6 and 12 December 1965, an average of 1186 men used the Reception Centres each night—a substantial reduction on the census five years previously (NAB, 1966, p. 265) and consistent with the falling numbers that had been noted throughout the post-war period. However, 965 people were found sleeping rough and approximately 9000 staying in lodging houses or hostels (NAB, 1966, pp. 169–170).

Despite this evidence of need, there was no obvious change to public opinion regarding single homeless people as there had been with homeless families—the limited change that appeared to come about was delayed until the 1970s. For the most part, the key causes of single homelessness were assumed to be individual factors. This was illustrated by the report of the study undertaken by the NAB, which echoed previous NAB publications in emphasising individual causes over structural ones.

The report argued that many of those who were found to be homeless had begun to live an unsettled life after the breakdown of a marriage or the death of a parent or a wife. It suggested that:

> some men in middle age find difficulty in coping with personal problems and at that stage start using Reception Centres or lodging-houses or sleeping rough and there is then a greater possibility that it will persist as a way of life. (NAB, 1966, p. 172)

Supporting evidence for this view was provided through the finding that 62% of those sleeping rough, 53% of those in lodging houses and 68% of those in Reception Centres said that they had no close relatives or had not been in touch with them for a year or more (NAB, 1966, pp. 174–175). The report argued that: "Another factor commonly thought of as causing men to sleep rough is that many of them have personalities which make it difficult for them to fit in with society and to co-operate with people trying to help them" (NAB, 1966, p. 173).

Less attention was given to structural factors, although there was clear evidence that they were important: although 29.3% of those sleeping rough said that they did so from preference, 24.5% said that they could not find any accommodation. Lack of money was given as the reason by 52.6% of those using Reception Centres, and 55% of those who sought assistance at the NAB's offices, who said that they sometimes slept rough (NAB, 1966, p. 173).

Much of the research undertaken into single homelessness in this period had a bias towards suggesting that single homeless people had major individual problems, as noted by Drake, O'Brien, and Biebuyck (1981, p. 9):

> [S]tudies conducted in specific, single agencies such as Reception Centres, night shelters and large hostels highlighted the large proportion of disturbed or disadvantaged people using these particular agencies. Single homelessness was a generic term for people concentrated in specific agencies who had severe problems in addition to their homelessness. Policies were largely concerned with treating or coping with these problems.

The use of the criminal law against homeless people perpetuated the public perception of them. In 1969, 366 people were convicted for sleeping rough and 412 for begging (Stewart, 1975, p. 130). However, convictions such as these were not sufficient to explain the relationship between homelessness and offending. From April to September 1969, an internal probation survey suggested that almost all of the single men coming before the courts in Manchester and Salford were 'effectively homeless'. Of those receiving a fine or a community order, 80% were homeless—and going to prison for even a week could mean that those who had accommodation would lose it (Stewart, 1975, p. 129). The relationship between homelessness and crime could be complicated by alcohol misuse: research conducted in a London soup kitchen in 1966 showed that 40 of 51 heavy drinkers had been in prison for drunkenness (Stewart, 1975, p. 131).

One policy factor that increased the number of single homeless people with needs beyond suitable housing was the discharge of many patients from psychiatric hospital. This policy change was initiated by the 1959 Mental Health Act; the development of injectable drugs had facilitated more effective control of the problematic behaviour of some people with mental health problems and so made it feasible that care could be provided 'in the community'. The lower cost of such treatment was an obvious attraction of this approach for policy makers. However, a failure to provide adequate 'community care' structures led to many former inpatients simply moving between homeless shelters and hospitals (Watson & Austerberry, 1986, p. 54). Concerns about the adequacy of services for discharged psychiatric patients were raised in the House of Lords by Lord Stonham:

> Part VI of the Mental Health Act gave responsibility for after-care to the local authorities. But few of them are even aware of the size of the need that exists, let alone attempting to satisfy it .... community work is left to the all too few social workers of various kinds, who just cannot carry the burden of discharged patients in addition to the out-patients who have never been in hospital... (HL Deb 04 July 1962 vol 241 cc1297)

Stewart (1975, pp. 107–109) identified a range of research that supported this conclusion. For example, a study of Bolton Salvation Army hostel suggested that all 51 residents had some form of mental health problem, with 34% having been in a psychiatric hospital at some point. In addition, research in a GP's surgery in Edinburgh in 1962–1963 suggested that 74.7% of consultations among lodging house dwellers were for psychiatric conditions compared to a figure of 1.3% for the general population.

So, the perception of single homelessness as having been brought about by individual factors—whether those associated with deviance or sickness—had some basis in reality. However, the belief that this was true for all single homeless people was problematic; the popularity of this belief did not appear to decline until the 1970s. Watson and Austerberry (1986, pp. 61–63) suggest that singleness itself began to be seen as a less unusual phenomenon in the 1970s due to factors such as a higher divorce rate, increasing age at marriage and an ageing population. Agencies began to question the distinction between family and single homelessness and there was a growing tide of radical opinion that policies for single homeless people should concentrate on their lack of housing rather than any assumed personal shortcoming on their part. It was recognised that housing problems were likely to affect the most vulnerable first, but that not all single homeless people had 'problems' beyond a lack of accommodation (Watson & Austerberry, 1986, pp. 61–63). Research and professional opinion began to acknowledge that one of the causes of single homelessness was difficulties in accessing housing. This view was reinforced by a report produced by the Greater London Council and the London Boroughs Association (quoted in Watson & Austerberry, 1986, p. 62): "The single homeless are not simply those with 'problems' of one kind or another other than housing problems…the evidence is overwhelming that the major cause of homelessness among single people…is a shortage of accommodation at prices they can afford."

Of course, more traditional views of single homelessness did not disappear. Page (1973) disguised himself as a homeless person (or 'down and out' as he put it) and described his experiences in a book entitled *Down Among the Dossers*. His account suggested a continuing high level of public disdain for rough sleepers (Page, 1973, p. 12).

Forms of Provision for Single Homeless People

The assumption that single homeless people must have needs beyond a lack of housing had a major bearing on the limited forms of provision that were made for them in this period. This was particularly evident in the NAB's refusal to expand the role of Reception Centres beyond the narrow remit established by the 1948 National Assistance Act, which specified that they should only accommodate those 'without a settled way of living'.

The NAB (together with London County Council) received a request for financial assistance in 1962 from the Salvation Army and the Church Army to expand their capacity for single homeless people. In refusing assistance, the NAB argued that its responsibilities were only to "persons without a settled way of living" and not to those whose need arose from housing shortage or low wages. It also suggested that many had chosen to sleep outside, or were doing so as a result of their own irresponsible choices (Noble, 2009, p. 141). In response to growing demand at Camberwell Reception Centre in early 1963, a team of NAB officials joined the London County Council resettlement officers there to steer those who did not appear to have an 'unsettled way of living' away from the Reception Centre (Noble, 2009, pp. 141–142).

People were considered by Reception Centres to have an unsettled way of living if they were regular users of centres and/or lodging houses, if they wanted to get to another place but were stranded without funds or had been turned out of accommodation with nowhere to go. They would be refused admission if they were drunk, or did not follow an unsettled way of living, or had the money to purchase a bed for the night (Stewart, 1975, p. 55). The perceived dangers of providing for those who were not yet unsettled, but might slip into this way of life, were illustrated by a review of Reception Centres conducted by the NAB and other government departments in the mid 1960s. The review recommended a reduction in the number of Centres; one reason given was that: "a network of Centres providing free accommodation could easily have a bad effect by encouraging the aimless wandering, which section 17 of the Act specifically sought to remedy" (NAB, 1966, p. 265). In 1965, 22 men received criminal convictions for persistently using Reception Centres while capable of maintaining themselves (Stewart, 1975, p. 60).

Stewart (1975, p. 155) notes that other options for single homeless people were similarly limited to those who fulfilled specific criteria:

> The local authorities and the SBC [*Supplementary Benefits Commission*] provide accommodation, but admission is reserved for people with some fairly specific type of need or problem (e.g. 'destitution'). Even voluntary bodies who provide accommodation often do so on a basis of selecting residents by some trait of character, such as a criminal record, alcoholism or mental illness. There remain the large Salvation Army hostels, municipal lodges and cheap private establishments who between them provide accommodation for the majority. This majority may contain many who could benefit from the specialist hostels.

The probation service taking over responsibility for homeless offenders from Discharged Prisoners' Aid Societies in 1965 (Goodman, 2012, pp. 182–185) illustrates the point that offenders were one group who could benefit from specific provision. However, for those who were without obvious additional needs, there were few services; local authorities housing stock consisted largely of three-bedroom properties that had been built for families (Raynsford, 2016, p. 27). Where local authorities had stock that was suitable for single people, they tended to allocate quotas of lettings to social services departments or voluntary organisations (Watson & Austerberry, 1986, p. 67). In the case of those who the National Assistance Board declined to steer towards Reception Centres, it could only on occasions provide money for accommodation in nearby lodging houses or with landladies (National Assistance Board, 1966, pp. 264–265).

Despite some changes to attitudes, provision for single homeless people in the 1970s continued to make assumptions about their additional needs. Watson and Austerberry (1986, pp. 65–68) note that the growth of the housing association sector, which followed the provision of extra finance under the Housing (Finance) Act 1974, led to the expansion of housing schemes for single people. However, the emphasis of such schemes remained on dealing with issues beyond a lack of housing:

> Through a combination of hostels, group homes, and self-contained units, a range of provision deemed to suit the 'special needs' of the single homeless was established. A central concept of this provision was to establish stages of housing along a continuum, with increasing self-containment as the 'special needs' of the residents subsided. Thus the institutionalised were given the opportunity of becoming gradually more autonomous in small, shared houses usually of a high physical standard. (Watson & Austerberry, 1986, p. 66)

Summary

This was a period in which the distinction between single homeless people and families with dependent children became an extremely important one, particularly as the 1977 Housing (Homeless Persons) Act came to provide much stronger legal protection to the latter group. The continuing negative assumptions about single homelessness were most clearly illustrated by the concerns of Reception Centre to limit their services only to those without a settled way of life and the fear that being more generous might encourage others to slip into this lifestyle. In contrast, while there remained assumptions of blame attached to homeless families, these became less prevalent as structural causes of their homelessness were more widely acknowledged.

This change in attitude to homeless families appears to be linked to several developments, one of which was the decreasing demand for, and popularity of, council housing. However, pressure on the provision of temporary accommodation remained and, while many local authorities improved services to homeless households, examples of hostile practices were by no means eliminated. The collation of more systematic evidence of such practices was a key element in the long drawn out process that eventually led to the passing of the 1977 Act.

The Act was part of a change of policy focus away from the primary prevention of homelessness through housebuilding. While concern was initially to meet the immediate needs of homeless families more effectively, this was to develop into a more sophisticated system of tertiary prevention in subsequent decades.

References

Bailey, R. (1973). *The squatters*. London, UK: Penguin.

Bailey, R., & Ruddock, J. (1972). *The grief report*. London, UK: Shelter.

Bartram, P. (1981). *David Steel: His life and politics*. London, UK: W.H. Allen.

Boughton, J. (2018). *Municipal dreams: The rise and fall of council housing*. London, UK: Verso Books.

Chinn, C. (2015, February 14). How 1960s film Cathy Come Home changed Birmingham's housing crisis forever. *Birmingham Mail*. Retrieved from https://www.birminghammail.co.uk/news/nostalgia/how-1960s-film-cathy-come-8639172

Clapham, D., Kemp, P., & Smith, S. J. (1990). *Housing and social policy*. Basingstoke, UK: Macmillan.

Crisis. (2017). *Not yet home: A history of Britain's attempts to tackle homelessness*. London, UK: Crisis.

Crowson, N. J. (2013). Revisiting the 1977 Housing (Homeless Persons) Act: Westminster, Whitehall and the homeless lobby. *Twentieth Century British History, 24*(3), 424–447.

Darke. (1991). Local political attitudes and council housing. In S. Lowe & D. Hughes (Eds.), *A new century of social housing* (pp. 159–174). Leicester, UK: Leicester University Press.

Dean, J., Goodlad, R., & Rosengard, A. (2000). Citizenship in the new welfare market: The purposes of housing advice services. *Journal of Social Policy, 29*(2), 229–245.

Department for Communities and Local Government. (2017). *50 years of the English Housing Survey*. London, UK: Department of Communities and Local Government.

Donnison, D., & Ungerson, C. (1982). *Housing policy*. Harmondsworth, UK: Penguin Books Limited.

Dorey, P. (2011). A rather novel constitutional experiment': The formation of the 1977–8 'Lib-Lab pact. *Parliamentary History, 30*(3), 374–394.

Drake, M., O'Brien, M., & Biebuyck, T. (1981). *Single and homeless*. London, UK: Department of the Environment.

Fitzpatrick, S., & Pleace, N. (2012). The statutory homeless system in England: A fair and effective rights-based model. *Housing Studies, 27*(2), 232–251.

Foord, M., Palmer, J., & Simpson, D. (1998). *Bricks without mortar*. London, UK: Crisis.

Foot, M. (1973). *Aneurin Bevan: A biography, volume 2 1945–1960*. New York: Atheneum.

Gibson, P. (1979). How Scotland got the Housing (Homeless Persons) Act. In H. M. Drucker & N. L. Drucker (Eds.), *The Scottish Government yearbook 1979* (pp. 36–42). Edinburgh, Scotland: Paul Harris Publishing.

Glastonbury, B. (1971). *Homeless near a thousand homes*. London, UK: George Allen and Unwin.

Glennester, H. (2000). *British social policy since 1945* (2nd ed.). Oxford, UK: Blackwell Publishers Ltd.

Goodman, A. (2012). *Rehabilitating and resettling offenders*. Chichester, UK: John Wiley and Sons.

Greene, J. (2014). Managing poverty, managing dissent: Homeless politics and collective action in London. *Policy and Politics, 42*(3), 315–331.

Greve, J., Page, D., & Greve, S. (1971). *Homelessness in London*. Edinburgh, Scotland: Scottish Academic Press.

Grimshaw, J. M. (2008). *Family homelessness: Causes, consequences and the policy response in England*. London, UK: The British Library.

Hilton, M., McKay, J., Crowson, N., & Mouhot, J. (2013). *The politics of expertise: How NGOs shaped modern Britain*. Oxford, UK: Oxford University Press.

Jones, A., & Pleace, N. (2010). *A review of single homelessness in the UK 2000–2010*. London, UK: Crisis and the University of York.

Kemp, P. (1991). From solution to problem? In S. Lowe & D. Hughes (Eds.), *A new century of social housing* (pp. 44–61). Leicester, UK: Leicester University Press.

Kemp, P. (1997). Burying Rachman. In J. Goodwin & C. Grant (Eds.), *Built to last?* (2nd ed.). London, UK: Roof Magazine, Shelter.

Kirkup, J. (2016). *The Lib-Lab pact: A Parliamentary agreement 1977–78*. Basingstoke, UK: Palgrave Macmillan.
Lowe, S. (1986). *Urban social movements*. Basingstoke, UK: Macmillan Education Limited.
Lund, B. (2016). *Housing politics in the United Kingdom*. Bristol, UK: Policy Press.
McDonnell, K. (1982). Working in housing aid. *Critical Social Policy, 2*(4), 63–77.
Michie, A., & Hoggart, S. (1978). *The pact: The inside story of the Lib-Lab government 1977–8*. London, UK: Quartet Books.
Montgomery, J. (1959). The Landlord and Tenant (Temporary Provisions) Act 1958. *Modern Law Review, 22*(1), 59–60.
National Assistance Board. (1966). *Homeless single persons*. London, UK: Her Majesty's Stationery Office.
Noble, V. A. (2009). *Inside the Welfare State: Foundations of policy and practice in Post-War Britain*. Abingdon, UK: Routledge.
O'Malley, J. (1977). *The politics of community action*. Nottingham, UK: Bertrand Russell Peace Foundation Ltd.
Page, R. (1973). *Down among the dossers*. London, UK: Davis-Poynter Limited.
Radford, J. (2004, February 11). The squatting campaign: Homes for families. *The Guardian*. Retrieved from https://www.theguardian.com/society/2004/feb/11/voluntarysector.comment1
Raynsford, N. (1986). The 1977 Housing (Homeless) Persons Act. In N. Deakin (Ed.), *Policy change in Government* (pp. 33–62). London, UK: Royal Institute of Public Administration.
Raynsford, N. (2016). *Substance not spin: An insider's view of success and failure in government*. Bristol, UK: Policy Press.
Richards, J. (1981). The Housing (Homeless Persons) Act 1977: A study in policy making. *Working Paper 22*, School of Advanced Urban Studies, University of Bristol, Bristol, UK.
Sandbrook, D. (2006). *White heat: A history of Britain in the swinging sixties*. London, UK: Abacus.
Somerville, P. (1994). Homelessness policy in Britain. *Policy and Politics, 22*(3), 163–178.
Stewart, J. (1975). *Of no fixed abode*. Manchester, UK: Manchester University Press.
Watchman, P. Q., & Robson, P. (1989). *Homelessness and the law in Britain*. Glasgow, Scotland: The Planning Exchange.
Watson, S., & Austerberry, H. (1986). *Housing and homelessness: A feminist perspective*. London, UK: Routledge and Kegan Paul.
Wilson, D. (1970). *I know it was the place's fault*. London, UK: Oliphants.
Wilson, D. (2011). *Memoirs of a minor public figure*. London, UK: Quartet Books Limited.
Young, M., Gavron, K., & Dench, G. (2006). *The new East End: Kinship, race and conflict*. London, UK: Profile Books.

CHAPTER 5

1979–1997: Homelessness and Ideological Conflict

Introduction

The implementation of the 1977 Housing (Homeless Persons) Act was followed quickly by the election of a Conservative government, under the Prime Ministership of Margaret Thatcher, in 1979. Her first election victory provided a small overall majority, but this was followed by landslide victories in 1983 and 1987. Now under the leadership of John Major, the Conservatives won again, with a substantially reduced majority, in 1992.

This was a period of huge social change as local authorities dealt with their new legal responsibilities to homeless households in a context where their stock of housing reduced for the first time in the post-war period. Growing inequalities, substantial increases in housing costs and a policy focus on economic growth rather than support for the poorest people were other factors that made this a particularly difficult period in which to be homeless.

Social Policy and Explanations of Social Problems

Social Policy

The election of Mrs Thatcher as Prime Minister in 1979 is widely assumed to have destroyed a cross party consensus over the role that the post-war welfare state should play (Pierson, 1998, p. 18). The Conservatives argued vigorously that the over-expansion of welfare that was a key cause of

J. Harding, *Post-War Homelessness Policy in the UK*,
https://doi.org/10.1007/978-3-030-22117-1_5

Britain's economic difficulties (McCarthy, 1989, pp. 1–6) and that individualism and self-reliance were key values that needed to be restored (Carlen, 1996, p. 22). While there were few specific references to the thinking of Charles Murray (discussed in Chap. 2), the rhetoric of Conservative politicians was often similar to his, blaming social problems such as unemployment on the people who experienced them and suggesting that over-generous social policies were counter-productive and encouraged dependency. The government's approach to social policy and other issues was sometimes referred to as representing a 'New Right' philosophy.

Employment and Social Security Policy

One of the key principles on which Beveridge had designed his blueprint for the welfare state—the need for full employment (Hill, 1993, p. 15)—was rejected by the New Right on the grounds that market forces should determine 'natural' employment levels: unemployment remained above 10% for much of the 1980s (Ellison & Pierson, 1998, p. 8). The increase in unemployment led to an increase in spending on social security, which the government sought to curb through reductions in the level of benefits (Andrews & Jacobs, 1990, p. 8). The greater inequality that arose from this approach was justified by the need to set entrepreneurs free, to remove the 'nanny state' (Hill, 1993, p. 129), to increase work incentives, to combat fraud, to reduce public expenditure, to reduce incentive to go on strike and to be fair to the taxpayers who paid for social security (Andrews & Jacobs, 1990, pp. 5–7). Mrs Thatcher's view of the danger of over-generous social security was reflected in her speech to the Small Business Bureau on 8 February 1984: "I came to office with one deliberate intent: to change Britain from a dependent to a self-reliant society; from a give-it-to-me to a do-it-yourself nation; a get-up-and-go instead of a sit-back-and-wait-for-it Britain" (quoted in Andrews & Jacobs, 1990, p. 3).

Young people bore the brunt of the growth of unemployment and cuts to benefits; they were a particular target of Conservative criticisms of those who were unemployed. The Youth Training Scheme (YTS) became a key instrument of the government's attempts to tackle a perceived culture of idleness and to ensure that families assumed more financial responsibility for young people. It began as a one-year programme in 1983, then was extended to two years in 1986 (Ashton, Maguire, & Spilsbury, 1990, p. 31). Allowances on YTS were deliberately set at a low level: the stated reason was to price school leavers back into jobs by lowering their wage aspirations (Lee, Marsden, Rickman, & Duncombe, 1990, p. 3). The assumption that families would make good the shortfall in income was made explicit in the 1981 White Paper *A New Training Initiative*:

> It is accepted that they [*students*] should continue to be dependent on their parents and that they should not have access to supplementary benefit in their own right. The same will apply to unemployed minimum age school leavers when they are guaranteed a place on this new scheme...parents will be expected to provide any necessary financial support to these trainees. (Quoted in Finn, 1987, p. 156)

The scheme effectively became compulsory for young people not in work or full-time education when entitlement to Income Support was removed from 16–17-year-olds in 1988 (Killeen, 1988, p. 1). The government guaranteed a YTS place to every school leaver who was not in work or education and Industry Secretary Lord Young made clear in 1987 that the state should not pay benefits to young people who "lay in bed" after consistently refusing YTS places (Andrews & Jacobs, 1990, p. 79). Another key change was that 18–24-year-olds ceased to receive a higher rate of benefits if living independently (making it more difficult to live away from the family home) and lost the amount of benefit representing their assumed contribution to their parents' housing costs if living at home (making it more difficult to live in the family home) (Harris, 1989, pp. 71–72).

The Conservatives and Local Authorities

The policies adopted in relation to homelessness in this period were strongly affected by the hostile relationship that existed between central and local government, with the centre seeking to exert more control than ever before. Local authorities had become more party political after local government re-organisation in 1974: uncertainty over which party would control newly defined authorities encouraged both Labour and the Conservatives to extend their operations into rural areas (Young & Davies, 1990, p. 18). Political polarisation brought with it a decline in the former consensus-based method of managing local government (Young & Davies, 1990, p. 42). Some urban Labour local authorities moved to the left, motivated by the weak socialist programme the party was felt to have offered at the 1979 general election, dissatisfaction with its performance in office in 1974–1979 and the emergence of more radical, middle-class activists (Byrne, 2000, pp. 540–541).

The move to the left on the part of some authorities was only one reason for them being the subject of hostility from the Thatcher governments, as noted by Gray (1994, p. 57):

> In general terms the government emphasised the importance of a successful economy, the need for a strong central government free from the demands of special interest groups (in particular, the trade unions), the superiority of the market over the state as an allocator of resources, and the central importance of the individual as the basis for government policy .... Given that SNG [*sub-national Government*] prior to 1979 was geared towards a public service orientation, emphasising the collective provision of goods and services, targeted towards distinct groups of consumers, and operating in a non-market fashion ... it is not surprising that it was not exactly loved by the Conservative government.

The Conservatives sought to implement policies with the minimum of interference from others who were involved in the process (Hill & Hupe, 2003, pp. 473–474)—most notably, local government. One tier of potential opposition was removed by the abolition of the Greater London Council and six metropolitan councils, together with the Inner London Education Authority (Stewart, 2014, p. 840). The assumption that local authority functions were best carried out by the authority itself was ended by the Conservative's introduction of Compulsory Competitive Tendering for many local authority services (Stewart, 2014, p. 844). Other measures also sought to take services out of local authority control: for example, giving schools powers to 'opt out' and become independently run (Gray, 1994, pp. 59–62).

All these measures were controversial, but possibly the greatest area of conflict was over the control of local authority spending by a government determined to cut public expenditure. Local authorities had become increasingly dependent on central government subsidy as they expanded in the post-war period, particularly from the mid-1960s onwards. Central government grants increased from 35% of local authority revenue in 1953–1954 to 45% in 1974–1975 (Stoker, 1991, p. 161). In their first term of office, the Conservatives spoke of 'overspending' by local authorities and 'value for money', developing several financial mechanisms to seek to control their expenditure (Stoker, 1991, pp. 161–165). In their second term, the government developed a system of rate-capping, whereby the Secretary of State for the Environment could limit the rates charged by named authorities (and so control their spending). The first list of 18 authorities to be rate-capped included 16 controlled by the Labour Party (Stoker, 1991, p. 170).

Wilks-Heeg (2009, p. 29) argues that, in their third term, the Conservatives articulated a clear vision of local authorities 'enabling not providing'. The 1988 Local Government Act substantially extended the number of areas where authorities were required to introduce Compulsory Competitive Tendering for services, the 1988 Housing Act (discussed further below) gave council tenants the opportunity to choose new landlords and the 1989 Local Government Finance Act introduced the poll tax or community charge with the aim of making more people aware of the impact of high local authority spending (Wilks-Heeg, 2009, p. 29).

There was local authority resistance to these changes, with the most high-profile reaction being the refusal of some councils to set a legal budget, resulting in the surcharging and disqualification of councillors in Liverpool and Lambeth (Smith, 2000). In addition, Alcock (1994, pp. 136–138) suggests that some authorities resisted Government policy through the introduction of 'local Socialism' and, in particular, anti-poverty strategies. Balloch and Jones (1990, pp. 40–54) suggest that there were four key types of activity: measures to increase income maintenance and support (e.g. insulating properties to reduce fuel costs), decentralisation, economic development (e.g. seeking to attract new employers to the area) and welfare rights work. Although homelessness was rarely mentioned as part of the discussion of anti-poverty strategies, it is possible that the substantial expansion of local authority services for homeless people in this period was part of an ideological commitment to protect the most disadvantaged people.

Voluntary Organisations

Both Margaret Thatcher and John Major spoke warmly about voluntary organisations (Kendall, 2000, p. 549) and the former Conservative Minister who was interviewed for this book spoke of these organisations "doing heroic work with rough sleepers". However, Kendall (2000, p. 550) argues that, while some commentators suggested that the 1980s was a period where voluntary agencies were turned to as an alternative to a welfare state in crisis, this was to exaggerate their role, with much policy discussion making a binary distinction between the 'public' and 'private' sectors. The state was happy to support voluntary organisations when it was politically convenient, and organisations were willing to respond when it was in their interests to do so, but there was no sense of these agencies being part of a 'sector'.

May, Cloke, and Johnsen (2006, p. 713) take a slightly different view, arguing that—following the Wolfenden Report of 1978, which encouraged voluntary organisations to see themselves as a 'sector'—new umbrella organisations emerged, working to co-ordinate services, disseminate good practice and encourage higher standards. As was noted in Chap. 4, organisations working for homeless people had formed themselves into a powerful political lobby from 1972 onwards. However, when it came to the provision of services, there was still limited co-ordination, as was noted by Jeremy Swain:

> It was very badly coordinated, so if you were sleeping along The Strand in central London at 6.00 you'd see Thames Reach, by 7.00 St Mungo's and 8.00 Salvation Army, and there was obvious duplication, poor coordination and we were doing a good job but not good enough.

Considering the advocacy element of voluntary organisations' work, Shelter continued to challenge local authorities about their practice during this period. Steve Hilditch recalled that they spent much of their energies ensuring that local authorities fulfilled their legal obligations, with free housing advice available to those who felt aggrieved by an authority's handling of their homelessness application, and campaigning to end the use of the worst forms of temporary accommodation. Greene (2014, p. 321) notes that Shelter was aware that people in bed-and-breakfast hotels were not among the 'visible' homeless and so launched advertising campaigns seeking to challenge the belief that local authorities would always provide for homeless families with children.

The political element of voluntary organisations' work was the subject of some debate, with Greene (2014, p. 318) arguing that the government was able to "channel activism into institutional structures of control and influence, even in the increasingly closed political environment of the Thatcher regime, and thus structured collective action away from contentious protest". However, Jeremy Swain took a different view, arguing that voluntary organisations found a way to work with the government while remaining critical:

> So by the 1990s we were actually having meeting with civil servants, before that we hadn't had meetings ... And government were saying to us, 'If we're going to give you this opportunity of building these units, if we're going to fund you directly to support people we do want to see results and we do want to see numbers [of rough sleepers] going down'. And it led to us working more collaboratively with government. That involves a degree of compromise, and also you've got to move away from the luxury of simply being a sector that vociferously campaigns against government. You still need to challenge and you still need to make sure that government feels under pressure from the sector, but you've also got to find a different way of working.

The role of voluntary organisations in the Rough Sleepers' Initiative (RSI) came under particular scrutiny, as will be shown in a later section.

The Social Rented Housing Sector

Despite the rhetoric, Mishra (1990, p. 23) argues that radical proposals in a number of areas of social policy were rejected by the Thatcher governments on the grounds that they would be electorally damaging. Ellison (1998, p. 33) argues that the Conservatives had to satisfy themselves instead with limited reforms designed to re-order the method of providing public services to ensure that they benefited from the disciplines of the market. However, it was in the area of housing that they were able to launch their most radical reforms.

Key concerns of Conservative housing policy were to increase the level of home ownership and to reduce the role of local authority housing departments, which were perceived to be inherently inefficient. The desire to increase home ownership was driven by the belief that free markets are more efficient than social planning, providing consumer choice and individual freedom (Monk & Kleinman, 1989, pp. 121–122). Secretary of State for the Environment Michael Heseltine told the Commons in 1980 that "There is in this country a deeply ingrained desire for home ownership. The Government believes that this spirit should be fostered" (quoted in Monk & Kleinman, 1989, p. 122). The 1987 White Paper *Housing—The Government's Proposals* presented the critique of local authority housing departments: they were too large, inefficient and paternalistic, with bureaucratic allocation methods resulting in unnecessarily long waiting times for housing (Kemp, 1991, p. 57).

The Government was able to achieve its twin objectives of increasing home ownership and reducing the role of local authorities through the Right to Buy council housing. It had been possible for local authorities to sell homes to tenants since the 1930s (Murie, 2016, pp. 14–15), but the 1980 Housing Act removed local discretion and gave all secure local authority tenants a right to buy the home that they lived in at a discount. By 1997, some 2 million properties had been transferred to owner occupation under the Right to Buy (Malpass & Murie, 1999, p. 79).

The role of local authority housing departments was further reduced by spending cuts. Central government expenditure on council housing construction and maintenance fell by 43% between 1980–1981 and 1990–1991 (Boughton, 2018, p. 175). Public sector housing was downgraded from being a major to a minor capital programme (Malpass & Murie, 1999, p. 105). As a result, the number of council house completions, which had been reducing through the 1970s, fell further from 88,590 new dwellings in 1980 to 3218 in 1995 (Malpass & Murie, 1999, p. 91).

The government hoped to make good the shortfall in new rented property through measures to encourage the growth of the housing association and private rented sectors under the 1988 Housing Act (discussed further below). Housing associations provided only 1.9% of dwellings in 1979 (Boughton, 2018, p. 168) and their stock grew under the Conservatives, but at a very modest rate compared to the reduction in local authority building: completions increased from 21,422 in 1980 to 39,178 in 1995 (Malpass & Murie, 1999, p. 91). The private rented sector reduced its share of the housing stock from 11.0% in 1981 to 9.7% in 1996, despite the de-regulation of rents under the 1988 Act. Taken alongside the right to buy, these developments demonstrate the substantial reduction in the number of rented dwellings available, for low-income households in particular. Many critics were to point to this factor as a reason for rising homelessness (e.g. Edwards, 1995, pp. 62–64).

One suggested further impact of the Right to Buy and the failure to significantly add to or refurbish the council housing stock was residualisation. As the most popular types of council properties in the most popular areas were bought by the most affluent tenants, the sector was left with unwanted types of accommodation in disadvantaged areas, occupied by the poorest and most disadvantaged tenants. Pearce and Vine (2014, pp. 657–659) argue that the process of residualisation involved the public sector becoming a 'safety net' for those who were unable to access private housing. It incorporated the physical decline of the accommodation in the sector and its increasing association with social exclusion and stigma. Between 1966 and 1989, the percentage of the population that identified renting from the council as their preferred housing tenure fell from over 20% to 12% (Boughton, 2018, p. 173). Malpass (1990, p. 29) suggests that the origins of residualisation can be traced back to the 1950s, although Jones and Murie (1998, p. 3) argue that the Right to Buy played a considerable part in accelerating the process.

While some parts of the residualisation thesis are difficult to evaluate, the increasing concentration of people on low incomes in the council housing sector can be evidenced. At a time when the sector was shrinking, the number of council tenants receiving Housing Benefit rose from 1,205,000 in 1979/80 to 3,053,000 in 1993/94. Between 1980 and 1992, the average gross incomes of owner occupiers with mortgages rose from £142 to £320 per week, while the average gross incomes of local authority tenants rose only from £68 to £110 per week (Wilcox, 1994). Between 1981 and 1998, the percentage of heads of household of council houses who were in full-time employment fell from 43% to 23% (Boughton, 2018, p. 211).

Whether or not residualisation was a specific aim of government, it fitted well with the aspirations for a reduced social rented sector, catering for those with needs beyond the provision of housing. Clapham and Smith (1990) noted the expectation of the government that social rented housing would be increasingly occupied only by those with 'special needs'. This view was made explicit by the Department of the Environment (DoE) (1994, p. 5):

> The Government recognises the complementary role that housing plays in the delivery of social welfare policies such as care in the community. It is committed to ensuring that accommodation will continue to be available for vulnerable individuals who cannot be expected to make their own arrangements for housing.

The re-housing of an increasingly high percentage of homeless households into local authority housing is often cited as one of the factors that contributed to the process of residualisation (e.g. Lund, 1996, p. 69). However, Forrest and Murie (1990, p. 109) see the pattern of cause and effect slightly differently, arguing that one impact of the right to buy was to force those who could not afford mortgages (including homeless people) into the most disadvantaged and stigmatised neighbourhoods. It is very difficult to evaluate whether residualisation contributed to homelessness, although it seems likely that people gave up tenancies due to difficult living conditions and/or failed to move into properties they were allocated in severely disadvantaged areas. Broader studies have found that concerns about antisocial behaviour and neighbourhood crime are major causes of housing dissatisfaction (Warnes, Crane, Whitehead, & Fu, 2003, p. 792).

While the government had no specific response to residualisation, there was some concern over inner city areas, where poor quality housing often existed alongside problems such as high concentrations of manual workers and rapidly declining manual employment opportunities (Harrison, 1985, pp. 22–23). The Government's Priority Estates Programme, followed by its Estate Action Programme, sought to bring about physical improvements to the most disadvantaged areas. By 1991, there were 350 Estate Action programmes in operation (Boughton, 2018, pp. 186–187)—10% of the 1986–1987 Estate Action budget was earmarked for the improvement of homes for homeless households (Foster, 1990, p. 13). City Challenge and the Single Regeneration Budget were to follow as regeneration programmes of the 1990s, providing funding to those local authorities that had the most attractive public–private partnerships (Bache & Catney, 2008, p. 414).

The 1987 Conservative Manifesto introduced a new element to policy on regeneration. It linked inner city decay to the perceived failures of council housing and announced plans for regeneration that were tied to giving council tenants a choice of landlord. The 1988 Housing Act provided the opportunity for local authority tenants in an area to transfer their property to another landlord—for example, a housing association—subject to a ballot (a policy referred to as tenants' choice). There were also provisions for the housing in run down areas to be transferred to new bodies, Housing Action Trusts, which would be given substantial funding to bring about improvements—again, this was subject to a ballot of tenants. Paradoxically, local authorities were the key to this policy producing changes: Housing Action Trusts were only created in areas such as Hull and Liverpool where they had the support of the local authority, and stock was only transferred via tenants' choice where this was initiated and encouraged by councils. Forty-nine authorities proposed transfers between

1988 and 1992 for a variety of reasons—to prevent further losses from the Right to Buy, to facilitate more borrowing or to avoid 'predatory' takeovers. However, two thirds of these authorities either abandoned their proposals or had them defeated in tenant ballots (Mullins & Pawson, 2010, p. 80)

Single Homelessness

The Conservatives' approach to homeless people, particularly those who were young, provoked fierce policy debate. The government was frequently accused of ignoring the needs of the most disadvantaged people in the drive to encourage home ownership (Malpass & Murie, 1994, p. 98). However, it consistently rejected the view that homelessness was a result of the reduced number of rental homes, with the DoE pointing out that the number of lettings had decreased less steeply than the total rental stock (Wilson, 1996, pp. 29–30) and Mrs Thatcher insisting that the Right to Buy reduced the demand as well as the supply of rental housing (Thatcher, 1993, p. 604). The government's policies for single people were to create particular controversy in the 1980s and early 1990s, with statutory homelessness becoming a major issue at a later stage, as will be demonstrated below.

Young Homeless People

The government presented its social security measures as solving social problems, by reducing the incentives for dependency, and claimed that its cuts to benefits for young people were tackling homelessness by encouraging them to remain in the family home rather than leaving prematurely. This argument fitted well with the New Right preference for the family and the voluntary sector as providers of social and material support (Clapham & Smith, 1990, p. 195). Mrs Thatcher's view that young people were responsible for their own homelessness was made clear in one of her most famous quotes:

> [T]oo many children and people have been given to understand 'I have a problem, it is the Government's job to cope with it!' or 'I have a problem, I will go to get a grant to cope with it!' 'I am homeless, the Government must house me!' and so they are casting their problem on society and who is society? There is no such thing! (Quoted in Lund, 2016, p. 219)

It followed that there should be no substantial response to youth homelessness as Mrs Thatcher made clear to the Commons in 1988: “There is a number of young people who choose voluntarily to leave home; I do not think that we can be expected, no matter how many there are, to provide units for them” (quoted in Hutson & Liddiard, 1994, p. 58). The preference for family over state provision was indicated again in 1989, when the Government's review of the homelessness legislation discussed “the need to avoid encouraging the break up of family life and the neglect of family duties” (DoE, 1989, p. 7, quoted in Anderson, 1993, p. 19).

The limited initiatives that were taken in the area of youth homelessness were largely consistent with the government's philosophy, focusing on young people who had no family to remain with (i.e. care leavers) and on those young people who wanted to find employment. The 1989 Children Act included measures intended to ensure that accommodation was available for care leavers. However, it should be noted that housing had a minimal role in the Act, which was intended to bring consistency and improvement to the law about bringing up and protecting children (Allen, 2006, p. 3).

The measures that were introduced by the Act in the area of housing were noted largely for the confusion that they created. Section 20 (1) placed a duty on local authorities to provide accommodation for a child in need whose parents were unable to accommodate them, without the age of the child being specified, and Section 20 (3) indicated that there was a duty to provide accommodation for a child in need who was aged over 16 and whose welfare was “likely to be seriously prejudiced” if accommodation was not provided (Allen, 2006, pp. 106–107). These clauses placed responsibilities on social services authorities and so created uncertainty as to whether they or housing authorities were responsible for assessing (and, where appropriate, accommodating) homeless 16–17-year-olds. This uncertainty persisted even after all 16–17-year-olds were placed into the priority need category of the homelessness legislation in 2002 (see Chap. 6). Several years later, some clarity was finally brought by a Supreme Court ruling in 2008 that social services could not avoid their responsibilities to provide social care to 16–17-year-olds by passing them to housing authorities. This was followed by a further ruling by Baroness Hale of the Supreme Court in 2009 that Southwark council's social services department had wrongly decided that a homeless 17-year-old-boy did not qualify for social services accommodation, and statutory guidance being issued in April 2010, indicating that all 16–17-year-olds in need should be assessed by social services departments “without exception” (Lloyd, 2013).

The introduction of foyers for young people fitted with Conservative concerns to ensure economic activity among this age group. The Employment Department's support for the development of foyers rested on the belief that they could achieve a number of objectives, that is, providing a safe place to go when young people first left home in search of a job and independence; providing the chance to mix with other young people; providing expert information and training in a wide variety of areas; giving an opportunity to develop the skills and earning power needed for living independently; and providing an environment that was encouraging and conducive to work (Gilchrist & Jeffs, 1995). The Director of Shelter proclaimed them to be "the housing innovation of the 1990s" (Gilchrist & Jeffs, 1995, p. 4).

An evaluation of the initial pilot foyer projects by Quilgars and Anderson (1995, p. 4) concluded that they could not address the deeper structural disadvantages experienced by young people but that they "provided a mechanism to help less able young people to compete for existing training, employment and housing opportunities". However, a much more critical evaluation by Gilchrist and Jeffs (1995) argued that the selection of certain young people for foyer places on the grounds that they wished to take advantage of services such as careers advice, debt counselling and training had historical overtones of identifying those who were deserving of assistance: "This approach is akin to a return to the nineteenth century workhouse test which demanded servility as a pre-condition for receipt of help" (Gilchrist & Jeffs, 1995, p. 7).

Finally, one small-scale initiative sought to ensure that young people from outside London did not become homeless in the capital. The Single Homeless Young People Initiative provided grants to voluntary organisations to work with young people outside London who were at risk of becoming homeless and moving there. Three million pounds was shared between 14 projects across the country for three years from 1991. Provision included drop in centres, support workers, direct access hostels, lodging schemes, move on housing from hostels, long-term housing, advice, education, training, co-ordination of statutory and voluntary services, and support and counselling for young women who had been sexually abused (Darke, Conway, Holman, & Buckley, 1993, p. 46). Like the development of foyers, this initiative appeared to represent a limited change of approach, acknowledging that there were some young people who could not live with their family.

Shared Housing for Single Homeless People and the Assumptions of Policy

In the case of single homeless people of all ages, there were less direct claims that they were to blame for their own circumstances, although Jones (1995, p. 5) notes that John Major as Prime Minister suggested on more than one occasion that people slept rough because they wanted to and described beggars as an eyesore who should be dealt with by the law. However, as in previous time periods, services were developed for single homeless people on the assumption that they had needs beyond the provision of housing. In 1980, housing associations were invited to bid for funding under the Hostels Initiative, which was intended to provide shared housing for people with special needs, including single homeless people (Garside, Grimshaw, & Ward, 1990, p. 8). In order to be eligible for funding under the initiative, schemes had to be designed with prescribed features such as communal space, shared facilities and accommodation for staff (DoE, 1971, 1974b, 1978 cited in Garside, 1993, p. 321). Garside (1993, p. 321) argues that making these requirements of schemes for single homeless people said much about their perceived needs:

> [R]esidents' own preference for the ordinary requirements of a home—notably seclusion, privacy and personal identity—were compromised in pursuit of design criteria originally evolved for other 'special needs' groups, notably children and the elderly. The kinds of designs that were adopted for accommodating single homeless people signalled the need to remedy not only their lack of housing but also their lack of family and community status.

New forms of provision also arose from the closure of the post-war Reception Centres (which, in later years, came to be known as Resettlement Units). The closure programme was announced in 1985 (Deacon, Vincent, & Walker, 1995, p. 347), with the Secretary of State for Social Security identifying a number of weaknesses of the units—their size and institutional character; their insensitivity to local circumstances, needs and services; their anomalous position in the welfare system, as other similar responsibilities rested with local authorities; the poor physical condition of many of the units; and their poor track record in resettlement work (Steele, 1989, p. 55).

In 1989, the Resettlement Units Executive Agency was created to work with local authorities and the voluntary sector to develop alternative provision with a view to the eventual closure of the units. Deacon et al.'s

(1995, pp. 359–360) study of the closure of one unit—Alvaston near Derby—noted that alternative provision was not able to meet the diversity of needs of former residents. While the alternatives provided were suitable for some, others ex-Resettlement Unit residents were excluded either by formal admission criteria or by the imposition of house rules that were inconsistent with their needs and capacities. The findings of the study echoed the critique of the Hostels Initiative: "…many of the former residents of Alvaston did not need 'special needs' housing as it is conventionally understood, other than for a short transitional period" (Deacon et al., 1995, p. 360).

The study indicated more favourable outcomes for those former residents who moved directly into independent accommodation (Deacon et al., 1995, pp. 356–357)—a finding that was replicated in the Pathways Housing First initiative in New York, which will be discussed further in Chap. 7.

The Rough Sleepers' Initiative

The most publicised initiative for single homeless people during the period of Conservative rule was the Rough Sleepers' Initiative, launched at a time of unprecedented concern over rough sleeping in London. Greene (2014, p. 332) notes that the late 1980s saw a large increase in the number of people—many of them young—street homeless and begging in Central London; this was the first time that hostel space could not be found for all of them. In 1990 and 1991, the government accepted that there were between 1000 and 3000 people sleeping rough in London on any one night.

There were a number of indicators of growing public concern over rough sleeping around this time. Shelter and Crisis saw their incomes from donations increase substantially, 30,000 people took part in National Sleepout week organised by St Mungos in 1991 and the Big Issue was launched (Greene, 2014, p. 323). During 1989–1990, there were numerous newspaper reports on this issue, local businesses complained about the impact of street homelessness on tourism, Members of Parliament were asked for money on their way to work and television documentaries portrayed life in 'Cardboard City' (Anderson, 1993, p. 22). Anderson (1993, p. 22) argues that, "Over a period of two years, a marginalised housing issue being championed by one or two pressure groups had become a hugely publicised social problem which had escalated beyond containment."

Part of the government's response focused on enforcement: between 1988 and 1990, the number of people prosecuted for begging in London increased threefold (Greene, 2014, p. 325). In her memoirs, Margaret Thatcher (1993, pp. 603–604) made clear her view that many rough sleepers were deviant:

> But I insisted that whatever Government did to help, there must be a stick as well as a carrot. Crowds of drunken, dirty, often abusive and sometimes violent men must not be allowed to turn central areas of the capital into no-go areas for ordinary citizens. The police must disperse them and prevent them coming back once it was clear that accommodation was available. Unfortunately, there was a persistent tendency in polite circles to consider all the 'roofless' as victims of middle-class society rather than middle-class society as victims of the 'roofless'.

Thatcher (1993, p. 601) acknowledged a shortage of direct access hostels but commented that: "Nor are behavioural problems solved by bricks and mortar." She rejected the suggestions of Social Security Minister Tony Newton and the Social Security Department that benefit regulations could become more generous to the under 25s on the familiar grounds that this would provide an incentive for them to move to London rather than continue to live with their families (Thatcher, 1993, p. 603).

Instead, the government introduced the Single Homeless Initiative in 1990, a programme to make more hostel bedspaces and move-on accommodation available to those sleeping rough in Central London. After John Major became Prime Minister, the initiative was extended, provided with additional funding and re-named the Rough Sleepers' Initiative (RSI) (Greene, 2014, p. 323).

The initiative had the very specific objective of making it unnecessary to sleep rough in Central London. The first phase (which ran from 1990 to 1993) was primarily concerned with providing hostel places in the capital (DoE, 1995, pp. 5–6). The second stage (1993–1996) sought to provide up to 3300 bedspaces of permanent accommodation, focusing on a smaller number of voluntary agencies, housing associations and geographical areas of Central London. The third stage of the initiative (launched in 1996 and continuing into the period of Labour government) concentrated on tackling homelessness among the hard core of people who continued to sleep rough—many of who experienced severe mental health problems (Wilson, 2015, pp. 2–4).

The rhetoric around the initiative avoided linking government policies to rough sleeping. When giving its reasons for taking action, the DoE (1995, p. 5) made no mention of any national shortage of rented housing, but instead suggested that there was a specific problem in Central London, where voluntary agencies indicated that hostel spaces had 'silted up' due to a lack of move on accommodation. Housing Minister Michael Spicer made clear that family breakdown was a key reason for the growth of street homelessness:

> The problem of rough sleeping in small but concentrated numbers is one that has begun to affect major cities throughout the western world. It has developed for complex reasons, involving in particular the break up of families and other social ties. (Spicer, 1990, p. 1 quoted in Anderson, 1993, p. 23)

The former Conservative Minister interviewed for this book suggested that the problem could sometimes be a logistical one of the different locations of rough sleepers and bedspaces:

> Somewhere in London there was a bed, which would have accepted them. So, eventually part of the system was that we approached people who were rough sleeping and provided transport from where they were to where the shelter was. We had some telephone based system.

The DoE (1995, p. 4) acknowledged that the motivation for the initiative was not just to meet the needs of homeless people but also to support the promotion of London as a good place for business and tourism.

The central role of voluntary organisations in the initiative was claimed to have two important political purposes. Cloke, May, and Johnsen (2010, p. 31) argue that it was important for the government to bypass local authorities, while Greene (2014, p. 324) notes that the government frequently pointed to the role of the voluntary agencies when the initiative was criticised. Nick Hardwick, the Director of Centrepoint Soho, was seconded to lead the initiative for the first six months (Greene, 2014, p. 324) and it was workers from voluntary organisations who sought to make contact with rough sleepers and to persuade them to take up places in hostels (Wilson, 2015, p. 2).

In 1993, the clearing of Lincoln's Inn Field, one of the most visible encampments of homeless people in the capital, was a major change brought about by the RSI, and one that was achieved with substantial support from voluntary organisations. The agencies involved were criticised in some quarters for their role, and it was suggested that they had become too close to the government (Greene, 2014, p. 326). However, Jeremy Swain offered a very clear justification for their actions:

> I have to say as an outreach worker working at Lincoln's Inn Fields I did not see that as a community. First of all people were turning over there a lot, in other words there wasn't a very stable group. But also you know, people were having their bashes, their boxes set on fire, there were rats there, there was fights, it was a really unpleasant scene .... And also you know, as an organisation working with the homeless our obligations do extend to the community, and frankly, Lincoln's Inn Fields was for a good part of the early evening and through the night not a place where people could use the park; it was really unpleasant because of the sheer volume of rough sleeping.

Voluntary organisations placed limits on the extent to which they co-operated with the government; they refused to assist when asked to help remove a 'hard core' of rough sleepers from the capital's 'black spots'. The task was taken on by the police alone, with the number of people arrested under various Vagrancy Acts in Central London rising from 192 in 1991 to 1445 in 1992 (Cloke et al., 2010, pp. 31–32). However, there were also examples of the police and voluntary organisations working together effectively, for example, when a new Homelessness Policing Unit was created in Charing Cross in 1992, acknowledging that homeless people could be exploited victims (Greene, 2014, p. 325).

Initiatives in the area of rough sleeping are inevitably judged mainly by numbers; Housing Minister Sir George Young was able to announce in 1992 that estimates of the number of rough sleepers in Central London had fallen from over 1000 when the initiative began to 420 in November 1992 (Wilson, 2015, pp. 2–3). Those who remained sleeping rough after the first phase of the initiative tended to have the most severe needs, often involving mental health and alcohol, and to have been sleeping rough for an extended period (Randall & Brown, 1993, p. 69).

However, critics were quick to point out that the reduction in numbers did not necessarily point to a positive experience for former rough sleepers, with difficulties reported in relation to both temporary and permanent accommodation. The evaluation of the first phase of the initiative noted that most hostel residents left within a month, with only a minority known to go on to long term, secure accommodation. Where residents did move onto permanent housing, this was sometimes a substantial distance from their established social contacts, leading to feelings of isolation. Many experienced serious difficulties in paying rent and other regular bills and said that they would have liked more support to move into their property, particularly advice about financial matters, housekeeping and furniture (Randall & Brown, 1993, pp. 69–70).

The evaluation at the end of the second stage of the initiative (1993–1996) was more positive in several ways and showed substantially more satisfaction. The long-term accommodation developed under the second phase was judged to be high quality and to meet the needs of clients. Only 11% of tenants said that they had not received enough resettlement support, compared to 40% in the first phase. A small group of longer-term rough sleepers had given up hope of ever finding a home, but even they could sometimes be persuaded to accept accommodation by outreach workers. Winter shelters, where the more relaxed management regime allowed dogs and alcohol, had some success in attracting in those who would not usually use services. The shelters varied as to how successful they were in resettlement work (Randall & Brown, 1996, pp. 1–2).

However, the initiative continued to be criticised for addressing the symptoms of the homelessness problem rather than the causes. Cloke et al. (2010, pp. 30–31) suggest that the value of the RSI to the government was that it was seen to be responding to the problem of rough sleeping without having to address the residual position of single homeless people within the welfare system. Anderson (1993, p. 22) similarly argues that the initiative did not tackle underlying causes and was motivated by media pressure and government embarrassment rather than a concern to meet needs.

The Homeless Mentally Ill Initiative

The Homeless Mentally Ill Initiative (HMII) was also launched in 1990 for reasons that were similar to those that lay behind the RSI. At the end of the 1980s, the Department of Health suggested that were a number of people who were homeless and also had significant mental health needs: approximately 300–500 people sleeping rough or in squats and as many as 2000–3000 staying in hostel accommodation (Croft-White, 1998, pp. 6–7).

A further stimulus to the HMII was the new arrangements made for community care under the 1990 NHS and Community Care Act, reflecting the government's desire that as many people as possible should live in the community rather than in institutions (Croft-White, 1998, p. 13). The HMII could help to alleviate some of the worst consequences when this policy was unsuccessful.

In addition, the HMII had the benefit of building on a Department of Health and Social Security (DHSS)-funded pilot project, which involved the creation of the Lewisham and North Southwark Psychiatric Team for Homeless People in 1987. This team of psychiatric, medical and social care professionals provided support to homelessness agencies in South-East London (Croft-White, 1998, p. 7).

The HMII was intended to "reintroduce homeless people with mental illness into mainstream services by encouraging them into temporary accommodation where they can be offered suitable care and assistance before they can be moved into community care" (Department of Health, 1990, quoted in Croft-White, 1998, p. 7). The initiative initially covered six London boroughs, with two more boroughs and ten areas outside London added subsequently. It provided high-care and medium-care temporary accommodation projects and, in later years, units of permanent move on housing (Croft-White, 1998, pp. 7–11). Hostels varied in the extent to which rehabilitation and 'moving on' were objectives, but all operated with a minimum of rules and regulations (Craig, Bayliss, Klein, Manning, & Reader, 1995, p. 122). Multidisciplinary teams made contact with people with mental health problems who were sleeping rough, but they also accepted referrals for former rough sleepers who were living in insecure accommodation (Croft-White, 1998, p. 16). These teams continued to work with service users through hostels and move on accommodation with the ultimate aim of resettlement and connection with appropriate 'mainstream' social and psychiatric support services (Craig et al., 1995, pp. 7–8).

An evaluation of the first five years of the initiative demonstrated that the needs of the client group, and the costs of providing services, were greater than had been anticipated: the clinical teams estimated that 84% of clients needed daily visiting in the first six months after resettlement and many needed assistance with daily tasks ranging from handling money to personal hygiene (Craig et al., 1995, p. 106). It was difficult to obtain suitably supported move on accommodation which would accept clients with high levels of need: for example, those with learning difficulties, alcohol/drug dependence and/or personality disorder (Craig et al., 1995, p. 122). The withdrawal of regular team input was often a trigger for resettlement breaking down (Craig et al., 1995, p. vii).

The evaluation provided one important parallel finding to the study of the closure of Alvaston Resettlement Unit (Deacon et al., 1995). Three times as many resettlement breakdowns occurred with clients who were living in supported accommodation placements (residential projects and group homes) than among those who moved into independent flats. This finding may be partly explained by the greater severity of disorder among those moving into shared accommodation, but there were also complaints that such accommodation was physically unsatisfactory, regulations were too difficult to adhere to and disposable income was too low after accommodation charges (Craig et al., 1995, p. vii).

A later evaluation found that by 1996–1997, the initiative was providing a service to over 1500 people, whose needs were often beyond those that conventional community-based services could meet (Croft-White, 1998, pp. 2–5). The evaluation noted that the initiative had not fully met the needs of some groups, most significantly those with problematic use of drugs or alcohol, those with undiagnosed mental health problems and those with an entrenched lifestyle due to many years of street homelessness (Croft-White, 1998, pp. 2–5): a finding consistent with evaluations of the RSI (Randall & Brown, 1996, pp. 1–2). In addition, accommodation could not always be found for clients who wished to be re-housed in an area that was familiar to them and some teams were not able to attract applications from consultant psychiatrists who could facilitate Mental Health Act assessments (Croft-White, 1998, pp. 2–5). However, the overall finding of the evaluation was that: "Over the past seven years the HMII has proved effective in making contact with and engaging a client group whose complex and different needs had largely been overlooked prior to its establishment in 1990" (Croft-White, 1998, p. 54).

Statutory Homelessness

Monitoring and Reviewing the Legislation

The Conservatives came to power with the 1977 legislation in its infancy. Despite major social policy changes in related areas, and a confrontational relationship with local authorities, there was surprisingly little attention paid to either the homelessness legislation itself or the manner in which authorities were putting it into practice. Neil Munslow recalled the level of monitoring when he took up his post in 1989: "At the time the main government measure of whether you were doing well or not was are you processing cases within 33 days." Similarly, the former Conservative Minister said of the local authority response to homelessness: "I don't recall us monitoring it very aggressively."

There were, however, several reviews of the legislation undertaken by the DoE. The first, which had been in progress since December 1978 to satisfy an undertaking of the previous Labour government, reported in 1982. It noted that the Conservative majority on the London Boroughs Association wanted to change the legislation, but that all other local authority associations were prepared to continue to operate it as it stood, albeit with requests for more resources. The review recorded a number of concerns about the operation of the legislation, most notably a widespread perception that it facilitated a degree of 'queue jumping'. However, it warned against making any change to the legislation on the grounds that this would leave the government "caught in a cross-fire between those who wanted to repeal or emasculate the Act on one side and those who wanted to strengthen it on the other" (Secretary of the State for the Environment and Secretary of State for Wales, 1982).

Margaret Thatcher expressed great disappointment with the review, particularly over its failure to recommend action in relation to queue jumping (Lund, 2016, p. 219). However, in 1982, Secretary of State for the Environment Michael Heseltine announced that the government had decided that there should be no change to the primary legislation but a number of other measures would be taken: the Code of Guidance would be tightened to limit the scope for local authority discretion, a new unified Housing Benefit system was intended to reduce homelessness due to rent arrears (although this proved highly problematic in practice), Housing Investment Programme financial settlements would take into account the number of homelessness acceptances by local authorities and there would be investment in hostels and low-cost home ownership schemes (Wilson, 1996, p. 12).

The government undertook a further review of the legislation in 1988–1989. The outcome was announced by Chris Patten, Secretary of State for the Environment, who stated that the Act sought an appropriate balance between those who were homeless and those in other forms of housing need. He suggested that local authorities were the right bodies to implement the legislation, but there were variations in practice. The Code of Guidance would be adjusted again to ensure improved standards in areas such as speed of processing applicants and efforts to avoid the use of bed-and-breakfast hotels (discussed further below). Extra funding was to be allocated to housing associations operating in London and the South East, where homelessness pressures were greatest (Wilson, 1996, p. 19). The changes to the Code of Guidance were made in 1991 (Wilson, 1996, p. 12).

Responding to Two Crises

In addition to raised public concern over rough sleeping among single homeless people in the late 1980s and the early 1990s, a less visible crisis—but one with greater financial implications—arose in relation to the provision of temporary accommodation for statutorily homeless households. The number of households accepted as statutorily homeless in England and Wales increased from 65,850 in 1980 to a peak of 154,620 in 1991 (Wilson, 1996, pp. 21–22). Although pressures were felt in most areas, they were particularly acute in London. By the end of the 1980s, approximately two thirds of local authority lettings in the capital were being made to statutorily homeless households, compared to slightly more than a quarter in England and Wales as a whole (Greve, 1991, p. 26). Evans and Duncan (1988, p. 2) found that three quarters of London authorities received over 1000 homelessness enquiries in 1985–1986 compared to an average of 521 per authority nationally.

As homelessness grew, so did the number of statutorily homeless households living in temporary accommodation—the 'year-end' figure increased from 9340 in 1983 to its highest level of 63,070 in 1992 (Wilson, 1996, pp. 21–22). In 1993, 60% of statutorily homeless households living in temporary accommodation were in London (Edwards, 1995, p. 63). The use of bed-and-breakfast hotels reached its peak in 1991, with 12,150 statutorily homeless households living in this form of accommodation at the end of the year, compared to 1640 in 1982 (Wilson, 1996, pp. 21–22). Evans and Duncan (1988, p. 2) found that the use of bed-and-breakfast accommodation was heavily concentrated in London. Steve Hilditch discussed working for the London Borough of Haringey in 1984, when the number of families in bed-and-breakfast hotels reached 100 for the first time, then finding that it was to reach 1000 within a few years, as a consequence of rising demand and declining supply during the 1980s. In addition to the financial costs, the severe consequences for families of being placed in bed-and-breakfast hotels were graphically described by Conway (1988).

Both central government and local authorities took action to seek to avert the crisis. Foster (1990, p. 6) notes that central government initiatives in the area of statutory homelessness tended to involve specific allocations of money for limited schemes. For example, a £250 million two-year programme announced in 1989 included support for the Cash Incentive Scheme, which provided council tenants with a cash incentive to buy a home on the open market so that the resulting vacancy could be used for a homeless household. A housing association version of the scheme—the Tenants' Incentive Scheme—followed in 1990 (Angle, Bellchambers, & Nuttall, 1995, p. 9).

Local authorities sought to make self-contained property available as temporary accommodation through private sector leasing, by which the authority took out long-term leases on private property. This became the dominant form of temporary accommodation for London's homeless households, albeit usually after an initial period in a bed-and-breakfast hotel. In 1986, approximately one fifth of London boroughs were leasing privately, but this had increased to four fifths in 1992—a trend aided by a downturn in the housing market (Edwards, 1995, pp. 63–64).

Government concerns over the cost of private sector leasing led to a change to capital expenditure rules that limited the maximum length of lease that could be taken to three years. A Housing Association Leasing Scheme was launched with some similar characteristics: a Housing Association took a lease with a private owner and the local authority had 100% nomination rights in return for a nomination fee (Edwards, 1995, p. 62).

While much of the temporary accommodation provided by leasing schemes was an improvement on bed-and-breakfast hotels in terms of both cost and quality, it still presented some difficulties. Edwards (1995) found that the properties leased by local authorities initially tended to be of a good standard, but, as the scheme expanded, concerns began to be raised about the quality of properties and people being accommodated a long way from their support networks. However, Niner (1989, p. 157) found that greater concerns were expressed over the hostel spaces that some local authorities had accessed as an alternative to bed-and-breakfast hotels, with concerns over the quality of properties, shared facilities and the standard of management.

The second statutory homelessness crisis, in the early 1990s, arose over mortgage repossessions and was embarrassing for a government that was so eager to advocate home ownership. The causes of the crisis were rapid house price rises in the late 1980s, followed by interest rate rises in response to inflationary pressures in the economy and rising unemployment. House prices fell every year from 1989 to 1993 and mortgage arrears—which had historically accounted for 2% or less of statutory homelessness cases—reached a peak of 12% in 1991 (Somerville, 1994, p. 173). The government responded by negotiating with lenders to be more flexible with those who fell behind with payments, introducing a 'mortgage rescue' scheme by which housing associations were able to purchase the property of a borrower in arrears and lease it back to them, and giving housing associations extra funding to buy up empty property (Stephens et al., 2008, pp. 6–7).

The government did not acknowledge that either of the crises in statutory homelessness had come about as a result of its own policies or a reduced supply of affordable housing (see, e.g. Foster, 1990, p. 6). Small initiatives to tackle specific problems were the theme of policy until the housing world was shocked by proposals for substantial legislative change.

The Change to the Legislation

Concerns that the homelessness legislation created an unfair advantage to those who were homeless, in comparison to those who were on waiting lists, had been a recurring Conservative concern since the passing of the 1977 Act. Various reasons have been suggested for the reluctance to change the legislation through the first 15 years of Conservative government and then for the surprise announcement in 1994 of proposals to make the local authority's obligation to homeless households one of providing temporary accommodation only (Somerville, 1994, p. 163).

Taking first the lack of any earlier change, Raynsford (2016, p. 30) suggests that the reasons were that the legislation had been accepted by the vast majority of local authorities, repeal of the 1977 Act would have risked a media storm over the hardship created prior to the legislation being passed, and the legislation fitted with a wider perspective that saw local authority housing as a safety net for the most disadvantaged, rather than a universal tenure. The former Conservative Minister interviewed for this book referred to the all-party support for the 1977 legislation and also suggested that there was a question of priorities: "The Department had other things on its plate at the time—we had rate capping, we had abolition of the GLC [*Greater London Council*], and quite a major programme on housing not on the homeless front."

Somerville (1999, pp. 41–42) argues that were three changes between 1979 and 1994 that prompted the proposal to change the legislation: a change in local authority attitudes towards homelessness, which made abuse of a temporary duty less likely; the assumed reviving of the private rented sector brought about by the 1988 Housing Act, together with fading memories of private landlords' abuses of tenants; and the ending of the perception that the local authority sector provided 'housing for life.' In addition, Lund (2016, p. 220) argues that the Conservatives suspected that Labour-controlled local authorities were accepting more people as statutorily homeless than they needed to because this would embarrass the government and also increases their funding—as noted above, the number of homeless acceptances had become a factor in determining the level of Housing Investment Programme funding given to authorities (Lund, 2016, p. 220).

A belief that the 1977 Act acted as an incentive to young unmarried women to become pregnant—echoing the thinking of Charles Murray (1990, pp. 47–48) in his discussion of the underclass—had frequently been voiced by Conservative politicians, including Margaret Thatcher (1993, p. 604). Fitzpatrick and Stephens (1999, p. 416) argue that the changes outlined in 1994 were part of an otherwise abortive attempt by John Major to re-assert traditional moral values through a 'back to basics' campaign. Major said in his 1993 speech to the Conservative Party conference:

> It is time to return to core values, time to get back to basics, to self-discipline and respect for the law, to consideration for the others, to accepting responsibility for yourself and your family—and not shuffling it off on other people and the state. (Quoted in Wintour & Bates, 1993)

At the same conference, the speech of Housing Minister Sir George Young addressed both this concern over core values, and the longstanding Conservative view of unfairness to those who were on waiting lists, when he discussed the shortcomings of the 1977 Act:

> How do we explain to the young couple … who want to wait for a home before they start a family … that they cannot be rehoused ahead of the unmarried teenager expecting her first probably unplanned child? How do we explain to parents that if they evict their children they may go to the top of the queue, and get secure accommodation? What signal about family responsibility does that send out? (Quoted in Fitzpatrick & Stephens, 1994, p. i)

The 1994 Consultation Paper *Access to Local Authority and Housing Association Tenancies* set out the Government's proposals for reforming the 1977 legislation. It began by arguing that the fear expressed in the parliamentary debate over the Act that it would become a "charter for scrimshankers and scroungers" had been justified and that there was now no incentive for people to take action to meet their own housing need:

> Someone who faces the possibility of homelessness will realise that anyone meeting the necessary criteria and taking no other action to find alternative accommodation will be accepted by the authority as statutorily homeless, and that the authority will be obliged to offer that individual and other members of their household permanent re-housing as soon as practicable and provide temporary accommodation in the interim. If, on the other hand, the person in question takes the initiative in finding alternative accommodation (which may be no different in character from the 'temporary' accommodation which the local authority would otherwise provide), the only route into a local authority or housing association tenancy is through the slower and less certain avenue of a waiting list. (DoE, 1994, pp. 3–4)

The view that waiting list applicants were unfairly disadvantaged was supported by citing their average waiting time of 1.2 years for housing, compared to 0.7 years on the part of those who were statutorily homeless. This difference, the paper suggested, could not be justified by different levels of need:

> Recent research conducted for the Department shows that people re-housed from the waiting list are in many important respects (such as income, employment status and previous tenure) similar to households re-housed through the homeless route. The housing needs of the two groups have much in common. But statutorily homeless households receive automatic priority over others on the waiting list in the allocation of tenancies. (DoE, 1994, p. 3)

The research to which this quotation referred consisted of three surveys: one of local authorities, one of waiting list applicants and one of new tenants. It showed that 29% of local authority allocations were made to people who were statutorily homeless, with this figure rising to 43% in London (Prescott-Clarke, Clemens, & Park, 1994, p. 11). The key piece of evidence on which the government based its conclusion of similarity between waiting list and statutorily homeless households was one table (in a 118 word report) which did indeed show that statutorily homeless applicants, non-statutorily homeless applicants and non-homeless applicants had almost identical levels of unemployment. However, one crucial difference was that the average number of children was 1.2 for those households who were statutorily homeless, compared to 0.6 for those who were non-statutorily homeless and 0.5 for those who were not homeless (Prescott-Clarke et al., 1994, p. 90). The limited evidence provided by the study suggested, therefore, that differences in the outcomes for households were largely a reflection of whether they had dependent children.

Fitzpatrick and Stephens (1994, pp. 6–13) add further reasons for questioning the use made of research in the Consultation Paper. For example, they argue that it failed to acknowledge that statutorily homeless households, although re-housed more quickly, tended to move into poorer quality properties out of a fear of losing their legal status if they were to refuse an offer.

Whatever the limitations of the evidence presented to support its argument, the main proposal of the Consultation Paper was that statutorily homeless households should qualify only for temporary accommodation as a result of their homelessness and should have to join the waiting list along with other households if they wished to be offered permanent local authority housing (DoE, 1994, p. 5) The Scottish Office produced its own consultation document which, although including more sympathetic wording than the DoE Consultation Paper, reiterated the key proposals (Fitzpatrick & Stephens, 1994, p. i).

There were nearly 10,000 written responses to the Consultation Paper, with the London Boroughs Association offering the only favourable response. Critics suggested that homeless households would be 'scapegoated' and had lost their safety net, and that the proposals were unnecessary, unjust and unworkable (Somerville, 1999, p. 44). Sir George Young defended the proposals in parliament in the following terms:

> Many of the responses did not address the actual proposals, but responded to misleading claims by lobby organisations. Others wrote in about hypothetical effects of policy … it is not and never has been the intention that families and other vulnerable people should be left to live on the streets or in unsatisfactory accommodation. (Quoted in Wilson, 1996, p. 36)

Parts 6 and 7 of the 1996 Housing Act embodied the thinking of the 1994 Consultation Paper with very few amendments (Somerville, 1999, pp. 49–50). Part 6 placed a duty on local authorities to allocate all housing from one housing register, with reasonable preference given to six categories of applicants, that is, people occupying insanitary or overcrowded housing or otherwise living in unsatisfactory conditions; people occupying accommodation which was temporary or occupied on insecure terms; families with dependent children; households consisting of or including someone who was expecting a child; households consisting of or including someone with a particular need for settled accommodation on medical or welfare grounds; and households whose social or economic circumstances were such that they have difficulty in securing settled accommodation.

Part 7 of the Act re-defined the responsibilities of local authorities to homeless households. The four tests to satisfy—that is, being homeless, not intentionally homeless, in priority need and with a local connection—remained broadly unchanged. However, if the local authority was satisfied that there was suitable alternative accommodation available, its duty was merely to provide advice and assistance to enable the household to access that alternative accommodation.

For households who had passed the four tests and for whom there was no alternative accommodation available, the local authority duty became to provide temporary accommodation for a two-year period. This duty ceased if an applicant refused an offer of accommodation having been told of the consequences of a refusal. There was a power for the local authority to continue to provide accommodation after the two-year period had ended, but temporary accommodation could only be provided in its own stock for two years in any three-year period (Somerville, 1999, p. 50). Homeless households would have the opportunity to put themselves onto the housing register and be considered along with others for permanent housing, provided that they were not excluded from the register—the Act gave legal backing to such exclusions, and they increased fourfold in the following year (Harding & Harding, 2006, p. 147).

The debate over the changing obligations to statutorily homeless households was complicated by a House of Lords Ruling in July 1995, in relation to the case of Victoria Awua. Lord Hoffman appeared to suggest that local authorities could discharge their duties to statutorily homeless households by making an offer of temporary accommodation, with no time period specified. The DoE issued an explanatory paper in October 1995, stating that the obligation to statutorily homeless households would be to secure accommodation for a minimum of one year (Wilson, 1996, p. 57)—this was later increased to two years as one of the few concessions that the government made to its critics.

Local Authority Responses to Homelessness

The improvement to local authority practice that had been noted before the passing of the 1977 legislation appeared to continue as they adjusted to their new responsibilities. The Association of District Councils had opposed the 1977 Act and local authorities in Scotland had resisted the extension of the legislation North of the Border (Lund, 2016, p. 245), but Somerville (1999, p. 35) notes that local authority opposition to the legislation had all but disappeared by the end of the 1980s. The evidence base for examining local authority practice improved during this period, with several significant studies. Although it remained difficult to gain a comprehensive view, examples of good practice appeared to become more commonplace.

However, in the years immediately following the Act, some housing authorities were challenged by judicial review for refusing to accept their new responsibilities. Others sought to minimise their responsibilities by arguing that people occupying emergency accommodation—such as night shelters and women's refuges—were not homeless in terms of the Act. Temporary accommodation continued to be a source of poor practice, with some authorities insisting that homeless households remained there for a fixed period of time before being made an offer of permanent housing. Accommodation provided on a temporary basis could consist of former poorhouses, hotels, guest houses, bed-and-breakfast accommodation, disused army camps, or—in one case—a 6 ft. by 4 ft. tent (Watchman & Robson, 1989, pp. 37–40). South Cambridgeshire District Council was quite explicit about selecting stock for temporary accommodation that was least desirable in terms of construction, facilities and location in order to deter applications from those who were not genuinely homeless (Thompson, 1988, pp. 69–70). A Housing Aid Centre worker from the time reported in interview the continuing struggle to persuade or force some local authorities to accept their new responsibilities under the legislation, for example: "I remember it took us quite a long time to get them to understand that the legislation didn't say somebody had to be so many months pregnant."

Unsympathetic practice had not disappeared by the 1990s, with Lidstone (1994, pp. 462–469) noting that some local authorities continued to find ways to ration the support provided to homeless households. Reception staff could advise applicants they did not consider to be in priority need not to seek an interview, information could be withheld about the local authority's legal responsibilities, investigations could be inadequately pursued due to lack of resources and a variety of measures could be used to deter applicants: they could be forced to wait to see staff, experience a humiliating interview process, forced to wait for a substantial period of time in temporary accommodation or re-housed outside the borough. The continuing use of deterrent measures was confirmed by Evans (1999, p. 148).

However, perhaps the clearest indication that the broad trend was towards local authorities meeting the needs of homeless applicants more effectively is provided by comparing a study of CHAR (the Campaign for the Homeless and Rootless, later the Housing Campaign for Single People) in 1983–1984 with later surveys of local authority practice. There was one finding where a direct comparison was possible—CHAR found that only five local authorities in England and Wales treated all 16–17-year-olds as being in priority need (Venn, 1985, pp. 18–20), while a study by Kay (1994, p. 14) approximately a decade later found that 23% of authorities (again in England and Wales) were taking this approach. In other areas, indirect comparisons pointed to the same trend. The study by CHAR found that 6% of responding authorities were implementing policies towards single homeless people beyond following the Code of Guidance and 11% were taking action to help single homeless people which was not formulated into policy (Venn, 1985, pp. 18–20). In contrast, Kay (1994, p. 20) found that 57% of housing authorities provided continuing support to 16–17-year-olds after they were re-housed, and a study in the same year by Butler, Carlisle, & Lloyd (1994, pp. 18–19) found that 56% of authorities in England provided outreach support to formerly homeless households of all ages.

There was local authority resistance to the limitations that the 1996 Housing Act sought to impose on the services that they provided to homeless households. Niner (1997, pp. 33–34), in case studies of responses to the Act, found that one authority housed statutorily homeless households in temporary, private sector accommodation and told them that support would be withdrawn if they had not made sufficient efforts to meet their own needs after two years. However, this was an atypical response as Mullins and Niner (1998, p. 187) note:

> [M]ost authorities had tried with some ingenuity to devise their Part VI priority schemes so as to replicate as far as possible the pre-existing balance between 'homeless' and other applicants in allocations, using the new rea-

> sonable preference categories. This was partly driven by the need to keep control of the amount and cost of temporary (two year duty) accommodation needed, but there seems also to have been recognition that homeless people merit priority because of their needs.

Similarly, Cloke, Milbourne, and Widdowfield (2000, p. 748) found that many authorities had adjusted their allocation policies to enable homeless households to be re-housed directly from the housing register, so avoiding the need for them to be given a temporary tenancy—another method of resisting the intentions of the legislation.

Variations in local authority practice during the period of Conservative rule were noted by Niner (1989, pp. 14–15), who studied the homelessness services of nine authorities and concluded that they could be divided into three groups. Three of the authorities (Birmingham, Newcastle and Nottingham) aimed to be 'generous and liberal' in their interpretation of the 1977 legislation, three (Gloucester, Islington and New Forest) sought an approach that was 'reasonably sympathetic' and fair and three (Cardiff, Hillingdon and Westminster) aimed at a stricter approach. Although the three 'generous and liberal' authorities were all Labour controlled, Niner (1989, p. 16) argued that the nature of the local housing market also had a significant influence on policy: "Use of temporary accommodation appeared to be related most directly to homelessness pressures, regardless of political control."

This finding demonstrates the continuing influence of housing demand on the services received by homeless households. Mullins and Niner (1996, pp. 103–113) note that the issuing of the new Code of Guidance in 1991 brought about a number of benefits—revisions to local authority policies and procedures and a better and fairer service to homeless applicants—but wide variations in practice remained.

Summary

This was the period of post-war history in which the debate about causes of homelessness was fiercest. In the case of statutory homelessness, the assumptions that the 1977 legislation was providing an incentive for some households to declare themselves homeless when there was no need to, while also rewarding young women who had children outside marriage, was among the factors that led to the weakening of statutory protection under the 1996 Housing Act. However, the ideologically driven debate about youth homelessness was the most intense, with the government insisting that bad choices on the part of the individual were the key cause, and rejecting claims that its policies were to blame because they reduced the supply of affordable rented housing and the disposable income available to young people. The rough sleeping crisis of the late 1980s, and the government response to it, further polarised the debate. Critics claimed that the initiatives taken did not tackle underlying causes of homelessness and that there was no acknowledgement of diversity among single homeless people—some were incorrectly assumed to require 'special needs' housing, while others could not access the higher levels of support that they needed.

The government's concern over homeless people having an unfair advantage in accessing the social rented sector seems slightly ironic, given that the popularity of this sector—already falling in the 1960s and 1970s—reduced substantially in this period. Although statutorily homeless households were re-housed into a sector of declining popularity, many benefitted from a greater range of services provided by local authorities. However, substantial differences remained between authorities, and there was a major divide between areas with high demand for housing (particularly London) and others.

While Mrs Thatcher insisted that cuts to the benefits of young people were a preventative measure designed to discourage them from leaving home unnecessarily, this was a period in which there were few primary or secondary prevention initiatives as conventionally understood. Instead, the focus of policy was on those households who were already homeless—with provision for rough sleepers becoming a central policy concern that would persist through subsequent changes of government.

References

Alcock, P. (1994). Welfare rights and wrongs: The limits of anti-poverty strategies. *Local Government Studies, 9*(2), 134–152.

Allen, N. (2006). *Making sense of the Children Act 1989* (4th ed.). Chichester, UK: John Wiley and Sons.

Anderson, I. (1993). Housing policy and street homelessness in Britain. *Housing Studies, 8*(1), 17–28.

Andrews, K., & Jacobs, J. (1990). *Punishing the poor: Poverty under Thatcher*. London, UK: Macmillan London Limited.

Angle, H., Bellchambers, A., & Nuttall, S. (1995). *Cash incentives to housing association tenants: A review of the tenants' incentive scheme*. London, UK: Department of the Environment.

Ashton, D., Maguire, M., & Spilsbury, M. (1990). *Restructuring the labour market*. Basingstoke, UK: Macmillan.
Bache, I., & Catney, P. (2008). Embryonic associationalism: New Labour and urban governance. *Public Administration, 86*(2), 411–428.
Balloch, S., & Jones, B. (1990). *Poverty and anti-poverty strategy: The local government response*. London, UK: Association of Metropolitan Authorities.
Boughton, J. (2018). *Municipal dreams: The rise and fall of council housing*. London, UK: Verso Books.
Butler, K., Carlisle, B., & Lloyd, R. (1994). *Homelessness in the 1990s*. London, UK: Shelter.
Byrne, T. (2000). *Local government in Britain*. London, UK: Penguin.
Carlen, P. (1996). *Jigsaw—A political criminology of youth homelessness*. Buckingham, UK: Open University Press.
Clapham, D., & Smith, S. (1990). Housing policy and 'special needs'. *Policy and Politics, 18*(3), 193–205.
Cloke, P., May, J., & Johnsen, S. (2010). *Swept up lives? Re-envisioning the homeless city*. Chichester, UK: John Wiley & Sons.
Cloke, P., Milbourne, P., & Widdowfield, R. (2000). *Change but no change: Dealing with homelessness under the 1996 Housing Act. Housing Studies, 15*(5), 739–756.
Conway, J. (1988). *Prescription for poor health: The crisis for homeless families*. London, UK: SHAC (the London Housing Advice Centre.
Craig, T., Bayliss, E., Klein, O., Manning, P., & Reader, L. (1995). *The homeless mentally ill initiative*. London, UK: Department of Health.
Croft-White, C. (1998). *Evaluation of the homeless mentally ill initiative 1990–1997*. London, UK: Department of Health.
Darke, J. Conway, J., & Holman, C. with Buckley, K. (1993). *Homes for our children*. London, UK: National Housing Forum.
Deacon, A., Vincent, J., & Walker, R. (1995). Whose choice, hostels or homes? Policies for single homeless people. *Housing Studies, 10*(3), 345–363.
Department of the Environment. (1994). *Access to local authority and housing association tenancies: A consultation paper*. London, UK: Department of the Environment, Her Majesty's Stationery Office.
Department of the Environment. (1995). *Rough sleepers initiative: Future plans*. London, UK: Department of the Environment.
Edwards, R. (1995). Making temporary accommodation permanent: The cost for homeless families. *Critical Social Policy, 15*(1), 60–75.
Ellison, N. (1998). The changing politics of social policy. In N. Ellison & C. Pierson (Eds.), *Developments in British Social Policy* (pp. 31–45). Basingstoke, UK: Macmillan.
Ellison, N., & Pierson, C. (1998). Introduction. In N. Ellison & C. Pierson (Eds.), *Developments in British Social Policy* (pp. 1–14). Basingstoke, UK: Macmillan.

Evans, A. (1999). Rationing device or passport to social housing? The operation of the homelessness legislation in Britain in the 1990s. In S. Hutson & D. Clapham (Eds.), *Homelessness: Public policies and private troubles* (pp. 133–154). London, UK: Cassell.
Evans, A., & Duncan, S. (1988). *Responding to homelessness, local authority policy and practice*. London, UK: Department of the Environment, Her Majesty's Stationery Office.
Finn, D. (1987). *Training without jobs*. Basingstoke, UK: Macmillan.
Fitzpatrick, S., & Stephens, M. (1994). Housing the homeless: Policy and legal issues. *Occasional Paper 2*, Centre for Housing Research and Urban Studies, University of Glasgow, Glasgow, Scotland.
Fitzpatrick, S., & Stephens, M. (1999). Homelessness, need and desert in the allocation of council housing. *Housing Studies, 14*(4), 413–441.
Forrest, R., & Murie, A. (1990). *Moving the housing market: Council estates, social change and privatisation*. Aldershot, UK: Avebury.
Foster, S. (1990). *No new homes*. London, UK: Shelter.
Garside, P. L. (1993). Housing needs, family values and single homeless people. *Policy and Politics, 21*(4), 319–328.
Garside, P. L., Grimshaw, R. W., & Ward, F. J. (1990). *No place like home: The hostels experience*. London, UK: Department of the Environment.
Gilchrist, R., & Jeffs, T. (1995). Foyers: Housing solution or folly? *Youth and Policy, 50*, 1–12.
Gray, C. (1994). *Government beyond the centre*. Basingstoke, UK: Macmillan.
Greene, J. (2014). Managing poverty, managing dissent: Homeless politics and collective action in London. *Policy and Politics, 42*(3), 315–331.
Greve, J. (1991). *Homelessness in Britain*. York, UK: Joseph Rowntree Foundation.
Harding, A., & Harding, J. (2006). Inclusion and exclusion in the re-housing of former prisoners. *Probation Journal, 53*(2), 139–155.
Harris, N. (1989). *Social security for young people*. Aldershot, UK: Avebury.
Harrison, P. (1985). *Inside the inner city*. London, UK: Penguin Books.
Hill, M. (1993). *The Welfare State in Britain*. Aldershot, UK: Edward Elgar Publishing Limited.
Hill, M., & Hupe, P. (2003). The multi-layer problem in implementation research. *Public Management Review, 5*(4), 471–490.
Hutson, S., & Liddiard, M. (1994). *Youth homelessness*. Basingstoke, UK: Macmillan.
Jones, C., & Murie, A. (1998). *Reviewing the right to buy*. York, UK: Joseph Rowntree Foundation Findings.
Jones, G. (1995). *Leaving home*. Buckingham, UK: Open University Press.
Kay, H. (1994). *Conflicting priorities*. London, UK: CHAR (Campaign for Single Homeless People) and the Chartered. Institute of Housing.

Kemp, P. (1991). From solution to problem? In S. Lowe & D. Hughes (Eds.), *A new century of social housing* (pp. 44–58). Leicester, UK: Leicester University Press.
Kendall, J. (2000). The mainstreaming of the third sector into public policy in England in the late 1990s: Whys and wherefores. *Policy and Politics, 28*(4), 541–562.
Killeen, D. (1988). *Estranged*. Edinburgh, Scotland: Shelter Scottish Campaign for the Homeless.
Lee, D., Marsden, D., Rickman, P., & Duncombe, J. (1990). *Scheming for youth*. Buckingham, UK: Open University Press.
Lidstone, P. (1994). Rationing housing to the homeless applicant. *Housing Studies, 9*(4), 459–472.
Lloyd, T. (2013, June 21). From pillar to post. *Inside Housing*. Retrieved from https://www.insidehousing.co.uk/home/home/from-pillar-to-post1-36030
Lund, B. (1996). *Housing problems and housing policy*. Harlow, UK: Longman.
Lund, B. (2016). *Housing politics in the United Kingdom*. Bristol, UK: Policy Press.
Malpass, P. (1990). *Reshaping housing policy: Subsidies, rents and residualisation*. London, UK: Routledge.
Malpass, P., & Murie, A. (1994). *Housing policy and practice* (4th ed.). Basingstoke, UK: Palgrave Macmillan.
Malpass, P., & Murie, A. (1999). *Housing policy and practice* (5th ed.). Basingstoke, UK: Macmillan.
May, J., Cloke, P., & Johnsen, S. (2006). Shelter at the margins: New Labour and the changing state of emergency accommodation for single homeless people in Britain. *Policy and Politics, 34*(4), 11–29.
McCarthy, M. (1989). *The new politics of welfare*. Basingstoke, UK: Macmillan.
Mishra, R. (1990). *The welfare state in capitalist society*. Hemel Hempstead, UK: Harvester Wheatsheaf.
Monk, S., & Kleinman, M. (1989). Housing. In P. Brown & R. Sparks (Eds.), *Beyond Thatcherism* (pp. 121–136). Buckingham, UK: Open University Press.
Mullins, D., & Niner, P. (1998). A price of citizenship? Changing access to social housing. In A. Marsh & D. Mullins (Eds.), *Housing and public policy: Citizenship, choice and control* (pp. 175–198). Buckingham, UK: Open University Press.
Mullins, D., Niner, P. with Marsh, A., & Walker, B. (1996). *Evaluation of the 1991 homelessness code of guidance*. London, UK: Department of the Environment.
Mullins, D., & Pawson, H. (2010). The evolution of stock transfer: Privatisation or towards renationalisation? In P. Malpass & R. Rowlands (Eds.), *Housing, markets and policy* (pp. 76–100). London: UK: Routledge.
Murie, A. (2016). *The right to buy? Selling off public and social housing*. Bristol, UK: Policy Press.

Murray, C. (1990). The emerging British underclass. In R. Lister (Ed.), *Charles Murray and the underclass* (pp. 23–53). London, UK: Institute of Economic Affairs Health and Welfare Unit.

Niner, P. (1989). *Homelessness in nine local authorities: Case studies of policy and practice.* London, UK: Department of the Environment, Her Majesty's Stationery Office.

Niner, P. (1997). *The early impact of The Housing Act 1996 and Housing Benefit changes.* London, UK: Shelter.

Pearce, J., & Vine, J. (2014). Quantifying residualisation: The changing nature of social housing in the UK. *Journal of Housing and the Built Environment, 29*, 657–675.

Pierson, C. (1998). New perspectives on welfare theory. In N. Ellison & C. Pierson (Eds.), *Developments in British Social Policy* (pp. 15–16). Basingstoke, UK: Macmillan.

Prescott-Clarke, P., Clemens, S., & Park, A. (1994). *Routes into local authority housing.* London, UK: Her Majesty's Stationery Office.

Quilgars, D., & Anderson, I. (1995). *Foyers for young people.* York, UK: Joseph Rowntree Foundation.

Randall, G., & Brown, S. (1993). *The rough sleepers initiative: An evaluation.* London, UK: Department of the Environment.

Randall, G., & Brown, S. (1996). *From street to home: An evaluation of phase 2 of the rough sleepers' initiative.* London, UK: Department of the Environment, Her Majesty's Stationery Office.

Raynsford, N. (2016). *Substance not spin: An insider's view of success and failure in government.* Bristol, UK: Policy Press.

Secretary of State for the Environment and Secretary of State for Wales. (1982, February 8). *Draft review of the Housing (Homeless Persons) Act and the Associated Code of Guidance.* Retrieved from the Margaret Thatcher Foundation website at: https://www.margaretthatcher.org/PREM19/1982/PREM19-0795.pdf

Smith, J. (2000, February 10). Death of the surcharge. *Local Government Chronicle.* Retrieved from https://www.lgcplus.com/death-of-the-surcharge/1390687.article

Somerville, P. (1994). Homelessness policy in Britain. *Policy and Politics, 22*(3), 163–178.

Somerville, P. (1999). The making and unmaking of homelessness legislation. In S. Hutson & D. Clapham (Eds.), *Homelessness: Public policies and private troubles* (pp. 29–57). London, UK: Cassell.

Steele, A. (1989). Towards a settled way of life. *Housing Review, 38*(2), 55–56.

Stephens, M., Ford, J., Spencer, P., Wallace, A., Wilcox, S., & Williams, P. (2008). *Housing market recession and sustainable home-ownership.* York, UK: Joseph Rowntree Foundation.

Stewart, J. (2014). An era of continuing change: Reflections on local government in England 1974–2014. *Local Government Studies, 40*(6), 835–850.

Stoker, G. (1991). *The politics of local government* (2nd ed.). Basingstoke, UK: Palgrave Macmillan.

Thatcher, M. (1993). *The downing street years.* London, UK: Harper Collins Publishers.

Thompson, L. (1988). *An act of compromise.* London, UK: Shelter.

Venn, S. (1985). *Singled out.* London, UK: CHAR (the Campaign for Single Homeless People).

Warnes, A., Crane, M., Whitehead, N., & Fu, R. (2003). *Homelessness factfile.* London, UK: Crisis. Retrieved from https://www.kcl.ac.uk/sspp/policy-institute/scwru/pubs/2003/Warnes-et-al-2003-Factfile.pdf

Watchman, P. Q., & Robson, P. (1989). *Homelessness and the law in Britain.* Glasgow, Scotland: The Planning Exchange.

Wilcox, S. (1994). *Housing finance review 1994/95.* York, UK: Joseph Rowntree Foundation.

Wilks-Heeg, S. (2009). New Labour and the reform of English local government, 1997–2007: Privatising the parts that Conservative governments could not reach? *Planning, Practice and Research, 24*(1), 23–39.

Wilson, W. (1996). Homelessness and housing allocations in the Housing Bill. *Research Paper 96/10.* House of Commons Library, Education and Social Services Section, London, UK

Wilson, W. (2015). Rough Sleepers Initiative (RSI) 1990–1999. *House of Commons Library Standard Note SN07121*, London, UK.

Wintour, P., & Bates, S. (1993, October 9). *Major goes back to the old values.* Retrieved from https://www.theguardian.com/politics/1993/oct/09/conservatives.past

Young, K., & Davies, M. (1990). *The politics of local government since Widdicombe.* York, UK: Joseph Rowntree Foundation.

CHAPTER 6

1997–2010: The Restoration of Rights, Social Exclusion and Meta-governance

Introduction

The year 1997 represents one of the most astonishing turning points in British political history as a Labour Party that had experienced four successive election defeats returned to power with a huge majority under Tony Blair. It was followed by an almost identical result in 2001, and a narrower victory in 2005, where Labour won a comfortable working majority despite receiving approximately 35% of the vote. During Labour's third term, Blair stepped down as Prime Minister to be replaced by Gordon Brown, whose period in office was largely defined by the economic crisis of 2007–2008.

Blair's electoral success was based partly on his claim to lead 'New Labour'—a party that was different from both the previous Conservative governments and the old Labour Party, with its unpopular policies such as increasing direct taxation. Instead, 'New Labour' represented a 'Third Way'. Fear of being too closely associated with approaches of the past was one reason why, despite their substantial majorities, the period of Labour government was marked by a cautious approach to adopting new social policies. However, homelessness was one area where there was substantial policy change.

Housing became a devolved power to Scotland, Wales and Northern Ireland in 1999. The process of devolution is discussed later in the chapter, but it is important to note here that many of the changes discussed applied only to England.

J. Harding, *Post-War Homelessness Policy in the UK*,
https://doi.org/10.1007/978-3-030-22117-1_6

Social Policy

Heffernan (2011, p. 166) notes that the Labour governments of 1997–2010 accepted most of the economic reforms introduced by their Conservative predecessors, acknowledging that high direct taxation, tight financial service regulation and extended state ownership were not viable options. However, a key difference with the Conservatives was that New Labour wished to see the proceeds of market-driven economic success used to improve public services and to expand the provision of the welfare state. Social justice was accepted as an objective of government by Tony Blair and, more enthusiastically, by Gordon Brown. In opposition, Labour's Commission on Social Justice had declared that social justice and economic efficiency were entirely compatible; business would benefit from a more just society (Powell, 2000, p. 43)

However, social justice is a concept that can have a number of meanings, as will be seen in Chap. 7. Previous social democratic objectives of equality of outcomes were dismissed as both impossible to achieve and undesirable, and were replaced by new policy goals based on equality of opportunity (Pautz, 2011, p. 193). Heron and Dwyer (1999, p. 91) argue that the Labour government also accepted much of the rhetoric of the Conservatives about the individual's responsibility for their own welfare. The welfare state was seen as a reciprocal arrangement, which imposed obligations on the individual as well as providing them with rights (Heron & Dwyer, 1999, p. 92). Balancing 'rights' and 'responsibilities' involved offering disadvantaged people opportunities to improve their situation, while insisting that it was their responsibility to accept those opportunities (Ellison & Pierson, 1998, p. 11).

Labour largely sought to take the ideological debate out of discussions of the welfare state and instead focus on technical issues of efficiency and delivery (Powell, 2000, p. 52). A 1999 White Paper on Modernising Government argued that the key to improvement was to adopt an evidence-based policy; a Centre for Management and Policy Studies was established within the Cabinet Office to ensure that better use was made of the research (Boswell, 2009, p. 3). Changes to policies tended to take the form of evolution rather than revolution: Conservative reforms that were judged to have worked were retained, while further reforms were applied to those that had failed (Powell, 2000, p. 53).

Social Exclusion

As it had rejected the goal of equality of outcomes, Labour needed a new language with which to express its concern for the poorest part of the community and so discussed inclusion and exclusion rather than inequality (Powell, 2000, p. 46). Social exclusion was a concept that gained support after the publication of Peter Townsend's classic study of poverty in 1979, which argued that people below a certain level of income were excluded from many of the activities that others regarded as customary (Welshman, 2013, pp. 189–190).

Levitas (2005, pp. 2–3) suggests that the Labour governments used three competing discourses around social exclusion: a redistributionist discourse, where the focus was on poverty; a moral underclass discourse, which explained exclusion in terms of the culture of excluded people; and a social integration discourse, which saw inclusion primarily in terms of labour force attachment. Labour quickly established a Social Exclusion Unit and Tony Blair's first speech as Prime Minister concentrated on this topic. Benn (2000, pp. 311–312) argues that it was a speech that demonstrated the elasticity of the social exclusion concept as Blair switched from discourse to discourse, declaring that poorer people would no longer be "forgotten people", before criticising their 'fatalism' and then discussing the impact on the middle classes of paying for their welfare.

Measure that were taken to tackle social exclusion included a series of 'New Deals' for marginalised groups (Manwaring, 2016, p. 249) and a number of measures for families with young children, such as the creation of the National Family and Parenting Institute (Home Office, 2000, p. 46). A flagship policy, Sure Start, was intended to break a perceived cycle of deprivation. As with the concept of social exclusion more generally, discussions of this cycle moved between a number of different assumptions as to why it existed—sometimes the focus was on culture, sometimes on conscious choices of poor people and sometimes on structural factors (Welshman, 2013, pp. 195–196).

The government's emphasis on employment led to it taking measures aimed at ensuring that low paid work offered greater financial rewards than unemployment. It sought to boost in-work disposable incomes through measures such as the introduction of the national minimum wage, reductions in tax and national insurance contributions for those on low incomes and the introduction of tax credits (Millar, 2003, p. 128).

Critics of the government's attempts to tackle social exclusion have sometimes concentrated on a number of disappointing outcomes (e.g. Manwaring, 2016, p. 429) and sometimes on the ambiguity of the concept. Welshman (2013, pp. 196–198) argues that from 2004 a range of government ministers—while not denying the impact of poverty and unequal life chances—increasingly linked social exclusion to factors such as poor parenting and the impact of growing up in workless households. The launch of the Respect initiative in January 2006 marked a further move towards the individualisation of social problems, with children and their families blamed for anti-social behaviour that led to a lifetime of exclusion and offending (Welshman, 2013, pp. 196–198).

By Labour's third term, both Blair and Hilary Armstrong, the Cabinet Minister for Social Exclusion, were arguing that programmes had failed to reach those in the greatest need of them (Welshman, 2013, p. 197). Blair argued in 2006 that there needed to be a change of focus to a smaller number of people who had not been reached by the new services: "… some aspects of social exclusion are deeply intractable. The most socially excluded are very hard to reach. Their problems are multiple, entrenched and often passed down the generations" (quoted in Welshman, 2013, p. 200). A number of social policy initiatives sought to identify and target children who were most at risk of a lifetime of exclusion (Welshman, 2013, pp. 200–203). The extent to which this approach was replicated for single homeless people will be considered below.

Quality Rather than Quantity in Social Rented Housing

The Labour governments put substantial resources into tackling the residualisation of the social rented sector, particularly the parts of the stock that were owned by local authorities. The (2000) Green Paper *Quality and Choice: A Decent Home for All* rejected the view of the social rented sector as a tenure only for the poorest people, while also indicating that there would be no return to Aneurin Bevan's view that it should provide accommodation for all:

> We do not believe that social housing should only be allocated to the poorest and most vulnerable members of the community. However, if social housing were available to anyone who wanted it, there is a risk that it could be denied to those who have no other choice. In order to prevent this, we

believe that priority for social housing should generally continue to be given to people in the greatest housing need and for whom suitable private sector housing is not an affordable option. (Department of the Environment, Transport and the Regions (DETR), 2000, p. 80)

The paper proposed a series of measures to tackle the problems of the sector including improving quality through increased investment, enabling more local authorities to transfer their stock to housing associations, trying new approaches to funding via the private finance initiative and Arm's Length Management Organisations (ALMOs—see below), moving to a fairer system of rents and developing new social housing to higher standards. This list of measures was followed by a statement that:

We believe that these reforms will help to turn social housing into a tenure where tenants have choices, where the image is no longer one of decline and decay, and in which problems of social exclusion, poor quality and poverty of opportunity are confronted and surmounted. (DETR, 2000, p. 57)

Raynsford (2016, p. 60) acknowledges that, with the benefit of hindsight, the 2000 Green Paper could be criticised for not giving sufficient attention to increasing the supply of housing. He suggests that three reasons for this were resource constraints, concern over abandonment and collapse of market confidence in areas of the North and Midlands, and pressures to restrain building on greenfield sites in order to protect the countryside and promote urban regeneration. In interview, he explained that:

Coming into government in 1997, we faced a huge obvious backlog of very poor condition in the housing sector. Quite clearly, the top priority had to be for renovation of the existing stock and that's what led through to the Decent Homes Programme .... It was pretty clear we had to and needed to expand the house building programme particularly in London and the south east and eventually it happened. But it took a long time mainly because the resources were being focussed on these other areas which, in my view, were priorities. But there was also, in the back of our minds, the fact that there was still this problem of abandonment and collapsing markets in large parts of the country... And in planning terms, we were moving to change planning policy to focus on inner-city rehabilitation, which was all part of the planning policy. That meant we had to restrain house builders who were trying to build on greenfield sites because that not only took greenfield land

> but it also had an adverse effect on inner-city regeneration. All of these factors contributed to the decisions that we took at the time, which were not to give top priority to new house investment. With hindsight, that was a mistake.

The problems of low demand and inner cities will be returned to below.

Improving Housing Quality in the Social Rented Sector

The scale of the difficulties inherited by the Labour government with regard to the quality of the social rented stock were demonstrated by the English House Conditions Survey of 1996, which indicated that £10 billion needed to be spent in order to tackle the problem of substandard council housing (Raynsford, 2016, pp. 57–58). The government established the Decent Homes Standard in 2000 as a benchmark for tackling these problems; it was updated in 2004 and 2006 (DCLG, 2006a, pp. 11–12). Although the standard was a modest one, it was estimated that 1.6 million homes in the social rented sector were failing to meet it in 2001, representing 39% of all social housing. Councils were offered three options to reach the standard: transfer of the housing stock to another landlord under the powers created by the Conservatives, the creation of an ALMO or borrowing from the private sector via the Private Finance Initiative (National Audit Office, 2010, p. 3).

The Green Paper *Quality and Choice* proposed that 200,000 council homes were transferred to new landlords each year, subject to a ballot of tenants and to the new Housing Inspectorate being satisfied that transfer would meet Best Value criteria (DETR, 2000, p. 61) (Best Value is discussed further below). ALMOs provided a new option for stock transfer; they were non-profit organisations that managed the stock on behalf of a local authority, while the authority retained ownership and strategic management. By 2010, ALMOs managed half of all council housing (Boughton, 2018, pp. 234–235).

The extent of improvement brought about through the various options offered by the government was demonstrated by the percentage of non-decent social rented homes falling to 14.5% by 2009. This was achieved with substantial investment: £22 billion was spent on improving 1.4 million local authority properties (National Audit Office, 2010, p. 4).

Low Demand and Abandonment

Low demand and abandonment of properties had been problems before the election of the first Blair government: between 1994 and 1997, 3500 council properties in Manchester, Leeds and Newcastle had been demolished or transferred to housing associations for demolition or improvement (Keenan, Lowe, & Spencer, 1999, p. 704). However, it was under Labour that these problems became a focus for policy.

Keenan et al. (1999), pp. 703–704) argue that the problem of abandonment was one that had not been much discussed by local authorities for political reasons; funding for housing from central government was obtained largely by indicating that there was a need for more accommodation. Gateshead Council was one of the first to announce a development plan (for 1999–2000) in which there was no new provision of housing, beyond some for people with special needs (Keenan et al., 1999, pp. 710–711).

Low demand and abandonment were not synonymous with residualisation because all tenures could be affected, but these problems tended to occur in poorer neighbourhoods with large amounts of rented housing. Power and Mumford (1999, pp. 8–17), in case studies of neighbourhoods in Newcastle and Manchester, concluded that city wide factors that had brought about low demand were loss of population and jobs in inner areas, where there were also higher-than-average percentages of manual workers, male unemployment and deprivation. Low levels of owner occupation within the neighbourhoods had led more affluent residents to leave for surrounding areas.

Keenan et al. (1999), pp. 704–709) noted that there was evidence of low demand and abandonment in areas as diverse as Coventry, Liverpool, Sheffield, Leeds, Teesside, the East Midlands and even a small number of boroughs in East London. The consequences included landlords competing for tenants, social housing providers being unwilling to invest in housing and residents lived in fear of crime and intimidation.

The Green Paper *Quality and Choice* acknowledged the differences between regions, with high demand and house prices in London and the South contrasting sharply with the situation that existed elsewhere (DETR, 2000, p. 71). The paper also noted that low demand was a difficulty that affected the owner-occupied (DETR, 2000, p. 35) and private rented sectors (DETR, 2000, p. 49), as well as social rented housing.

While having areas of low housing demand might be assumed to offer more options for homeless households, Neil Morland echoed the views of many in the social rented sector at the time by noting that simply having accommodation to go to, particularly in an area with major social problems, would not meet the needs of many non-statutorily homeless people:

> I think it would be very easy for people to find a home.... What I don't think low demand did was help homeless people who were single homeless or street homeless who never would have been owed a duty because I think their support needs still prohibited them from obtaining social housing, because their support needs were so obvious, so manifest, that I think social landlords, irrespective of low demand, were still reluctant to let homes to them because of the consequential problems that that would cause.

In April 2002, the government launched the Housing Market Renewal Initiative in nine 'pathfinder' areas in the North and Midlands where low demand was judged to be a problem. Areas were selected on the basis that their housing market was failing and there was a risk that this failure might spread to adjacent areas. Five hundred million pounds was made available for the first three years of the programme, with this sum increasing in later years (Cole & Nevin, 2004, p. viii). The nine areas encompassed 800,000 properties in total, for a programme of selective demolition, refurbishment and new build (Boughton, 2018, pp. 237–238).

To give an example of the balance between different types of measure taken under the initiative, in Liverpool it funded the construction of 2746 housing units, the refurbishment of 20,384 and the demolition of 4290 (Couch, Lord, & Crocks, 2015, p. 468). Evaluations of the initiative faced technical difficulties, but all agreed that the gap in prices between the areas affected and surrounding areas narrowed (Couch et al., 2015, pp. 471–472). The number of properties experiencing 'low demand' appeared to fall and some of the most problematic housing was demolished, although the process was hindered by people buying properties simply to benefit from compulsory purchase orders. All of the Pathfinder areas experienced an increase in population in the period 2001–2008, largely among working people aged 16–24, but there was a continued decline among people aged 25–49 and children, suggesting that the areas were largely housing mobile populations for a limited period (Leather & Nevin, 2012, pp. 862–866).

The Housing Market Renewal Initiative was only one part of a broader approach to tackling neighbourhood deprivation and the associated problems of residualisation: Tony Blair announced early in his first administration that, within 10 to 20 years, no one should be "seriously disadvantaged by where they live". Goals were set to reduce worklessness and crime, and improve health, skills, housing and the physical environment, both in absolute terms (with minimum standards set) and relative to more affluent areas. Sure Start Centres and Neighbourhood Warden posts were examples of measures concentrated on the most disadvantaged areas (Lupton, 2013, pp. 1–2).

Taking a very broad view, Power, Ploger, and Winkler (2010, pp. 28–32) use a number of international case studies—including Sheffield and Belfast—to argue that a period that broadly coincided with the rule of the Labour governments was one in which there was a trend towards the regeneration of inner city areas in the United States and Western Europe. New civic leaders emerged and public–private partnerships brought new jobs and physical regeneration to inner urban areas.

Turning to the specific factors believed to contribute to the process of residualisation, Pearce and Vine (2014, p. 670) note that, while income differences between people in social rented housing and other tenures increased sharply between 1970 and 1990, they remained stable between 1990 and 2010. From 2002 onwards, the numbers on local authority waiting lists increased (Ministry of Housing, Communities and Local Government, 2018), suggesting some revival in the popularity of the social rented sector. In addition, a range of evidence suggested that conditions in the most difficult areas improved under the Labour governments. The number of burglaries in disadvantaged neighbourhood fell by almost half, at a greater rate than in other neighbourhoods, and there were also more substantial falls in litter and vandalism. Surveys of areas covered by Labour's New Deal for Communities—a programme concentrated on the most disadvantaged neighbourhoods—showed statistically significant improvements in factors such as perceptions of the environment, being a victim of crime and satisfaction with the area. Worklessness decreased faster in disadvantaged neighbourhoods than others (Lupton, 2013, pp. 5–6). Lupton (2013, p. 8) argues that:

> the Coalition government in 2010 inherited fewer physical and environmental problems than its predecessors. Many poor neighbourhoods had a new stock of fit-for-purpose public buildings. Fewer neighbourhoods were coping with problems of widespread housing abandonment, dereliction and dilapidation.

Housing Supply

Despite the positive changes to disadvantaged neighbourhoods, Steve Hilditch suggested that concerns over low demand had a distorting influence over policy:

> Central government seems to work a few years behind the reality. They discovered low demand quite slowly and late, and by the time they'd reacted and developed an agenda for it, it was much less true than it was. So I think they were caught behind the curve again as demand started to rise.... But London never had low demand; I think it was almost wished for by the treasury so they could say, 'We don't need more money for new social housing because there isn't enough demand for what already exists'.

Labour's commitment to following the spending plans of the Conservatives in its first two years of office meant that the provision of new social housing initially fell below that of the Major government (Boughton, 2018, p. 249). A 2004 Review of Housing Supply commissioned by the government from Kate Barker concluded that 23,000 social rented homes were needed per year, although the government committed to only 10,000. However, it announced a target of building 200,000 homes annually in 2005—this figure was increased to 240,000 in 2007 when Gordon Brown became Prime Minister. A total of 224,680 homes were built across all sectors in 2007: a year that was also notable as the first since 1981 when the number of new social rented homes was greater than those lost under the Right to Buy (Boughton, 2018, p. 249). Nick Raynsford said of the record of the Labour governments on housing output:

> In the end, by 2007, housing output had got to a level of just over 200,000 new units in terms of net additions to the stock, which was in line with what we now know is the need at that point in time. So, towards the end of the Labour government it looked as though we were going in the right direction. Then, of course, the recession hit and everything went off a cliff edge.

In total, 7870 council homes and 350,000 housing association homes were built under the Blair and Brown governments (Boughton, 2018, p. 248). By the third term, the supply of housing and levels of homelessness were being more directly linked by ministers, with Secretary of State for Communities and Local Government Ruth Kelly saying in 2006:

> That is why I am personally committed to doing my utmost in the fight against homelessness and the causes of it. We cannot talk about social justice without this commitment ... Of course, part of the long-term solution has to be in making more homes available. That's why we are aiming to build 75,000 new social rented homes between 2005/06 and 2007/08. (DCLG, 2006b)

Statutory Homelessness

The Legislation

The 1997 Labour Manifesto had promised to increase protection for unintentionally homeless households in priority need (DETR, 2000, p. 87), and the new government took swift action to deal with some of the implications of the 1996 Housing Act for homeless households. In November 1997, regulations were introduced to ensure that those owed a homeless duty were added to the categories of people who should be given a reasonable preference for allocations from housing registers. A further measure required local authorities to ensure that any suitable alternative accommodation judged to be available to homeless households must be available for at least two years (Mullins & Niner, 1998, p. 188).

However, the government's main priority on its election was rough sleeping (as discussed further below), with more substantial changes to the homelessness legislation not announced until 2000 in the Green Paper *Quality and Choice*. This paper proposed that priority in social housing allocations should be given to three broad categories of people: those who were homeless, those who were living in housing conditions that were not reasonably tolerable and those who needed to move to a particular location for reasons such as securing or retaining a job (DETR, 2000, p. 81). The Green Paper suggested that homeless people should be offered the same types of choice as other housing applicants and that local authorities should only make a final offer once there had been some time to exercise this choice (DETR, 2000, p. 88).

Major changes to the homelessness legislation were proposed in a Housing Bill of 2001 that failed to progress through Parliament because of the calling of the 2001 General Election. However, the proposals—now appearing in legislation of their own, because of the abandonment of plans to introduce 'seller's packs' for owner occupied housing—were enacted in the 2002 Homelessness Act. The Act abolished the two-year limit for the provision of accommodation to statutorily homeless households—effectively reinstating the duty to secure permanent accommodation—and specified that the main homelessness duty could not be fulfilled through an assured shorthold tenancy with a private landlord unless the homeless household was satisfied with this (Lund, 2016, p. 223). It removed the requirement for authorities to consider whether suitable alternative accommodation was available before making an offer themselves, and gave a new power (but not a duty) to secure accommodation for those who were unintentionally homeless but not in priority need (http://www.legislation.gov.uk/ukpga/2002/7/notes).

These measures, despite largely reversing those made by the Conservative Government only six years previously, faced very little opposition. The former Conservative Minister noted that homelessness was not a controversial issue under the Labour governments:

> It is interesting, housing was a big issue in the 1990s, with Sheila McKechnie [*director of Shelter from 1985 to 1994*] and it was right up there on the policy agenda, and each quarter, the Homeless Acceptance figures were published. There would be a lot of interest in the House of Commons about the numbers and all the rest. By the time we got to this Century, housing seemed to have fallen away and other issues were far higher up the agenda.

This view is supported by an analysis of the debate on the second reading of the 2001 Homelessness Bill (which was to become the 2002 Act) (HC Deb 02 July 2001 vol 371 cc33-114). In a debate lasting over five hours, there were only three contributions that made any form of reference to the dangers of over-generous provision for homeless households—all were made by Conservative MPs. Tony Baldry advanced the historical argument that waiting list applicants were unfairly disadvantaged by the priority given to statutorily homeless households (HC Deb 02 July 2001 vol 371 cc 62), Julian Brazier suggested that the 1996 Act had provided more opportunities to non-homeless applicants (HC Deb 02 July 2001 vol 371 cc100-101) and Andrew Turner raised concerns over people moving into an area and applying as homeless there (HC Deb 02 July 2001 vol 371 cc87).

However, these were isolated voices. Indeed, Nigel Waterson, the Shadow Minister for Local Government, announced that "The Opposition broadly welcome the Bill …" (HC Deb 02 July 2001 vol 371 cc44), and there were a number of observations by Labour and Liberal Democrat members that the Conservatives had changed their position since the passing of the 1996 Act. Almost all the contributions to the debate focused on how services could more effectively meet the needs of homeless people, with the tone set by the first few contributions that followed the presentation of the Bill by Stephen Byers, the Secretary of State for Transport, Local Government and the Regions. Julian Lewis (Conservative) asked about joint working with the Department of Health in the case of homeless people with mental health problems (HC Deb 02 July 2001 vol 371 cc33); Mike Hancock (Liberal Democrat) asked about the definition of affordable housing (HC Deb 02 July 2001 vol 371 cc34); Jeremy Corbyn (Labour) expressed concern over the provision of affordable housing in London (HC Deb 02 July 2001 vol 371 cc34-35); Brian Cotter (Liberal Democrat) asked about difficulties in releasing empty properties (HC Deb 02 July 2001 vol 371 cc35); and David Drew (Labour) raised concerns over hidden homelessness in rural areas (HC Deb 02 July 2001 vol 371 cc36).

In addition to re-establishing local authorities' duties to provide permanent housing to statutorily homeless households, the government also took action to broaden the range of households that should be considered statutorily homeless. The 2002 Homelessness (Priority Need for Accommodation) (England) Order brought into the priority need category people aged 16–17, care leavers to the age of 21, people vulnerable as a result of leaving prison, people vulnerable as a result of having served in the armed forces and people fleeing domestic violence (http://www.legislation.gov.uk/uksi/2002/2051/pdfs/uksi_20022051_en.pdf). This change had been announced in the 2000 Consultation Paper (DETR, 2000, p. 89) and, as with the 2002 Homelessness Act, met with little opposition. However, not all the groups benefitted substantially: Harding and Harding (2006, pp. 148–149) note that, although 1000 people were found to be vulnerable as a result of having spent time in custody in 2003, this was a very small proportion of released prisoners who experienced housing difficulties.

Prevention/Bed and Breakfast

The number of households in bed-and-breakfast hotels, and the cost both to them and to public finances of this form of provision, was one of the most frequently occurring themes of the debate on the 2001 Homelessness Bill and was soon to become a government priority. Homeless acceptances had been increasing even before the 2002 Order broadened the priority need categories, with corresponding increases in the numbers in temporary accommodation in general and bed-and-breakfast hotels in particular. The number of statutorily homeless households living in bed-and-breakfast accommodation increased from 4100 in 1997 to 13,240 in 2002. A Bed and Breakfast Unit was created, later to be merged with the Rough Sleepers' Unit (RSU—which is discussed further below), to become the Homelessness Directorate within the Office of the Deputy Prime Minister. The Directorate was charged with ensuring that, by March 2004, homeless families with children did not stay in bed-and-breakfast hotels except in an emergency, and then for no more than six weeks (Lund, 2004, pp. 18–19).

Nick Raynsford explained the reasoning behind setting the six-week limit:

> I remember talking about even shorter limits than six weeks at one stage—but if you set too tight a limit, this could result in people being denied access because the authority couldn't clear it in time. So, that was one of those pragmatic discussions about how do you encourage good practice but not perversely encourage malpractice in order to meet targets?

Two means were used to enforce the six-week limit. A Best Value Performance Indicator was introduced for the average length of stay in bed-and-breakfast accommodation for households with dependent children or a pregnant woman (Office of the Deputy Prime Minister, 2003, section 2.3). This had an immediate effect: between June 2002 and June 2003, the number of homeless households with children in bed-and-breakfast hotels declined by 44%, although the numbers in other forms of temporary accommodation continued to grow (Lund, 2004, pp. 18–19). The Homelessness (Suitability of Accommodation) (England) Order 2003 (SI 2003/3326) came into force in April 2004. This brought into law the requirement that households with dependent children or a pregnant member should not be put into bed-and-breakfasts hotels except in an emergency, and even then for no more than six weeks. Local authorities that failed to comply with this order placed themselves at risk of judicial review proceedings (Wilson & Barton, 2018a, p. 12).

Efforts to end the use of bed-and-breakfast hotels were linked to a broader concern to reduce the number of statutory homelessness acceptances—and hence the use of all forms of temporary accommodation—through prevention measures. From 2003 to 2004, the government began to provide specific grant funding to local authorities for secondary prevention activities that fell into three categories: those that helped a household to remain in their current accommodation, those that delayed a household's need to move until an alternative could be found and those that helped a household to find alternative accommodation (Pawson, 2007, pp. 868–870). The government gave examples of the types of prevention activity that might be most effective, such as encouraging other agencies to identify households whose homelessness might be prevented by negotiating with their landlord and family mediation services to prevent young people from being forced to leave the family home (Pawson, 2007, p. 872). A Best Value Performance Indicator was introduced in 2005 for the number of cases where homelessness was prevented through housing advice casework (ODPM, 2005, p. 26).

Labour's (2005) strategy document *Sustainable Communities: Settled Homes; Changing Lives, A Strategy for Tackling Homelessness* (produced shortly before the 2005 general election) reinforced the commitment to preventions and advocated the 'housing options' approach (Lund, 2016, pp. 223–224). This approach involves local authorities giving thought to solutions to housing need that go beyond social rented housing and providing 'housing options' interviews to all applicants, separate from the homelessness application process (Pawson, 2007, pp. 872–873).

The prevention agenda had a substantial impact on practice. Department of Communities and Local Government figures for 2009–2010 showed that local authorities had been involved in 165,200 homelessness prevention and relief activities, a substantial increase on the 123,370 the previous year. Over half of these activities—88,800—involved help to find accommodation in the private rented, housing association or supported housing sector, or in a hostel or house in multiple occupation. Less common were activities to enable people to remain in their own home: there were 6600 negotiations (or instances of legal advocacy work) to enable a household to remain in the private rented sector, 5800 examples of conciliation work including home visits, 5400 examples of debt advice and 5300 resolutions of debt problems (Jones & Pleace, 2010, p. 52).

Despite some concerns over the lack of robust evidence for its effectiveness (Jones & Pleace, 2010, p. 52), the prevention agenda is widely assumed to have been the main cause of a very substantial decrease in the number of homelessness acceptances. By the end of 2006, acceptances had fallen by a remarkable 50% from 2003 (Pawson, 2007, pp. 877–878). The number of households in temporary accommodation, having exceeded 100,000 for the first time in 2004, subsequently fell, although it remained at historically high levels (Wilson & Barton, 2018b, p. 12). In 2006, Ruth Kelly felt able to state that the bed-and-breakfast crisis was over (DCLG, 2006b).

Despite this apparent success, the prevention agenda faced criticisms. Some professionals argued that prevention was focusing on those who would otherwise be statutorily homeless, at the expense of other groups (Jones & Pleace, 2010, p. 53). In 2004, Shelter published a survey of 60 local authorities, which showed that over half felt under pressure from central government to reduce the number of households accepted as homeless. Shelter suggested that this pressure had led to some people being prevented from applying as homeless, although this claim was rejected by the Office of the Deputy Prime Minister (Hetherington, 2004). The Local Government Ombudsman warned local authorities in 2006 that the rights of homeless applicants and potential homeless applicants should not be compromised by the pressure created by homelessness applications and by government targets to reduce the use of temporary accommodation (Pawson, 2007, p. 872).

The role of housing options came under particularly close scrutiny, with Steve Hilditch arguing:

> Housing options became a filter rather than anything else. So I know in one local authority I looked at in London people who went into the housing options service hardly ever became homeless applicants. Sometimes they were given a list of private rented accommodation and not told their full rights under the Act and discouraged from applying.

A Court of Appeal decision (Robinson v London Borough of Hammersmith and Fulham, July 2006) confirmed that homelessness prevention activities should take place alongside a homelessness assessment rather than replacing it (Pawson, 2007, p. 874). Following this ruling, the government issued guidance to local authorities, insisting that reductions in homelessness should be achieved by more effective help rather than by gatekeeping activities that prevented or discouraged applications (Pawson, 2007, p. 875). Further guidance on prevention was issued in 2009, including support for the housing options approach (Lund, 2016, p. 246).

Single Homelessness

While hugely significant changes to the services provided to statutorily homeless households aroused relatively little comment or analysis, the attempts of the Labour governments to tackle rough sleeping were given a higher profile, more closely linked to the social exclusion agenda and more thoroughly evaluated by commentators. Tony Blair had indicated the high priority to be given to this issue before becoming Prime Minister, explaining in an interview with the *Big Issue* magazine (No. 214, 6–12 January 1997) how he saw a balance of rights and responsibilities working out for those who were sleeping rough:

> [Y]es it is right to be intolerant of people homeless on the streets. But the way to deal with that is you make sure that when those people come off the streets that you're doing the other part of the equation. You're providing them with somewhere to go.

Nick Raynsford described rough sleeping as "probably the most visible evidence" of social exclusion in explaining why it was such an immediate priority for the government. The first report of the Social Exclusion Unit had rough sleeping as its subject; it set a target of reducing the number of rough sleepers by at least two thirds by 2002 and recommended the setting up of a Rough Sleepers' Unit (RSU) (Lund, 2016, p. 224).

The Homelessness Action Programme

Labour's initial approach from 1997 to 1999 was to extend the scope of the Rough Sleepers' Initiative (RSI) that it inherited from the Conservatives. It created a Rough Sleepers Revenue Fund to support the expansion of rough sleeping work beyond the capital, with funding for voluntary organisations and housing associations in Manchester and selected towns and cities in the South and Midlands. The Homeless Mentally Ill Initiative was also expanded beyond Central London and a small amount of money was made available to organisations working with homeless people with addiction problems through a Drug and Alcohol Specific Grant (Wilson, 2015, p. 4). In a significant change of approach to that of the Conservative governments, local authorities were encouraged to work with hostels to develop a more strategic approach in areas where there was a perceived lack of co-ordination (Wilson, 2015, p. 5).

The RSU was created in 1999; its strategy document *Coming in from the Cold* set out an approach with two central ideas. The first was that the focus should be on prevention, achieved by addressing the reasons for rough sleeping, with particular reference to care leavers, offenders and former members of the armed services. The second was the importance of everybody accepting their responsibilities, including rough sleepers. Tony Blair's introduction to the report noted that: "... this approach will only succeed as part of a genuine partnership between central and local government, the voluntary sector, statutory bodies, businesses, community groups and rough sleepers themselves" (Rough Sleepers Unit, 1999, p. 2).

The document suggested that previous attempts to tackle rough sleeping had failed to concentrate sufficiently on its causes, to target or co-ordinate services effectively and to focus on services that sought to bring people off the streets, rather than supporting them to remain there. It suggested that "daytime street culture" was a growing problem. The theme of rights and responsibilities was evident in the six principles that the document identified as underpinning its strategy: tackling the root causes of rough sleeping; pursuing approaches that helped people off the streets and rejecting those that sustained a street lifestyle; focusing on those most in need; never giving up on the most vulnerable; helping rough sleepers to become active members of the community and being realistic about what could be offered to those who could help themselves (Rough Sleepers Unit, 1999, pp. 2–4).

Arising from this new approach was the Homelessness Action Programme, which ran from 1999 to 2002, and eventually provided funding to 113 towns and cities in England, Wales and Scotland, with a total budget of £134 million (Cloke, May, & Johnsen, 2010, p. 32). The programme was widely judged to be a success, with its target of reducing rough sleeping by two thirds being achieved ahead of schedule so that, from 2001, the aim of policy became maintaining the lower numbers (Pawson, 2007, p. 871). Various reasons were suggested for the success of the programme: Nick Raynsford attributed it in interview to a clear objective, high government priority, a good level of funding and co-operation between central government, local government and the voluntary sector. Cloke et al. (2010, pp. 37–39) similarly note the role of voluntary organisations, alongside the emphasis on welfare, care and prevention.

An evaluation of the programme (Randall & Brown, 2002, pp. 46–48) suggested that the style of outreach work was particularly effective, with features such as an assertive and persistent style that discouraged continued rough sleeping, detailed action plans for individuals and close working with the police and hostels. The police and local authorities worked effectively with homelessness agencies to tackle drinking, drug dealing and begging. Access to hostels improved, with no shortage of places in some areas.

Despite this largely positive picture, there were criticisms of the programme. Cloke et al. (2010, p. 243) quote one service provider who suggested that it was largely motivated by the need to attract tourists and Jones and Pleace (2010, p. 40) note that the target of cutting the number of rough sleepers by two thirds was not achieved in London, where the numbers began to increase again by the end of Labour's term in office. Randall and Brown's (2002, pp. 46–48) evaluation identified a number of shortcomings: there was often inadequate support for service users with the greatest needs, there were too many instances of eviction or abandonment of hostel places, some low-standard night shelters with dormitory accommodation remained, some people with high support needs continued to face difficulties in accessing accommodation, there was inadequate pre-tenancy work and exclusions from local authority registers could be particularly problematic if there was no stock earmarked for former rough sleepers.

Perhaps a more fundamental criticism is that, despite the aspirations of the *Coming in from the Cold* document, there was no substantial evaluation of the extent to which homeless people had been enabled to achieve objectives beyond accessing accommodation. Nonetheless, the reduction in rough sleeping achieved by the programme is frequently held up as one of the most striking successes of Labour's period in office.

Later Initiatives

While there were no further developments of the scale or impact of the Homelessness Action Programme, initiatives for single homeless people continued to be introduced throughout the lifetime of the Labour governments. The Hostels Capital Improvement programme (also known as the Places of Change programme) was introduced in 2005. The aim was to improve the quality of the physical environment and services within hostels and day centres in order to facilitate more positive moves from them, that is, moves to more secure housing alongside the taking up of training or work opportunities (Jones & Pleace, 2010, p. 41).

The programme lacked robust evidence to demonstrate its effectiveness but was widely welcomed by those working in the field (Jones & Pleace,

2010, p. 41). For example, Neil Munslow identified the advantages of improved physical conditions and services:

> At that time, we had a lot of evictions and a lot of people churning around because of four or five people sharing a room, some had come out of prison and this understandably caused problems. Is it any wonder that they were going to have fall outs? And the lack of dignity of no privacy. ... So, that step to modernising our offer, giving people more dignity and space to change through having their own room, and access to training and support, and facilities. It helped a lot. I don't think it was enough, but it meant that we got rid of all shared rooms in Newcastle.

After the initial success in reducing numbers, later initiatives in the area of rough sleeping concentrated on the 'entrenched' group who were hardest to resettle (Cloke et al., 2010, pp. 242–243): a development that mirrored broader concerns under the social exclusion agenda to reach out to those who had not benefitted from the first wave of services. A very small pot of money was made available for the Adults Facing Chronic Exclusion (ACE) pilot programme in 2007 to find new ways to achieve positive outcomes for both the most excluded adults and the broader community. Work took place to help individuals to make contact with appropriate services and to move between services. In addition, changes were sought to the way such services were provided and commissioned where this was judged to be necessary (Jones & Pleace, 2010, p. 42). An evaluation of the pilots gave a cautiously positive verdict overall, indicating that they had succeeded in targeting those in the greatest need:

> The client groups comprised some of the most chaotic or isolated individuals in a local community, who were hard to reach and difficult to engage. Seven clients at one Adults facing Chronic Exclusion site have a total of 79 years of care, hospital and prison between them, yet the oldest one is only 40 and three are still in their 20s. (Cattell & Mackie, 2011, p. 1)

Similarly, the London Delivery Board targeted London's 205 most entrenched and difficult-to-reach rough sleepers with intensive, personalised support to move into housing where few demands were placed on them. By 2010, only 41 of the original 205 were still sleeping rough (Jones & Pleace, 2010, p. 42). Finally, the government's *No One Left Out* strategy, launched in 2008, set the goal 'to end rough sleeping once and for all' (DCLG, 2008a, p. 7). This strategy targeted those with the most chaotic lifestyles (often involving substance misuse and mental health problems), in addition to other groups such as young people and newly arrived migrants.

Homelessness and Anti-social Behaviour

Anti-social behaviour was to be a recurring theme of the Labour governments. A key part of the building of the identity of the New Labour occurred in the area of youth crime, with Tony Blair (as shadow Home Secretary and then leader of the opposition) presenting the Conservatives as being out of control on this issue. He famously promised that a Labour government would be "tough on crime, tough on the causes of crime" (Pitts, 2003, p. 87). Anti-Social Behaviour Orders (ASBOs) were created by the 1998 Crime and Disorder Act and their powers extended by the 2003 Anti-Social Behaviour Act, whereupon the number of ASBOs reached a peak in 2005 (Ministry of Justice, 2011). The issue of anti-social behaviour was given new impetus when Tony Blair launched the Respect Action Plan as his key third term social policy initiative in 2006 (Tempest, 2006). Critics of this approach noted that those accused of anti-social behaviour were often the most vulnerable in society (Parr, 2009) and argued that the policies seemed unconcerned with mental health problems, addictions and other personal mitigating factors that are common features of anti-social behaviour cases (Brown, 2004).

The 2002 Homelessness Act took away the powers of local authorities to issue 'blanket' exclusion policies against classes of applicant. Instead, only individuals who had neglected their responsibilities through the most severe case of anti-social behaviour could be denied a place on the housing register (Harding & Harding, 2006, p. 148). However, Harding and Harding (2006, p. 148) suggest that informal blanket bans continued to operate in some areas, with a particularly severe impact on homeless people who had spent time in prison.

In the case of rough sleepers, Cloke et al. (2010, pp. 37–39) argue that, from 2003 onwards, the focus of policy moved away from tackling their social exclusion and towards a concern to 'take control of the streets' (Cloke et al., 2010, pp. 37–39). There were two linked elements of policy that could be viewed in this context: attempts to forcefully persuade homeless people to accept the services that were available and measures to tackle anti-social behaviour among those who slept rough. The RSU's *Coming in from the Cold* document had hinted that coercion could be applied to rough sleepers who refused to accept the services that were available: "Once we are satisfied that realistic alternatives are readily available, we and the public at large are entitled to expect those working on the streets to seek to persuade people to take advantage of them. This includes the police…" (RSU, 1999, p. 14).

From 2003, the Home Office's Anti-Social Behaviour Unit was asked to tackle 'problem street culture'. Begging was subsequently made a recordable offence (Cloke et al., 2010, p. 37) and ASBOs were used disproportionately against homeless people (Whiteford, 2013, pp. 14–15). These changes coincided with the establishment of 'Business Improvement Districts', which created new ways of managing urban spaces (Cloke et al., 2010, pp. 37–39). The focus on the role of city centres in urban regeneration may also have created pressure to curb the perceived anti-social tendencies of street homeless people.

Johnsen and Fitzpatrick (2007, pp. viii–ix) note that, although the government provided the tools for enforcement activities against rough sleepers, it was local authorities that decided which action should be taken. A number of authorities took measures designed to discourage people from staying on the streets and to stop the provision of services that were perceived as maintaining a street lifestyle. For example, Westminster Council sought to dissuade voluntary organisations from organising soup runs (Carvel, 2003) and Nottingham City Council urged organisations not to give out blankets to homeless people, pointing to empty capacity in hostels and discarded blankets being found with syringes in them (Wainwright, 2002).

Operation Poncho was a controversial campaign in the City of London, which involved workers encouraging rough sleepers to access places in hostels and/or drug and alcohol services. If they refused, police officers instructed them to move on and road cleaners 'wetted down' the place where they had been sleeping. Other areas also adopted 'wetting down' approaches. Benjamin (2008) argues that this measure was a response to government pressure on local authorities to achieve the target of eliminating rough sleeping by 2012.

Johnsen and Fitzpatrick (2007, pp. viii–ix) argue that measures such as the creation of controlled drinking zones, environmental measures to 'design out' street homeless activities (e.g. putting arm rests in the middle of benches to prevent people lying on them) and using ASBOs (or the threat of ASBOs) could be effective in stopping activities that caused concern in city centres. However, positive responses from street homeless people were much more likely where enforcement activities were accompanied by the offer of intensive support. Otherwise, the activities could bring them no benefit and could simply 'displace' problematic activity, for example, a person prevented from begging could raise funds through shoplifting instead.

None of the respondents interviewed for this book agreed with the analysis that, in the later stages of the Labour governments, the focus was on the anti-social behaviour of rough sleepers rather than attempts to meet their needs. Steve Hilditch said that such a view did not take account of differences between areas and was 'oversimplified'—there was a balance struck between measures to support rough sleepers and to tackle anti-social behaviour. Neil Morland said that his discussions with the government were always focused on providing support and Jeremy Swain noted a tension between support and enforcement but recalled that there were:

> occasions when we were eager for antisocial behaviour orders to be used, and particularly where we saw very vulnerable people on the street being exploited by other people and we were happy to be part of that because there's nobody more vulnerable than somebody sleeping rough.

Nick Raynsford made clear his strong disagreement with any suggestion that anti-social behaviour measures had been used disproportionately against homeless people:

> [T]he idea that anti-social behaviour is the preserve of just poor people or just homeless people is absolutely wrong. But there was rightly a wish to discourage anti-social behaviour wherever it occurred and the ASBO was the chosen mechanism, which I think had quite a lot of success. Not entirely successful but I think it did help. And the focus on reducing anti-social behaviour, I think, helped. But I don't think—I certainly don't feel that this was anything to do with homelessness policy. It certainly wasn't at that time, in the early years when I was involved and I don't recall it in the later years of the Labour government.

Youth Homelessness

In contrast to the previous period of Conservative rule, youth homelessness was not a major political issue under the Labour governments and changes to services for young homeless people were largely welcomed. The extension of the priority need categories to bring all unintentionally homeless 16–17-year-olds within the definition of statutory homelessness was a major reversal of the philosophy of the 1979–1997 period, where the prevailing view was that more generous provision could encourage young people to leave the family home unnecessarily. However, the government also acknowledged that leaving home was not a necessary or desirable step for many young people; the prevention agenda incorporated an expectation that family mediation would be explored with young people who were homeless or at risk of homelessness. Further measures in the area of youth homelessness included the YMCA and Centrepoint being charged with setting up a network of supported lodging schemes and the creation of a panel of formerly homeless young people to advise ministers (Quilgars, Johnsen, & Pleace, 2008, pp. 1–2).

The government, like its Conservative predecessors, sought to provide greater protection to care leavers in a number of areas, including housing. It increased to 18 the age to which local authorities were required to pay for accommodation for young people in their care, which removed the financial advantage to the authority of a young person moving to independent accommodation and claiming Housing Benefit. The extension of the priority need categories of the homelessness legislation to care leavers aged 18–20 represented a further layer of protection. There were also new responsibilities to create pathway plans for young people in care to the age of 21 (or 24 if they remained in education) (Quilgars et al., 2008, p. 3).

The foyer movement continued to grow under the Labour governments; its philosophy fitted well with the focus on rights and responsibilities and by 2010 there were 130 foyers, mainly operated by housing associations. They continued to house large numbers of young people who had experienced various forms of disadvantage and to operate on an assumption that these young people should actively seek to improve their own circumstances (Hillman, 2010, pp. 40–41).

The Labour Governments, Local Authorities and Voluntary Organisations

There were major changes to the relationship between central government, local authorities and voluntary organisations in this period, which had implications for the services provided to homeless people. In opposition, Labour had created the Commission for Local Democracy whose report had focused on the need to restore local autonomy (Wilks-Heeg, 2009, pp. 27–28). Labour's (1997) manifesto made a number of statements that could be read as commitments to return to local authorities some of the powers that had been lost under the Conservatives. For example, it argued that "local decision-making should be less constrained by central government, and also more accountable to local people" (quoted in Laurie, 2004, p. 51).

Once elected, Labour's commitment to 'modernise' local government was shown to incorporate two elements—measures to create new enthusiasm for local democracy and reforms to improve the delivery and performance of public services (Wilks-Heeg, 2009, pp. 27–28). Travers (2004, pp. 92–93) argues that there were tensions between these two elements, as moves towards increased local autonomy were in conflict with the government's desire to exercise greater control over service delivery.

Wilks-Heeg (2009, p. 28) argues that the measures that sought to create new interest in local democracy were largely unsuccessful in England. The 1999 Greater London Act created a strategic authority for the capital for the first time since the abolition of the Greater London Council in 1986 (Wilks-Heeg, 2009, p. 27). However, attempts to create regional assemblies were abandoned after a referendum in the North East of England in which only 22.1% voted in favour of the creation of such an assembly (Knock, 2006, p. 685).

Devolution and Homelessness

The failure to devolve power in England was in sharp contrast to the experience in other parts of the United Kingdom. A referendum on the creation of a Scottish Parliament—a proposal supported by Labour, the Liberal Democrats and the Scottish National Party—was held in September 1997. 74% voted in favour of creating the Parliament and 63% in favour of it having tax raising powers. A week after the Scottish referendum, there was a similar one on the creation of a Welsh assembly, with more limited powers. Again, the proposal was supported by Labour, the Liberal Democrats and the relevant nationalist party (Plaid Cymru), but here the vote was much closer, with 50.3% in favour. The first elections to the Scottish Parliament and the Welsh Assembly took place in 1999.

The arrangements were much more complicated in Northern Ireland, as they were part of a broader peace process. The Good Friday Agreement was reached in April 1998 and elections to the power-sharing Northern Ireland Assembly took place in the same year. The transfer of powers was then delayed by difficulties over the decommissioning of terrorist weapons (Tomaney, 2000, pp. 682–684). However, despite there being different processes, housing became a devolved power for the Scottish Parliament, the National Assembly for Wales and the Northern Ireland Assembly in 1999 (Jones & Pleace, 2010, p. 32).

The Scottish Parliament was the first of the devolved bodies to develop a distinctive approach to tackling homelessness. Mooney and Scot (2012, p. 2) argue that, whichever party or parties have been in power, the Scottish Parliament has always claimed social justice as a distinctive Scottish value. Homelessness was a key part of this agenda from the beginning, with a task force established in 1999 (McKee & Phillips, 2012, pp. 226–227). The Housing (Scotland) Act 2001 introduced new duties for the greater protection of homeless households: registered social landlords were required to comply with requests from local authorities to house statutorily homeless households and authorities themselves were given a number of new duties, including one to provide temporary accommodation to non-priority homeless households (McKee & Phillips, 2012, pp. 227–228).

A more radical change was introduced by the 2003 Homelessness etc. (Scotland) Act, which made provision for the gradual phasing out of the distinction between 'priority' and 'non-priority' need, so that by the end of 2012 all unintentionally homeless people would be entitled to 'settled' accommodation (Wilson & Barton, 2018c, p. 13). This measure increased the number of households in temporary accommodation and the percentage of lettings by social landlords to statutorily homeless households rose from 26.8% in 2004–2005 to 44.5% in 2010–2011 (Lund, 2016, p. 245). Concerns were expressed in some areas that homelessness had become the only access route into social rented housing (McKee & Phillips, 2012, p. 230).

The Scottish Executive set a target of eliminating "the need to sleep rough" and extended the existing Rough Sleepers' Initiative, increasing the level of funding and seeking better integration between housing and other services (Fitzpatrick, Pleace, & Bevan, 2005, pp. 6–7). The evaluation of Fitzpatrick et al. (2005, p. 2) suggested that the initiative had largely achieved its objectives, with a major factor in this success being the adoption oflocal authority homelessness strategies which coordinated Supporting People plans (see later section) and health and homelessness action plans.

In Wales, secondary legislation introduced in 2001 added people who were homeless following release from custody and people who were homelessness after leaving the armed services to the list of priority need groups (Jones & Pleace, 2010, p. 33). The Welsh Assembly also made a commitment to eliminating the need for anyone to sleep rough by 2003 and funded schemes targeted at rough sleepers and other homeless people, such as emergency accommodation and advice and resettlement services (Jones & Pleace, 2010, p. 39). In 2003, the Assembly set an objective to eliminate the use of bed-and-breakfast hotels for homeless households (Welsh Assembly Government, 2003). Limits were set for the amount of time that some groups, for example, 16–17-year-olds, could spend in this form of temporary accommodation (Quilgars et al., 2008, p. 21).

A much more conservative approach was adopted in Northern Ireland, which continued to subject homeless applicants to an extended eligibility for assistance test, covering immigration status and any previous 'unacceptable behaviour' in a Northern Ireland Housing Executive tenancy (Wilson & Barton, 2018c, p. 16). Although a 1999 Northern Ireland Office report failed to find any evidence of rough sleeping, it was a problem that was increasingly recognised through Labour's period in office. The Northern Ireland Housing Executive's Strategy of 2002 made a commitment to address rough sleeping in Belfast and a rough sleepers' strategy was introduced in Derry/Londonderry in April 2010 (Jones & Pleace, 2010, p. 40).

Improving the Delivery and Performance of Public Services

The element of Labour's modernisation agenda that focused on greater efficiency was to have major implications for local authorities in England. The government's aim to improve the delivery and performance of public services was closely tied to its desire to shed the Old Labour image—accountability was a key Third Way principle (Wilks-Heeg, 2009, pp. 25–26) and 'prudence' was identified as one of Chancellor Gordon Brown's most important objectives. The need to spend public money wisely was reflected in numerous initiatives to ensure that government departments, appointed bodies and local government operated more efficiently (Travers, 2004, p. 92).

As was identified in Chap. 2, the approach taken by the Labour governments to local authorities and other organisations is sometimes characterised as meta-governance, where hierarchical relationships remain in place but the state rarely exercises power overtly, preferring to use more subtle methods, sometimes through third parties (Kelly, 2006, p. 607). Some of the more overtly controlling and confrontational measures of the Conservatives were revoked: the surcharge and disqualification of councillors were abolished as penalties in 2000 (Smith, 2000). However, the Conservative system of capping the council tax charged by local authorities was retained in a modified form, penalising councils that raised council tax by more than 4.5% per year (Travers, 2004, p. 91). A proposal to phase out capping, beginning with those authorities who achieved the highest performance rating, created political difficulties when the average proposed council tax rise for 2003–2004 was 13%, at a time when inflation was running at approximately 2% (Travers, 2004, p. 92). As a result, the capping system was retained.

The 1999 Local Government Act abolished Compulsory Competitive Tendering and replaced it with a system of Best Value (Wilks-Heeg, 2009, p. 27), which encouraged (rather than required) local authorities to consider alternative forms of provision (Stewart, 2014, p. 844). Many councils opted to continue to put service out to tender, partly as a result of strong government pressure to use private finance for capital projects (Travers, 2004, p. 91). Authorities faced having some of their functions taken from them in the event of poor performance, but this power was rarely used (Kelly, 2006, pp. 603–604).

Best Value required local authorities to seek continuous improvement in their services against a set of detailed performance indicators (Sanderson, 2002, p. 10). The extensive use of the indicators was justified by a need to reduce inequalities in service provision—often referred to as a 'postcode lottery' (Wilks-Heeg, 2009, p. 32). However, by 2004, even the Treasury was acknowledging that their use had become excessive (Travers, 2004, p. 92).

In addition, local authorities were required to review their performance across all areas on a five-year cycle, produce a Local Performance Plan and numerous strategies, and be subjected to a rigorous regime of audit and inspection (Sanderson, 2002, p. 10). A Comprehensive Performance Assessment graded them as 'excellent', 'good', 'fair', 'weak' or 'poor' (Travers, 2004, p. 92). While it is not clear whether such measures improved services, there is broad agreement that they had a centralising effect (Wilks-Heeg, 2009, p. 28).

There were also 'softer' measures that offered incentives for good practice. The Audit Commission had been established in 1983 to assess the effectiveness of public spending; one of its roles under the Labour governments was to persuade local authorities to accept the government's policy objectives and to create models of best practice (Kelly, 2006, pp. 603–604). The Beacon Council scheme was introduced to encourage local authorities to learn from their peers who were performing best in specific areas. To be selected as a Beacon, a council needed to demonstrate innovation or excellence in their chosen area (with homelessness being one of the options), be judged to have good corporate performance overall and have a plan for disseminating their good practice to other local authorities if they were selected (Wilson & Lilly, 2016, p. 3).

In 2005 a total of £3 million was made available to councils for achieving Beacon status, with an additional £2 million available to those Beacon Councils that wanted to offer peer support to other local authorities (Wilson & Lilly, 2016, p. 2). Downe, Hartley, and Rashman (2004, p. 552) evaluated the Beacon scheme and were unable to determine whether it was sustainable or had brought about cultural change but were able to conclude that "Beacon scheme events are a successful means of sharing good practice and encouraging inter-organisation change and learning in local government." Similarly, creating 'Regional Champions' was judged to be a positive method of spreading good practice by local authorities and other agencies dealing with homelessness (Moseley & James, 2008, pp. 125–126).

Nick Raynsford identified the Beacon council scheme as a measure that typified the approach of the Labour governments to local authorities:

> A lot of the work of the Social Exclusion Unit was all about highlighting best practice and trying to encourage it and, similarly, we did that in relation to housing policy and other local government services. It was very much our belief that carrot is better than stick if possible, but sometimes stick is necessary ... central government wanted local government to be adequately funded, wanted it to be able to do its job properly, wanted to give it incentives and certainly wasn't going to put up with appalling failure.

Steve Hilditch offered a more critical assessment, suggesting that: "Labour did not trust local government and that was reflected in a lot of the things it did. It was still quite controlling of local government and was too prone to tell people what to do."

When considering homelessness specifically, Neil Morland and Neil Munslow agreed that the government's approach was to seek to encourage rather than to coerce local authorities to adopt good practice. However, Neil Munslow identified a negative consequence of this approach: Newcastle City Council, under pressure from the government, sought to re-house more homeless people in the private rented sector when there was no need to and despite evidence showing loss of private rented accommodation to be one of the main causes of homelessness.

Homelessness Strategies and Supporting People

In addition to changes to the legal obligations to homeless households, the 2002 Homelessness Act required local authorities to carry out a review of homelessness in their area and to formulate and publish a homelessness strategy based on this review. Homelessness strategies were required to include plans for the prevention of homelessness, for ensuring that sufficient accommodation was available for those who were (or might become) homeless and for ensuring that support was available for those who might become homeless or return to homelessness. Strategies were to be renewed every five years or sooner (Department of Transport, Local Government and the Regions (DTLR), 2002, p. 14). The guidance provided by the Department of Transport, Local Government and the Regions on how to write a homelessness strategy was extensive, stretching to 11 chapters and 87 pages (DTLR, 2002). The first strategies produced by local authorities largely reflected the government's wish for a more pro-active approach: for example, 80% included commitments to improved housing advice and two thirds discussed the development of closer liaison with private landlords to prevent homelessness (Pawson, 2007, p. 873). Research commissioned by Shelter suggested that these strategies had a positive effect, enabling authorities to identify gaps in their knowledge and strengthening both inter-departmental and inter-agency working (Dudleston, Alty, Henthorne, & Credland, 2004, p. 7).

Closely linked to the requirement to form a Homelessness Strategy was the Supporting People programme, which was launched in April 2003. It gave local authorities control over funding for housing-related support provided to single homeless people and other groups. This funding had previously been available through Housing Benefit. In the case of single homeless people, Supporting People spending by local authorities was primarily focused on prevention and resettlement services (Jones & Pleace, 2010, p. 37). Similar arrangements were made in Scotland and Wales, with the programme in Northern Ireland being administered through the Northern Ireland Housing Executive (Jones & Pleace, 2010, p. 37). Although there were some complaints about a loss of autonomy for voluntary organisations, Neil Munslow praised the Supporting People programme for facilitating more effective coordination of services by local authorities: "Commissioning gave us some power really, to try and rationalise the system from 27 competing providers to more of a system that was meant to help the people."

The Supporting People programme had a larger than expected budget initially; Jeremy Swain argued that this had a positive effect on services:

> It allowed us particularly to develop tenancy support services, floating support services in different London boroughs, which I think were fundamental in terms of supporting people in a low key way and helping them to get their life sorted out, to reconnect with family and friends, get skilled, get into work.

However, Nick Raynsford suggested that subsequent cuts to the budget were to mean that many of the benefits of Supporting People were lost:

> When it *[the Supporting People budget]* went below a certain level, it really ceased to have the benefits that it did have of ensuring adequate funding for a lot of specific specialist units doing very, very important work and then you began to see the closure of units and housing associations pulling out of supporting housing work and so on. So, I think the Supporting People history is a very interesting case study of a brilliant idea that started well and then just was allowed to wither.

Initially, many Supporting People funded resettlement services for single homeless people were delivered along traditional lines of seeking to provide 'daily living skills'. Such an approach was critiqued in Chap. 5; research continued to suggest that it was not the most effective method of working with this group (Jones & Pleace, 2010, pp. 59–60). However, after reviews in England and Scotland in 2007, new directions began to be taken. Some services focused on secondary prevention for groups believed to be at risk of homelessness, others on employment, training and education, and there were also attempts to develop low-cost support models (e.g. housing support workers negotiating a package of support from other services). In 2008–2009, 37% of the Supporting People budget was spent on supported housing, 30% on direct access accommodation and night shelters, 22% on floating support, 5% on women's refuges, 4% on outreach services, 2% on foyers and 1% on supported lodgings (Jones & Pleace, 2010, pp. 58–60).

Pilots in 2008–2009 resulted in Supporting People being one of a number of specific grants incorporated into Area Based Grant, meaning that the ring fence around the budget was lost. The Government announced a presumption in favour of non-specific grants to increase local control over resources and reduce reporting requirements (Department of Communities and Local Government, 2008b, pp. 4–5).

The ending of the ring fence for Supporting People produced a mixed response from interview respondents, with Jeremy Swain suggesting that one hoped for outcome was greater integration between housing support and other services: "So it made sense not to just limit a pot around housing support, but clearly the people we were working with needed other forms of support for mental health issues."

In contrast, Steve Hilditch saw the ending of the ring fence in entirely negative terms:

> Whatever the principles behind it, in practice it was a terrible decision. I recall at the time homelessness projects tended to miss out quite badly, but there were a number of less popular groups that people didn't like spending money on. So money disappeared from Supporting People into other programmes.

The ending of the ring fence came close to a change of government, so it was difficult to differentiate its impact from that of major cuts to local authority spending from 2010.

Greater Consistency in Local Authority Homelessness Practice

Although direct comparisons with previous time periods are not possible, there is some evidence to suggest that the range of measures used by the government achieved greater consistency in local authority homelessness practice in England, at least in terms of the focus on prevention. When the government undertook a review of homelessness services in 2005, 87% of responding local authorities said that they provided rent deposit and/or bond schemes, 81.4% provided prevention services through Citizens Advice Bureaux, 79.8% provided mediation services, 77.8% provided tenancy support aimed at prevention, 75.7% provided home visits and 74.6% provided tenancy support aimed at resettlement (ODPM, 2005, p. 14).

When taking a broader view, the evidence is less clear. In 2009–2010, the regions with the highest rate of statutory homelessness acceptances (London, the North East and Yorkshire and the Humber) tended to also have higher rates of homelessness prevention and relief. However, there were exceptions to the trend: the West Midlands had the highest rate of acceptances of any region but reported the lowest rate of activity in the areas of prevention and relief (DCLG, 2009, p. 10).

More specific evidence of differing practice was provided by examining data from eight core English cities (Birmingham, Bristol, Leeds, Liverpool, Manchester, Newcastle, Nottingham City and Sheffield) for 2009–2010 (cited in Harding, Irving, Fitzpatrick, & Pawson, 2013, p. 15) and comparing it to population data from the 2011 census. Some of the differences between cities were striking—most notably Sheffield made 3.9 homeless assessment decisions per 1000 population, while Bristol made 0.8. However, Bristol accepted 83% of homeless applicants, compared to a figure of 44% in Sheffield. While the figures cannot indicate the reasons for these differences, they suggest that there were wide variations in practice. Using a more qualitative approach, Cloke et al. (2010, p. 183) note the very different responses to homelessness between one local authority that had a longstanding commitment to tackle the issue and another where the commitment was more recent, with the authority having previously relied on people moving to a nearby city.

Even where similar services were provided, there could be quite different outcomes. The Association of London Government (2005, cited in Quilgars et al., 2008, p. 67) found that the proportion of young people remaining at home or returning home after receiving family mediation services varied between 38% and 96% in different London boroughs.

So, although Labour's period in office was widely acknowledged to have brought about improvement and greater consistency in some areas of local authority practice, substantial differences remained in others.

The Third Sector

The government's focus on collaborative working had important implications for the agencies that it liked to refer to as the 'Third Sector'; a collective noun that incorporated the voluntary sector (charities, housing associations, campaigning organisations, etc.), the community sector (small and locally organised groups) and businesses with social objectives (e.g. credit unions and community interest companies). The importance of the sector under the Labour governments was, to some degree, a function of its size: the number of charities expanded hugely from 1991 to 2004, partly as a result of the creation of trusts to run former public services (Haugh & Kitson, 2007, pp. 974–977). However, more importantly, the sector's involvement in the delivery of public services provided a method of reconciling Conservative enthusiasm for markets in public services with Labour's historic commitment to social justice (Haugh & Kitson, 2007, p. 982). Third Sector organisations were expected (and supported) to deliver public services within a 'mixed economy' of welfare, in addition to promoting civic engagement and supporting community action (Alcock, Kendall, & Parry, 2012, pp. 349–350). They were believed to bring important attributes into this mixed economy such as public trust, closeness to local communities and concern with issues such as social exclusion and the environment (Haugh & Kitson, 2007, p. 983).

The government launched a 'Compact' with voluntary organisations in 1998, promising to provide strategic funding, adequate consultation and better working relationships. In return, organisations were required to be accountable, to promote good practice and to inform and consult more widely with members, users and supporters (Lewis, 2005, pp. 121–123). Alcock et al. (2012, p. 348) argue that Labour's relationship with voluntary organisations reached a high point when the Office of the Third Sector was created in 2006, with the aim of promoting good policy and practice. As economic difficulties came to dominate Labour's third term, a series of recession summits were held with the sector and further financial support was provided (Alcock et al., 2012, p. 348). Spending on voluntary organisations doubled to £11 billion per year during Labour's period in office (Davies, 2011, p. 643).

However, although voluntary organisations were largely pleased with the government's approach, the nature of the funding received raised some questions about their role. Grant income increased, but there was a greater increase in income from public service contracts, raising concerns that some local authorities were replacing grant aid with competitive tendering (Davies, 2011, p. 645). Contracts to provide public services were seen to be moving voluntary organisations towards government-driven targets, enforced by measures of performance (Alcock et al., 2012, p. 349). The government itself acknowledged that: "A narrow focus on financial efficiency and value for money in the delivery of public services may have unintended consequences for the third sector's ability to help transform public services" (HM Treasury and Cabinet Office, 2006, p. 42, quoted in Haugh & Kitson, 2007, p. 990).

There were concerns that voluntary organisations might be unwilling to criticise the policies of public bodies for fear of losing funding (Davies, 2011, pp. 646–647). Lewis (2005, p. 122) argues that there is no clear evidence that the role of the sector in the development of policy increased under the Labour governments.

Voluntary Organisations Dealing with Homelessness

Cloke et al. (2010) express similar concerns to those above when considering specifically voluntary organisations dealing with homelessness. Organisations receiving funding from the Homelessness Action Programme were tied by contract to the RSU and were required to demonstrate that they were meeting a number of conditions—working with other organisations, focusing on rough sleeping and having suitable outreach and resettlement programmes. Those that rejected the approach of the RSU were considered 'unprofessional' and denied further funding opportunities (Cloke et al., 2010, pp. 33–34). Cloke et al. (2010, p. 244) argue that these measures "undermine a fundamental role of the voluntary sector: namely, to act as an advocate of homeless people and, where necessary, a critic of government".

However, a more positive view was taken by the people interviewed for this book. Steve Hilditch recalled that Shelter had a very active role in the shaping of the 2002 Homelessness Act:

> There was open discussion about the ways of improving the legislation, improving the rights and so on, which is how it was driven. Chris Holmes, the then Shelter director, was very heavily engaged with ministers and civil servants in drawing up the Bill and implementing the Act.

Jeremy Swain described the surprise of voluntary organisations when, having asked for a substantial sum of money to tackle rough sleeping and a dedicated unit, headed by someone with experience of the voluntary sector, the incoming Labour government provided what had been asked for. Funding was increased and Louise Casey (a former deputy director of Shelter) was appointed to head the RSU. There were expectations of voluntary organisations in return: "So we asked for it, we got it and then the government said, 'All right, you want it, we're giving it to you, stop whingeing, bring down rough sleeping'."

Both Jeremy Swain, from his experience at Thames Reach, and Neil Morland, from his time at Potteries Housing Association, evaluated positively the active role that the Rough Sleepers' Unit took in engaging with the voluntary sector. Neil Morland said, "They were very pro-active, that's absolutely for sure"; he found the advice of the unit helpful because its aims were aligned with those of the association. Jeremy Swain similarly said that:

> The Rough Sleepers' Unit was very, very directly engaged, so members of the Rough Sleepers' Unit used to go out on to the street with outreach workers to if you like experience and test the system to see whether it was working effectively and to do things if they were finding blocks. So typically they'd go on the street and try to refer people into hostels themselves and find out what happened directly and then respond if they weren't getting the response they expected.

The greater monitoring that went with the increased resources was acknowledged to have brought about major change. Neil Morland commented that voluntary organisations experienced a

> shift in relationship with the state from one of being a hands-off relationship with the state, you know, almost begging the state to be interested in the issue of homelessness, to one where the state were then very, very interested.

Steve Hilditch saw both positives and negatives, saying of the voluntary sector: "… to be very honest it did need sharpening up. It didn't really need to be told what to do. It needed sharpening up so it could do what it was meant to do better".

Local Authorities and Voluntary Organisations

In addition to areas where the government exerted direct influence, there were several examples of it working with local authorities to direct voluntary organisations in a manner consistent with the concept of meta-governance (Kelly, 2006, p. 67). For example, the Quality Assessment Framework created by the Homelessness Action Programme provided a mechanism by which local authorities could monitor the performance of agencies providing hostels and night shelters (May, Cloke, & Johnsen, 2006, p. 715). Projects providing emergency and supported housing were required to adhere to the standards of the National Housing Federation's "Framework for Housing Care and Support" in order to be eligible for Supporting People funding and to face regular monitoring by the responsible local authority (May et al., 2006, p. 724).

Neil Munslow spoke very positively about the changes to the relationship between local authorities and other agencies during the time of the Labour government:

> [N]ew Labour started to create those aspirations of place building, a perception of local authorities being the lynchpins to bring together the rest of the public sector, part of the requirements in the Homelessness Act 2002, and an ongoing aspiration of joining things up ... it becomes increasingly, hopefully a more consensual evidential approach that encourages providers to do what they can and provide good value within the resources they've got. This helps us to better understand what beyond access to accommodation causes homelessness. In Newcastle this often relates to complex drug and alcohol, mental health problems that homeless hostels struggle to manage.

However, Neil Morland suggested that there was a mixed response among voluntary organisations to the changed relationship with local authorities:

> Some voluntary organisations were very happy to do that and could do that very well. Some voluntary organisations struggled with having to explain what they were doing with the money and couldn't give a good explanation as to what they were doing with the money. So, I think it very much varies in terms of how local authorities embraced the changes depending on their culture.

Evaluation of the Approach to Voluntary Organisations

The evidence that is available suggests that the Labour governments were partially successful in their efforts to ensure that more voluntary agencies worked in partnership with central and local government and operated to agreed standards. Moseley and James (2008, pp. 131–133) found that the use of legislation did not ensure genuine co-operation between agencies, although could be used as a tool by local authorities to pressurise other organisations to fulfil their legal responsibilities. May et al. (2006, p. 719) note that there were limits to the financial influence of local authorities over voluntary organisations, with providers of accommodation obtaining funding from a wide variety of other sources including health authorities, the probation service and individual donations. When considering specific services, the Government succeeded in approximately halving the number of soup runs—services that were seen to be maintaining rough sleeping (Cloke et al., 2010, pp. 94–95). However, pressure on day centres to offer services only to those who expressed some form of commitment to change their lifestyle and behaviour was judged to have produced minimal impact (Cloke et al., 2010, p. 121). So, as in other areas, the government brought about change, but not the complete transformation of services that had been hoped for.

Summary

When considering the five key factors influencing homelessness policy, it is clear that the desire to create a New Labour identity had more influence in some areas than others. The adoption of social exclusion as the conceptual framework for discussions of rough sleeping neatly combined elements of the individualistic explanations of the Conservatives and the focus on inequalities of Old Labour. This framework was relevant because it influenced the types of services that were encouraged and discouraged. However, the government's programme was widely regarded as a success because of a reduction in the numbers sleeping rough, with other objectives such as increasing employment opportunities being little evaluated. There was less explicit discussion of causes of statutory homelessness, but the restoration of a right to settled housing, together with the inclusion of 16–17-year-olds in the priority need categories, demonstrated a different view to the one favoured by previous Conservative governments.

While some of the more confrontational measures of the Conservatives were abandoned, the Labour governments' concern to ensure that public money was well used was reflected in a range of measures that sought to control or influence the work of local authorities and voluntary organisations. One clear example of success in this area was the manner in which authorities embraced the prevention agenda, which represented a significant shift in focus from tertiary to secondary prevention. The most obvious example of a primary prevention measure—the building of new property—was a low priority for much of Labour's period in power. However, although the decline in numbers of social rented dwellings that had occurred under the Conservatives was not reversed to any significant extent, there were major improvements to the quality of the properties and to the disadvantaged neighbourhoods in which many of them were located, resulting in higher demand for housing in the sector. So, more homeless households were able to access a considerably improved social rented sector, indicating that this period represented a high point in the response to homelessness in England, with Scotland taking advantage of the devolution of powers to provide an even more generous service.

References

Alcock, P., Kendall, J., & Parry, J. (2012). From the third sector to the Big Society: Consensus or contention in the 2010 UK General Election? *Voluntary Sector Review, 3*(3), 347–363.

Benjamin, A. (2008, September 24). Cleaned out. *The Guardian*. Retrieved from https://www.theguardian.com/society/2008/sep/24/homelessness.rough.sleepers

Benn, M. (2000). New Labour and social exclusion. *Political Quarterly, 71*(3), 309–318.

Boswell, C. (2009). *The political use of expert knowledge*. Cambridge, UK: Cambridge University Press.

Boughton, J. (2018). *Municipal dreams: The rise and fall of council housing*. London, UK: Verso Books.

Brown, A. P. (2004). Anti-social behaviour, crime control and social control. *The Howard Journal of Crime and Justice, 43*(2), 203–211.

Carvel, J. (2003, December 17). Westminster fights flood of soup runs. *The Guardian*. Retrieved from https://www.theguardian.com/society/2003/dec/17/homelessness.uknews

Cattell, J., & Mackie, A. (2011). *Adults facing chronic exclusion programme: Evaluation findings*. London, UK: Department for Communities and Local Government.

Cloke, P., May, J., & Johnsen, S. (2010). *Swept up lives? Re-envisioning the homeless city*. Chichester, UK: John Wiley and Sons Ltd.

Cole, I., & Nevin, B. (2004). *The road to renewal: The early development of the Housing Market Renewal programme in England*. York, UK: Joseph Rowntree Foundation.

Couch, C., Lord, A., & Crocks, M. (2015). Questioning the concept of market failure in housing: The case of Housing Market Renewal in Liverpool. *International Journal of Housing Policy, 15*(4), 461–490.

Davies, S. (2011). Outsourcing, public sector reform and the changed character of the UK state-voluntary sector relationship. *International Journal of Public Sector Management, 24*(7), 641–649.

Department for Communities and Local Government. (2006a). *A decent home: Definition and guidance for implementation June 2006—Update*. London, UK: Department of Communities and Local Government. Retrieved from https://

www.gov.uk/government/publications/a-decent-home-definition-and-guidance

Department for Communities and Local Government. (2006b) *Tackling the changing face of homelessness*. Speech by Ruth Kelly MP at the Andy Ludlow Awards on 14 November 2006. Retrieved from http://webarchive.nationalarchives.gov.uk/20070701134647/http://www.communities.gov.uk/index.asp?id=150446

Department for Communities and Local Government. (2008a). *No one left out: Communities ending rough sleeping*. London, UK: HM Government.

Department for Communities and Local Government. (2008b). *Area based grant, general guidance 2008*. London, UK: Department for Communities and Local Government.

Department for Communities and Local Government. (2009). *Homelessness prevention and relief: England 2009/10 experimental statistics*. London, UK: Department of Communities and Local Government. Retrieved from https://www.gov.uk/government/uploads/system/uploads/attachment.../1698295.pdf

Department of the Environment, Transport and the Regions. (2000). *Our future homes*. London, UK: Department of Environment, Transport and the Regions.

Department of Transport, Local Government and the Regions. (2002). *Homelessness strategies: A good practice handbook*. London, UK: Department of Transport, Local Government and the Regions.

Downe, J., Hartley, J., & Rashman, D. (2004). Evaluating the extent of inter-organizational learning and change in local authorities through the English beacon council scheme. *Public Management Review, 6*(4), 531–554.

Dudleston, A., Alty, C., Henthorne, K., & Credland, S. (2004). *The Act in action: As assessment of homelessness reviews and strategies*. London, UK: Shelter.

Ellison, N., & Pierson, C. (1998). Introduction. In N. Ellison & C. Pierson (Eds.), *Developments in British Social Policy* (pp. 1–14). Basingstoke, UK: Macmillan.

Fitzpatrick, S., Pleace, N., & Bevan, M. (2005). *Final evaluation of the rough sleepers' initiative*. York, UK: University of York, Centre for Housing Policy.

Harding, A., & Harding, J. (2006). Inclusion and exclusion in the re-housing of former prisoners. *Probation Journal, 53*(2), 139–155.

Harding, J., Irving, A., Fitzpatrick, S., & Pawson, H. (2013). *Evaluation of Newcastle's 'co-operative' approach to prevention and management of homelessness in light of changing government policy*. Newcastle-upon-Tyne, UK: Northumbria University.

Haugh, H., & Kitson, M. (2007). The Third Way and the third sector: New Labour's economic policy and the social economy. *Cambridge Journal of Economics, 31*(6), 973–994.

Heffernan, R. (2011). Labour's New Labour legacy: Politics after Blair and Brown. *Political Studies Review, 9*(2), 163–177.

Heron, E., & Dwyer, P. (1999). Doing the right thing: Labour's attempt to forge a new welfare deal between the individual and the welfare state. *Social Policy and Administration, 33*(1), 91–104.

Hetherington, P. (2004, December 13). Charity claims housing law bent. *The Guardian*. Retrieved from https://www.theguardian.com/society/2004/dec/13/homelessness.politics

Hillman, S. (2010). The Foyer Federation: Aiming to transform the institutions and policies that currently help young people. *Criminal Justice Matters, 80*(1), 40–41.

Home Office. (2000). *Listen Up*. London, UK: Home Office.

Johnsen, S., & Fitzpatrick, S. (2007). *The impact of enforcement on street users in England*. York, UK: Joseph Rowntree Foundation.

Jones, A., & Pleace, N. (2010). *A review of single homelessness in the UK 2000–2010*. London, UK: Crisis and the University of York.

Keenan, P., Lowe, S., & Spencer, S. (1999). Housing abandonment in inner cities—The politics of low demand for housing. *Housing Studies, 14*(5), 703–716.

Kelly, J. (2006). Central regulation of English local authorities: An example of meta-governance? *Public Administration, 84*(3), 603–621.

Knock, K. (2006). The North East referendum: Lessons learned? *Parliamentary Affairs, 59*(4), 682–693.

Laurie, E. (2004). The Homelessness Act 2002 and housing allocations: All change or business as usual? *Modern Law Review, 67*(1), 48–68.

Leather, P., & Nevin, B. (2012). The Housing Market Renewal Programme: Origins, outcomes and the effectiveness of public policy interventions in a volatile market. *Urban Studies, 50*(5), 856–875.

Levitas, R. (2005). *The inclusive society? Social exclusion and New Labour* (2nd ed.). Basingstoke, UK: Palgrave Macmillan.

Lewis, J. (2005). New Labour's approach to the voluntary sector: Independence and the meaning of partnership. *Social Policy and Society, 4*(2), 121–131.

Lund, B. (2004). Housing policy: Coming in from the cold? In N. Ellison, D. Bauld, & M. Powell (Eds.), *Social policy review 16: Analysis and debate in social policy* (pp. 13–28). Bristol, UK: Policy Press.

Lund, B. (2016). *Housing politics in the United Kingdom*. Bristol, UK: Policy Press.

Lupton, R. (2013). Labour's record on Neighbourhood Renewal in England, Social Policy in a Cold Climate. *Summary Working Paper 6*. London School of Economics and Political Science, London: UK. Retrieved from http://sticerd.lse.ac.uk/dps/case/spcc/WP06_SUMMARY.pdf

Manwaring, R. (2016). From new/labour to Rudd/Gillard—Transferring social policy. *Policy Studies, 37*(5), 426–439.

May, J., Cloke, P., & Johnsen, S. (2006). Shelter at the margins: New Labour and the changing state of emergency accommodation for single homeless people in Britain. *Policy and Politics, 34*(4), 711–729.

McKee, K., & Phillips, D. (2012). Social housing and homelessness policies. In G. Mooney & G. Scott (Eds.), *Social justice and social policy in Scotland* (pp. 223–228). Bristol, UK: Policy Press.

Millar, J. (2003). From wage replacement to wage supplement: Benefits and tax credits. In J. Millar (Ed.), *Understanding social security: Issues for policy and practice* (pp. 123–143). Bristol, UK: Policy Press.

Ministry of Housing, Communities and Local Government. (2018). *Local authority housing statistics: Year ending March 2017*. Retrieved from https://www.gov.uk/government/statistics/local-authority-housing-statistics-year-ending-march-2017

Ministry of Justice. (2011). *Statistical notice: Anti-Social Behaviour Order (ASBO) statistics England and Wales 2010*. London, UK: Ministry of Justice.

Mooney, G., & Scot, G. (2012). Devolution, social justice and social policy: The Scottish context. In G. Mooney & G. Scott (Eds.), *Social justice and social policy in Scotland* (pp. 223–228). Bristol, UK: Policy Press.

Moseley, A., & James, O. (2008). Central state steering of local collaboration: Assessing the impact of tools of meta-governance in homelessness services in England. *Public Organization Review, 8*, 117–136.

Mullins, D., & Niner, P. (1998). A price of citizenship? Changing access to social housing. In A. Marsh & D. Mullins (Eds.), *Housing and public policy: Citizenship, choice and control* (pp. 175–198). Buckingham, UK: Open University Press.

National Audit Office. (2010). *The Decent Homes Programme, summary report by the comptroller and auditor general*. HC 212. Session 2009–2010. Retrieved from https://www.nao.org.uk/wp-content/uploads/2010/01/0910212es.pdf

Office of the Deputy Prime Minister. (2003). *Best value in housing and homelessness framework*. Retrieved from http://webarchive.nationalarchives.gov.uk/20120920035507/http://www.communities.gov.uk/documents/housing/pdf/157311.pdf

Office of the Deputy Prime Minister. (2005). *Survey of English local authorities about homelessness*. London, UK: Homelessness and Housing Support Directorate, Office of the Deputy Prime Minister.

Parr, S. (2009). Confronting the reality of anti-social behaviour. *Theoretical Criminology, 13*(3), 363–381.

Pautz, H. (2011). New Labour in government: Think-tanks and social policy reform, 1997–2001. *British Politics, 6*(2), 187–209.

Pawson, H. (2007). Local authority homelessness prevention in England: Empowering consumers or denying rights? *Housing Studies, 22*(6), 867–883.

Pearce, J., & Vine, J. (2014). Quantifying residualisation: The changing nature of social housing in the UK. *Journal of Housing and the Built Environment, 29*(4), 657–695.

Pitts, J. (2003). Youth justice in England and Wales. In R. Matthews & J. Young (Eds.), *The new politics of crime and punishment* (pp. 71–99). Cullompton, Devon: Willan Publishing.

Powell, M. (2000). New Labour and the third way in the British welfare state: A new and distinctive approach? *Critical Social Policy, 20*(1), 39–60.

Power, A., & Mumford, K. (1999). *The slow death of great cities? Urban abandonment or urban renaissance.* York, UK: Joseph Rowntree Foundation.

Power, A., Ploger, J., & Winkler, A. (2010). *Phoenix cities: The fall and rise of great industrial cities.* Bristol, UK: Policy Press.

Quilgars, D., Johnsen, S., & Pleace, N. (2008). *Youth homelessness in the UK: A decade of progress?* York: UK: Joseph Rowntree Foundation.

Randall, G., & Brown, S. (2002). *Helping rough sleepers off the street.* London, UK: Office of the Deputy Prime Minister, Homelessness Directorate.

Raynsford, N. (2016). *Substance not spin: An insider's view of success and failure in government.* Bristol, UK: Policy Press.

Rough Sleepers Unit. (1999). *Coming in from the cold.* Retrieved from https://webarchive.nationalarchives.gov.uk/20120920014720/http://www.communities.gov.uk/documents/housing/pdf/roughsleepersstrategy.pdf

Sanderson, I. (2002). Performance management, evaluation and learning in 'modern' local government. *Public Administration, 79*(2), 297–313.

Smith, J. (2000, February 10). Death of the surcharge. *Local Government Chronicle.* Retrieved from https://www.lgcplus.com/death-of-the-surcharge/1390687.article

Stewart, J. (2014). An era of continuing change: Reflections on local government in England 1974–2014. *Local Government Studies, 40*(6), 835–850.

Tempest, M. (2006, January 10). Blair launches 'respect' action plan. *The Guardian.* Retrieved from https://www.theguardian.com/politics/2006/jan/10/immigrationpolicy.ukcrime

Tomaney, J. (2000). End of the empire state? New Labour and devolution in the United Kingdom. *International Journal of Urban and Regional Research, 24*(3), 675–688.

Travers, T. (2004). Labour's local record. *New Economy, 11*(2), 90–94.

Wainwright, M. (2002, December 10). Cold ends blanket ban for homeless. *The Guardian.* Retrieved from https://www.theguardian.com/society/2002/dec/10/homelessness.uknews

Welsh Assembly Government. (2003). *National homelessness strategy.* Cardiff, Wales: Welsh Assembly Government.

Welshman, J. (2013). *Underclass.* London, UK: Bloomsbury Publishing plc.

Whiteford, M. (2013). New Labour, street homelessness and social exclusion: A defaulted promissory note? *Housing Studies, 28*(1), 10–32.

Wilks-Heeg, S. (2009). New Labour and the reform of English local government, 1997–2007: Privatising the parts that Conservative governments could not reach? *Planning, Practice and Research, 24*(1), 23–39.

Wilson, S., & Lilly, A. (2016). *Beacon Councils scheme case study*. London, UK: Institute for Government. Retrieved from https://www.instituteforgovernment.org.uk/sites/default/files/beacon-councils-scheme.pdf

Wilson, W. (2015). Rough Sleepers Initiative (RSI) 1990–1999. *House of Commons Library Standard Note SN07121*, London, UK.

Wilson, W., & Barton, C. (2018a). Households in temporary accommodation (England). *House of Commons Briefing Paper Number 02110*, London, UK.

Wilson, W., & Barton, C. (2018b). Statutory homelessness in England. *House of Commons Library Briefing Paper Number 01164*, London, UK.

Wilson, W., & Barton, C. (2018c). Comparisons of homeless duties in England, Wales, Scotland and Northern Ireland. *House of Commons Library Briefing Paper Number 7201*, London, UK.

CHAPTER 7

The Conservative-Led Administrations from 2010: Familiar Policies in New Rhetoric

Introduction

The general election of 2010 resulted in a hung parliament. The Conservatives, who were the largest party, formed a coalition with the Liberal Democrats, with David Cameron as Prime Minister, which was to last a full parliament. The Conservatives then won a small overall majority in 2015, but Cameron resigned as Prime Minister a year later, when Britain voted in a referendum to leave the European Union. Theresa May won the subsequent Conservative leadership election, but she also was not able to enjoy her success for long, calling a snap general election in 2017 only to find that the Conservatives overall majority disappeared, and they were once again the largest party in a hung parliament. She continued in government after reaching an agreement with the Democratic Unionist Party.

Although the Liberal Democrats were able to list specific achievements from the 2010 to 2015 Parliament, their influence was widely perceived to be negligible, and the direction of social policy appeared to change as much following David Cameron's succession by Theresa May as it did after the general election of 2015. While May's government did not specifically blame its immediate predecessors for the growth of homelessness, there were a number of hints in its rough sleeping strategy that welfare reform had aggravated the problem, with the discontinuation of some reforms further strengthening this inference. This book is being completed at the start of 2019, when domestic policy has almost ground to a

J. Harding, *Post-War Homelessness Policy in the UK*,
https://doi.org/10.1007/978-3-030-22117-1_7

standstill amidst the debate over the European Union. In addition, Mrs May has indicated that she will not be Conservative leader at the next general election. So, as it is not clear how many of her policies will be implemented, the direction taken under her Premiership will be discussed only briefly.

David Cameron and the New Conservatives

The direction given to the Conservative Party by David Cameron following his election as party leader in 2005 marked the culmination of a long period of change. Pautz (2012, pp. 366–367) argues that by the mid-1990s Conservatives were acknowledging that social policy issues had been neglected during their years in government and that policies needed to be found to deal with demographic change, increasing demand for health care and the need to improve schools.

After eight years of opposition, Cameron perceived the need to establish the party as 'nice' and to develop policy positions to reflect this new image. He sought to underpin policies with new ideas such as the 'Big Society', 'localism' and 'compassionate Conservatism' (Pautz, 2012, p. 364). Cameron urged the party to think of prosperity not simply as being about economic growth and wealth creation but also about ending poverty (Pautz, 2012, p. 371). Conservative leaning think tank the Policy Exchange led a shift in thinking to give importance to issues of poverty and social exclusion and former party leader Iain Duncan-Smith acknowledged that poverty had been a "difficult issue" for the party in the past (Pautz, 2012, pp. 366–368). Cameron accepted that there was such a thing as society, but differentiated this from the state and argued for enhanced roles for active citizens and voluntary organisations (Pautz, 2012, p. 365).

The extent to which these developments represented a genuine change to thinking is difficult to establish because the prolonged recession that followed the financial crisis of 2007–2008 led to a more traditionally Conservative style of leadership and policy (Pautz, 2012, p. 364). Once in power, the Conservatives oversaw increased privatisation, outsourcing of public services and a stringent programme of welfare reform (Kerr & Hayton, 2015, p. 121). Smith and Jones (2015, p. 229) argue that some of the social policy approaches adopted were similar to those of the previous Labour governments—such as increasing the role of choice, markets and the private sector—but the crucial difference was that Labour took these measures in the context of increasing public spending, while the coalition government was reducing spending through austerity measures.

There were two key factors that enabled Cameron to present the Conservatives as a changed party while pursuing many traditional policies. One was a greater commitment to some forms of equality. The Conservatives' candidate selection process for parliamentary seats was adjusted to improve the opportunities for female, gay and ethnic minority candidates. Cameron was able to appeal to both modernising and traditional Conservatives by presenting his support for the 2013 Marriage (Same Sex Couples) Act as being consistent with traditional Conservative views, arguing that the institution of marriage was strengthened by making it available to more people. However, a majority of Conservative MPs voted against the Act; it passed with Labour and Liberal Democrat support (Hayton & McEnhill, 2015, pp. 136–137).

The second factor was described by Kerr and Hayton (2015, p. 213) in the following terms: "Cameron arguably proved to be ideologically entrepreneurial in pinning themes of social justice and liberal conservatism onto a pre-existing commitment to neo-liberalism." The language and redefinition of key concepts that made possible this reconciliation between traditional policies and a modern image is considered further below.

Re-defining Social Justice

The Centre for Social Justice, a centre-right think tank co-founded by Iain Duncan Smith in 2004 (Pautz, 2012, p. 371), was central to Cameron's claim to have put social justice at the heart of Conservatism. It produced three reports on the subject while the Conservatives were in opposition (Page, 2015, pp. 130–132) and, after eight years in office, felt able to claim that: "Since its inception, the CSJ has changed the landscape of our political discourse by putting social justice at the heart of British politics. This has led to a transformation in government thinking and policy" (Centre for Social Justice, 2018, p. 2).

However, crucial to this claim was a radical re-definition of social justice. It is a concept that has always had a range of definitions, although most have centred on addressing marginalisation through the redistribution of resources, supported by policy and legislative changes (Harley, Alston, & Middleton, 2007, p. 41). However, the Department for Work and Pensions' (DWP) Social Justice Strategy, launched in 2012, re-defined the concept in line with traditional Conservative values and policies. The strategy tied poverty closely to family breakdown and suggested that maintaining strong families was the way to ensure better outcomes for children. Income inequality was seen as a 'symptom' rather than a 'cause' of poverty and disadvantage. Poverty could be ended by tackling the individual 'flaws' that were associated with poor people such as low levels of educational achievement, alcohol and substance misuse, and long-term unemployment. Measures such as increasing the conditions that had to be fulfilled in order to receive benefits, work placement schemes and the re-assessment of people on disability benefits were all presented as encouragement to people to improve their lives by promoting inclusion and self-fulfilment (Hayton & McEnhill, 2015, pp. 140–141).

The switch from focusing on income to behaviour was made very clear in the government's key policy document *Social Justice: Transforming Lives*, produced in 2012, where Iain Duncan Smith's introduction stated that "We can no longer sustain a strategy based on maintenance alone, more concerned with pushing people just above the poverty line than changing their lives" (DWP, 2012, p. 1).

The point that poverty was a consequence of bad life choices was made clear elsewhere in the document:

> Though low income is a useful proxy measure, it does not tell the full story of an individual's well-being. Frequently, very low income is a symptom of deeper problems, whether that is family breakdown, educational failure, welfare dependency, debt, drug dependency, or some other relevant factor. (DWP, 2012, p.10)

As will be seen below, this revised concept of social justice provided the justification for a programme of substantial cuts to social security benefits referred to as welfare reform.

The Big Society and Civil Society

As a re-defined form of social justice provided the justification for cuts to social security benefits, substantial reductions in local authority spending were framed by two concepts—the Big Society and localism. The Big Society was the key idea by which Cameron sought to distance the Conservatives from the focus on the individual under Thatcher (Page, 2015, pp. 132–133). It was linked to his claim in opposition that British society was broken and that individuals were no willing to take responsibility for improving it. The cause of this problem was too much state involvement: people were turning first to the government for solutions to social problems, rather than to families, neighbourhoods and communities (Bulley & Sokhi-Bulley, 2014, p. 455). Instead, individuals and groups should be encouraged to undertake activities for the common good (Page, 2015, p. 133). However, critics once again suggested that the key difference with Labour's approach was a reduction in resources:

> [T]he most important difference between the Big Society and the partnership and participation policies of New Labour lies in its zero-sum concept of the relationship between civil society and the state, whereby more 'society' involvement equates to less 'state' activity. Indeed, civil society activity is seen not just as filling gaps left by a retreating 'nanny state' but also as offering innovative and independent alternatives to meeting social need. (Lowndes & Pratchett, 2012, p. 32)

Cameron himself indicated in 2011 that Big Society activities could replace state provision, asking the rhetorical question: "If there are facilities that the state can't afford to keep open, shouldn't we be trying to encourage communities who want to come forward and help them and run them?" (quoted in Smith & Jones, 2015, p. 234).

Four Big Society vanguard areas were created but one of them, Liverpool, withdrew from the pilot on the grounds that cuts were being made to support for the voluntary sector at a time when it was needed most (Lowndes & Pratchett, 2012, p. 30). Indeed, the voluntary sector estimated that it saw a £3.3 billion cut in its funding from government between 2010 and 2015–2016 and a growing number of voluntary organisations reported reducing the level of services that they could provide as a result (Smith & Jones, 2015, p. 235).

Smith and Jones (2015, p. 235) suggest that the concept of the Big Society was based not so much on existing voluntary organisations but on "an assumption of spontaneous voluntary action filling the gaps created by the reduction of state spending". Various mechanisms were put in place to try to encourage communities to take up this role, and there were some successes in volunteers taking over facilities such as parks, libraries, shops and pubs (Smith & Jones, 2015, p. 234). However, Hastings, Bailey,

Bramley, Gannon, and Watkins (2015, p. 25) found that this was not a consistent pattern:

> The Coalition Government has emphasised the potential for voluntary sector and civil society groups to step in and fill gaps where local authority services have been withdrawn. The evidence showed that civil society/community groups did not always have the capacity to do this, and there was an overall absence of detailed strategies for developing activity in a coherent and comprehensive manner.

The Big Society concept appeared to have fulfilled its purpose by the end of 2013, after which it was not mentioned by Cameron again and disappeared from government discourse (Butler, 2015). There were some echoes of it in the civil society strategy that was launched under Theresa May's premiership in 2018. This strategy proposed to use funds from dormant bank accounts to support community organisations, to increase efforts to get disadvantaged people into employment, and to involve local people in the commissioning of services. However, as with the Big Society, there were criticisms that this strategy was a totally inadequate remedy to the decline of public services brought about by reductions in funding to local authorities and voluntary organisations (Butler, 2018a).

Localism

The principle of localism was particularly politically convenient for Cameron and the Conservatives because it was supported by the Liberal Democrats and could be presented by both coalition partners as a means of returning power to communities (Griggs & Sullivan, 2012, p. 496). However, once again, there were issues over definitions, with the two parties attaching different meanings to localism: the Conservatives were happy to sidestep local authorities in their efforts to devolve powers to communities while the Liberal Democrats were concerned to free local councils from central government control (Lowndes & Pratchett, 2012, p. 35).

Despite these differences, a number of significant steps were taken that affected the role of local authorities. The 2011 Localism Act included measures that sought to involve local people in the planning of services through mechanisms such as Neighbourhood Development Forums (Holman & Rydin, 2013, p. 72). There were also specific measures in relation to homelessness, which are discussed further below. New powers were offered to cities and surrounding regions, including some relating to regeneration (Shaw & Tewdwr-Jones, 2017, pp. 216–217). An overlapping development announced after the 2015 general election was the creation of 'Combined Authorities', where further responsibilities and funding could be devolved to several local authorities working together. For example, the creation of the Greater Manchester Authority in 2015 meant that the ten local authorities of the Greater Manchester area operated as one body in some areas of policy (Shaw & Tewdwr-Jones, 2017, p. 218).

A further development saw six new mayors elected in May 2017, with three of them making homelessness a major commitment—Andy Burnham in Greater Manchester, Andy Street in the Combined Midlands Authority and Steve Rotherham in Liverpool City Regions. As these mayors had no formal powers in the area of homelessness, it was thought that their most important contribution could be to raise the profile of the issue (Fitzpatrick et al., 2018, p. 31).

The Audit Commission, Comprehensive Area Assessments and the Place Survey (which compared local authorities according to 18 national indicators) were all abolished by the coalition government. Local authorities and other public bodies were instead expected to devise their own performance measures focused on issues of concern to their communities (Lowndes & Pratchett, 2012, p. 26). Local Strategic Partnerships and Community Strategies were allowed to 'wither on the vine', without funding or authority (Lowndes & Pratchett, pp. 29–30). The government presented such measures as saving both money and local authority time (Department for Communities and Local Government (DCLG), 2010a) but Lowndes and Pratchett (2012, p. 36) suggest another agenda:

> [T]he removal of the comprehensive audit regime for localities can be seen as another politically expedient manoeuvre, making it difficult, if not impossible for localities to be benchmarked or compared. Consequently, there will be no high profile failures being published by government but only quietly deteriorating localities in the more socially and economically disadvantaged parts of the country.

More fundamentally, the localism agenda was criticised because of the financial context in which it was put into practice. Lowndes and Pratchett (2012, p. 28) suggest that claims to provide a greater level of local independence seemed implausible in in an environment where central government controlled 75% of local government spending—the Liberal

Democrats failed to fulfil their manifesto pledge to reform local government finance. In addition, the commitment to localism went alongside major reductions to the funding available to local authorities. Shaw and Tewdwr-Jones (2017, p. 213) argue that devolved powers are often associated with austerity, with sub-national government left to make choices about reductions in services. Similarly, Hastings et al. (2015, p. 5) suggest that localism can simply be a method of moving responsibility for difficult decisions:

> There is a risk that, under a localist agenda, central government absolves itself of responsibility for supporting delivery of critical local services while at the same time cutting local budgets to such an extent that local services are inescapably affected.

So accepting devolved powers increased the risk that blame for cuts to services would be placed at a local level.

Cuts to Local Authority Spending

There were clear reasons for local authorities being the target for major reductions in government funding. The coalition's commitment to cut public expenditure—alongside its desire to maintain spending on health, schools and pensions—meant that less popular public services would inevitably face severe cuts. Local authority services, and benefits for working aged people, were major targets for reductions to expenditure, despite being seen by many as crucial to the prevention of homelessness.

An emergency budget in June 2010 sought to address the financial deficit with £30 billion of spending cuts; the subsequent October spending review went further and brought total spending reductions to £81 billion over four years. Local authority budgets were cut by 27% as part of this process (Lowndes & Pratchett, 2012, p. 23). At the start of 2011, Liberal Democrat leader Nick Clegg and senior councillors from his party attacked the speed and scale of cuts to local authorities, but to no avail (Lowndes & Pratchett, 2012, p. 35) The poorer authorities, that raised less from local taxation and depended more on government grant, were particularly heavily hit. Among all purpose authorities (those that provide the full range of local authority services), the most deprived saw cuts in spending of £220 per head of population, while the least deprived saw cuts of £40 per head (Hastings et al., 2015, p. 6).

Significantly increasing council tax was not a realistic option to make good the shortfall in government funding. The 2011 Localism Act removed direct capping but required a local referendum on any spending above a government-defined level (Stewart, 2014, p. 843). Experiences of previous local referendums suggested that they were likely to result in increases being rejected (Lowndes & Pratchett, 2012, pp. 27–28).

So, local authorities had no option but to seek to manage the cuts. There was a 58% increase in outsourcing of local authority services, often in 'back office' areas such as human resources (Smith & Jones, 2015, p. 240). Some authorities sought to reduce service by targeting individuals rather than vulnerable groups, with others opting for area-based, spatial approaches to the provision of services (Daly, 2018, p. 67). However, with time sustained cuts became increasingly difficult to manage: Hastings et al. (2015, p. 4) found that local authorities were working hard to find efficiency savings and to cushion service users from the impact of cuts, but argued that the extra pressures on staff were not sustainable. By 2018, the National Audit Office (NAO) was warning that authorities were using their financial reserves at a rate that could not be maintained for more than three years (Tinson, Ayrton, & Petrie, 2018, p. 5). Conservative run Northamptonshire County Council ran into such severe financial difficulties that, in November 2018, the government had to change its accounting rules—allowing the council to sell its headquarters and use the proceeds to fund day-to-day services—to prevent it from making cuts so severe that it could not meet its statutory obligations (Butler, 2018b).

Welfare Reform

In the area of social security, both the coalition government and the brief Cameron led administration of 2015–2016 adopted familiar themes from previous periods of Conservative rule. They expressed concerns over welfare dependency, perverse incentives and the 'choice' to depend on benefits rather than to work. In contrast to the protection that was offered to the incomes of pensioners, social security benefits for people of working ages were treated as problematic (Edmiston, Patrick, & Garthwaite, 2017, pp. 253–254), particularly in the light of the unemployment figure of 2.45 million people in September 2010 (Lowndes & Pratchett, 2012, p. 24). The 2015 Conservative Manifesto (p. 25) outlined the stated reasons for the welfare reform programme:

> Under Labour, those who worked hard found more and more of their earnings taken away in tax to support a welfare system that allowed, and even encouraged, people to choose benefits when they could be earning a living. This sends out terrible signals: if you did the right thing, you were penalised—and if you did the wrong thing you were rewarded, with the unfairness of it all infuriating hardworking people.

There is insufficient space here to list the details of all the cuts to benefits made by the coalition and Conservative governments, so the discussion is limited to those that had the greatest potential to influence the level of homelessness. In 2012, the government amended previous legislation to increase the level of sanctions that could be applied to two key benefits (Jobseeker's Allowance and Employment and Support Allowance) if a claimant failed to satisfy the conditions for them: for example, if they left employment voluntarily, failed to participate in a work programme or failed to attend an adviser interview without good reason. In April 2013, 77,056 sanctions were applied in England, Scotland and Wales, compared to 30,789 in April 2009 (Harding, Hugman, & Irving, 2015, pp. 8–11).

Universal Credit was introduced to replace six means-tested benefits for working age households: Jobseeker's Allowance, Income Support, Housing Benefit, Employment and Support Allowance, Working Tax Credit and Child Tax Credit. In addition to simplifying the process of claiming, the aims of this measure included encouraging people into work by increasing incentives, increasing requirements to search for work and reducing fraud and error. Work began on the project in 2010 with an original completion date of 2017, which had been progressively pushed back to 2023 by the time of writing—as the benefit was trialled in different areas, large numbers of difficulties emerged (NAO, 2018, p. 5).

A benefit cap was established in 2013 for all out-of-work households below pensionable age, with some exemptions for those with disabilities. This was intended to ensure that the total income received by workless households could not exceed that of households where one or more people were working (Fitzpatrick et al., 2018, p. 36).

The benefit cap was most likely to affect larger families in the South East, who were in expensive privately rented property and so received large amounts of Housing Benefit. In contrast, the 'bedroom tax' reduced the amount of benefit paid to people in social rented housing who were below pensionable age and who were judged to be under-occupying the property, for example, because children had grown up and moved away. It was presented as a means of meeting need by encouraging smaller households to move to more appropriately sized properties, so freeing up larger dwellings for families with children (Page, 2015, p. 140).

Perhaps the most significant changes to Housing Benefit were reductions to Local Housing Allowance (LHA), which represents the maximum Benefit that can be paid towards private sector rents. LHA was first changed to the 30th percentile of market rent levels in an area rather than the median, then its uprating was reduced to 1% in 2014–2015 and 2015–2016 (below the rate of inflation) and finally its level was frozen for four years from 2016–2017 (Fitzpatrick et al., 2018, p. 34). A targeted Affordability Fund was made available in those areas most affected by the freeze (Fitzpatrick et al., 2018, p. 36).

The welfare reform programme was widely criticised and blamed for an increase in foodbank use by groups as diverse as the Child Poverty Action Group, the Church of England, Oxfam GB and the Trussell Trust (the largest umbrella organisation for foodbanks in the United Kingdom) (Perry, Williams, Sefton, & Haddad, 2014). The National Audit Office (NAO) (2018), p. 46) demonstrated that foodbank usage increased faster in areas where universal credit had been rolled out than in other comparable areas. Their report also showed that four in ten claimants who had been through the transition to universal credit were experiencing financial difficulties, and one in five claimants did not receive their full payment on time (NAO, 2018, pp. 7–8). David Cameron did not accept these criticisms, arguing that the increase in foodbank usage was due to the government allowing job centres to advertise their availability, in contrast to the previous Labour administration (Wintour, 2013). However, in a sign of change under Theresa May's leadership, Amber Rudd, the Secretary of State for Work and Pensions, acknowledged that:

> It is absolutely clear that there were challenges with the initial rollout of universal credit, and the main issue that led to an increase in foodbank use could have been the fact that people had difficulty accessing their money early enough. (Quoted in Walker, 2019)

The evidence to link these changes to homelessness will be considered below.

The Social Rented Sector

The number of social rented dwellings did not change substantially under the Cameron governments. Changes to the balance of tenures largely reflected trends that had begun in the previous decade: owner occupation reached a peak of 69% of dwellings in the United Kingdom in 2005, falling to 65.5% in 2010 and then to 62.6% in 2016. In contrast, private rented dwellings increased from 11.3% of the stock in 2005 to 16.4% in 2010 and 19.7% in 2016. There was a modest change to the balance between the two main parts of the social rented sector, with housing association dwellings increasing from 8.1% of the stock in 2005 to 9.4% in 2010 and 10.1% in 2016, while local authority dwellings fell from 10.6% in 2005 to 8.4% in 2010 and then 7.4% in 2016 (Stephens, Perry, Wilcox, Williams, & Young, 2018, table 17d). Output in the social rented sector remained largely stationery and at a low level, with 3130 local authority starts in the United Kingdom in 2010–2011 and 3100 in 2016–2017, compared to 30,040 in the housing association sector in 2010–2011 and 31,500 in 2016–2017. In contrast, output in the private sector increased from 138,220 starts in 2010–2011 to 197,290 in 2016–2017 (Stephens et al., 2018, table 19k).

However, the figures for outputs hide a reduced role for government in funding social rented housing. The coalition reduced the affordable housing grant from £8.4 billion for the period from 2008 to 2011 to £4.5 billion for the period from 2011 to 2015, with higher rents intended to make up the shortfall in subsidy (Pearce & Vine, 2014, p. 662). In 2011, government guidelines allowed social landlords to let property at less subsidised 'affordable rents', which could be up to 80% of private market rents (Centre for Social Justice, 2018, p. 7). However, there appeared to be a change of direction in 2016 when Chancellor of the Exchequer George Osborne introduced a measure meaning that all registered providers of social housing must reduce their rents by 1% per year for four years (Wilson, 2018, p. 3): a move that he acknowledged was motivated by a desire to reduce the Housing Benefit bill (Boughton, 2018, p. 267). This was a major change to the existing financial models (Murie, 2016, pp. 126–127) and had an impact on the levels of service that social landlords could provide.

Faced with the decrease in subsidy, some local authorities began to find their own solutions: by March 2017, 180 authorities were providing new housing via one of 27 financial models, very few of them involving the traditional means of the Housing Revenue Account (Boughton, 2018, p. 282). By 2018 the Chartered Institute of Housing (2018, p. 22) were arguing that only 50,290 genuinely affordable homes had been built in the previous five years, with the number falling to 5380 in 2016–2017. Two thirds of these were built by social landlords without any government subsidy.

David Cameron and George Osborne made clear that their view of social rented housing was a sector that benefited from subsidies and should only be there to meet short-term needs. A plan to raise the rents of tenants of social housing to the same level as private rents if they earned above a certain level, announced by Osborne in 2015, was eventually dropped (Boughton, 2018, p. 261). However, the 2011 Localism Act encouraged, and then the 2016 Housing and Planning Act required, local authorities in England to let properties on a fixed term basis. One of the government's stated reasons for this change was that experiencing housing need at one time should not be a reason for living in housing at below market rents for life. Another was that homeless households should spend less time in temporary accommodation as more tenancies become available (Fitzpatrick & Watts, 2017, pp. 1022–1026). Boughton (2018, p. 257) argues that measures such as these demonstrate that residualisation—a partly unintended consequence of policies adopted under Margaret Thatcher's Premiership—was a conscious goal of the administrations led by David Cameron. In contrast, after she became Prime Minister, Theresa May urged politicians and others to no longer 'look down on social housing' (Walker, 2018).

May also expressed enthusiasm for the expansion of the social rented sector, although, at the time of writing, it is unclear how far her plans will be put into practice. Her government set a target of providing 250,000 new affordable homes over five years (Fitzpatrick et al., 2018, pp. 10–11); a figure that was still considerably lower than the Chartered Institute of Housing's (2018, p. 21) estimate that 145,000 affordable homes were required per year. The 2018 Rough Sleeping Strategy (Ministry of Housing, Communities and Local Government, 2018, p. 4) acknowledged that affordable housing was essential if rough sleeping was to be eliminated and discussed creating "a new generation of council housing" with increased government funding.

Increases in Homelessness

All the available indicators point to an increase in homelessness after the change of government in 2010, although demonstrating that this increase was a result of specific policies is difficult. National figures were collected for the number of rough sleepers from 2011, with all local authorities required to provide counts or estimates, although this methodology was questioned (see Chap. 1). Despite the limitations of the figures, they suggest a clear trend, with 1767 rough sleepers recorded in 2011 (Lund, 2016, pp. 226–227) and 4751 in 2017 (Ministry of Housing Communities and Local Government (MHCLG), 2018, p. 9).

Statutory homelessness figures also increased: 59,100 homeless acceptances in 2016–2017 represented a 19,000 increase from 2009–2010. London was the key to the rising national figure, with a 91% increase in acceptances in the capital (Fitzpatrick et al., 2018, pp. 60–61). This was despite an even greater focus on prevention, with three quarters of potentially homeless applications experiencing a prevention intervention in 2014 (Lund, 2016, p. 227). The end of an assured shorthold tenancy was identified as the reason for homelessness in 15% of cases in 2010–2011 but 31% of cases in 2016–2017 (Wilson & Barton, 2018a, p. 7).

It was widely perceived among professionals working in the area of homelessness that the increases in different forms of homelessness were at least partly due to cuts to government spending, especially in the area of social security. In Newcastle upon Tyne, close working between the homelessness section and the welfare rights service provided Neil Munslow with the data needed to argue that: "18% of the 535 people who received debt advice in 2017–18, did not have sustainable budgets. They can only meet that through work. If they can't secure work, then they are at risk of homelessness …."

At a national level, the evidence that homelessness increased as a result of welfare reform emerged slowly. Beatty, Foden, McCarthy, and Reeve (2015) found some evidence to link homelessness to benefit sanctions. The Oakley review of the sanctions system in 2014 identified poor communication, particularly with those in temporary accommodation, as a major weakness. In response, the government gave discretion for homeless claimants of Jobseeker's Allowance to be relieved of the expectation to seek employment for up to four weeks (Harding et al., 2015, pp. 8–11).

Fitzpatrick et al. (2018, p. 87) found that 74% of professional respondents felt that the full roll out of Universal Credit would 'significantly' increase homelessness in their area by 2020, while 19% thought it would increase it 'slightly'. This view found support from the NAO (2018), p.44), which argued that rent arrears had increased across all tenures since the introduction of Universal Credit. Their report noted that some private landlords were refusing to let to Universal Credit claimants as a result of the difficulties. The Department for Work and Pensions (DWP) responded by changing rules so that those moving onto Universal Credit from March 2018 would continue to receive Housing Benefit for two weeks (and so have their housing costs met twice for this period). It also put in place measures making it easier for private landlords to request that the element of Universal Credit covering housing costs should be paid directly to them, rather than to the tenant.

The Department for Communities and Local Government (DCLG) acknowledged in 2017 that affordability in the private rented sector was a key issue, although it also argued that the growth of the sector was part of the reason for the increase in homelessness arising from the end of an assured shorthold tenancy (Wilson & Barton, 2018a, p. 8). However, the NAO (2017, pp. 7–8) was more critical, arguing that the government had not fully assessed the impact of its Housing Benefit reforms on homelessness. It suggested that changes to LHA, alongside rent rises in the private rented sector that outstripped wage rises, were likely to have contributed to the growth in homelessness. Private landlords were more likely to end tenancies as a result of cuts to Housing Benefit. The House of Commons Public Accounts Committee (2017, pp. 5–7) was similarly critical of the government for failing to measure the impact of changes to LHA on homelessness, in addition to failing to tackle the lack of affordable housing. In its response to the committee, the government committed to explore the feasibility of a study, jointly commissioned by DCLG and DWP, into the wider causes of homelessness, including households' experiences of the welfare system, housing affordability and relationship breakdown (HM Treasury, 2018, p. 31).

The 2018 Rough Sleeping Strategy, produced after Theresa May became Prime Minister, came close to acknowledging that welfare reforms had increased the number of rough sleepers:

> There have been a number of reforms to the welfare system over recent years that have been designed to create a welfare system that supports the most

> vulnerable, helps to support people into work wherever possible, and is fair to the taxpayer. It is clear that the highly complex needs of some people who sleep rough can make it difficult for them to navigate the welfare system. (MHCLG, 2018, p. 36)

The strategy announced that new policy options would be considered when the freeze on LHA came to an end in 2020 (MHCLG, 2018, p. 10).

It was also difficult to demonstrate that cuts to local authority services were responsible for an increase in homelessness. However, the NAO (2017, pp. 8–10) identified the key difficulties faced by local authorities in seeking to respond to increased homelessness as a reduced social housing stock, decreasing number of private landlords who were willing to work with them, some private landlords rejecting long-term leases in favour of a more lucrative nightly rate, a 21% reduction in spending on housing services since 2010 and a 59% cut in real terms in funding for Supporting People services over the same period.

Central Government Responses to Homelessness

The rhetoric of social justice was largely reflected in the Cameron governments' discussions of homelessness. While using sympathetic language and acknowledging some role for structural factors, the view was made clear that homelessness arose largely from individual problems:

> Many people in society, as part of everyday life, face experiences, or triggers that could lead to homelessness, such as a relationship breakdown or the ending of a tenancy. In most cases individuals cope and find suitable accommodation using their own resources. But for others it is these life events that tip them into homelessness: either because they lack the resources to tackle the immediate challenge—for example enough money for a deposit; or because they suffer more underlying problems—such as an addiction or mental health problem—which makes it hard for them to deal with their situation. (DCLG, 2012, p. 8)

Homelessness was linked to the Government's Troubled Families programme, where the focus was on the 'chaotic' lives of the families concerned:

> The Government is working with local agencies to support a group of troubled families whose lives are so chaotic they cost the Government some £9

> billion in the last year alone. Many of these families will be living in poor quality and unstable housing or be at risk of homelessness. (DCLG, 2012, p. 13)

The limited role attributed to structural causes of homelessness was consistent with a government response consisting of a plethora of small-scale initiatives, involving levels of funding which in no way compared to the amounts cut from local authority and social security budgets. Many of these initiatives were specific to rough sleeping.

Rough Sleeping

Rough sleeping became an important issue for the Conservatives in opposition: Grant Shapps (who was to become Housing Minister) slept rough to attract publicity, the party set up a Homelessness Foundation with the leading voluntary organisations represented and the Labour Government's rough sleeper counts were condemned as inaccurate for omitting people who were living in short-term accommodation or 'sofa surfing' (Lund, 2016, p. 255). Lund (2016, p. 225) argues that concentrating on rough sleeping was a logical tactical move for the Conservatives under David Cameron's leadership because it helped to shed the party's 'nasty' image, addressed what many in the party saw as the 'real' homelessness problem and could be tackled with minimal expenditure. It was an issue increasingly associated with East European people, with counts in 2012 suggesting that 25% of rough sleepers came from countries that had joined the European Union after 2004.

The most significant initiative of the coalition government, certainly in terms of demonstrating its thinking on rough sleeping, was the No Second Night Out initiative, which was launched in London in 2011 and then rolled out nationally. It targeted people who were new to the streets and sought to move them away as quickly as possible. The premise of the initiative was that there was a street homelessness 'culture' that people should be prevented from falling into. The initiative sought to provide to new rough sleepers, at the earliest opportunity, an assessment of needs, advice on options, access to emergency accommodation, access to other services such as health care and reconnection with their area of origin for those who were migrants (Homeless Link, 2015a, p. 3).

While the initiative could be criticised for reflecting the thinking of Charles Murray that homeless people have a different set of values to the rest of society, the government was able to boast that 84% of people who had slept rough and accessed a No Second Night Out service in 2016–2017 did not sleep rough again in the following year. However, it acknowledged that there were only 70 spaces in No Second Night Out hubs while rough sleeper counts totalled 1137 in the capital (MHCLG, 2018, pp. 43–44). Jeremy Swain praised the philosophy of No Second Night Out and the role of Rick Blakeway, Deputy Mayor to Boris Johnson:

> And one thing that happened was we realised that as a group of organisations working on the street with rough sleepers there were some people who we were just not getting to quickly enough. Now some of those people then found their own way out of homelessness, but others were getting stuck on the street. So we became much more sophisticated in terms of reflecting on the different needs on the street. So No Second Night Out was an attempt to get to people earlier.

Among the other initiatives launched under David Cameron's premiership, the most substantially funded was the Homeless Change Programme, which provided £42.5 million to improve hostel accommodation and created new and refurbished bedspaces for rough sleepers. It later received an extra £55 million to focus on improving the physical and mental health of rough sleepers (DCLG, 2015, p. 7).

Smaller amounts of funding were allocated to a number of initiatives. The Streetlink service encouraged members of the public to raise alerts for outreach teams to go out to meet rough sleepers (MHCLG, 2018, p. 52). A Homeless Hospital Discharge Fund provided £10 million in short-term grants to extend intermediate care and create more effective partnerships between local authorities, the voluntary sector and the NHS (Cornes et al., 2018, p. 346). Finally, the Homeless Transition Fund fitted with Big Society thinking about the desirability of a voluntary sector operating without state support; it provided £20 million of grants to support projects to develop innovative ways of tackling rough sleeping and to become financially independent through business development activities (Homeless Link, 2015b, p. 3).

In contrast to these piecemeal initiatives, Theresa May sought to develop a co-ordinated approach, creating a Rough Sleeping and Homelessness Reduction Taskforce, a Rough Sleeping Advisory Panel, and a Rough Sleeping Strategy. May pledged to halve rough sleeping by 2022 and eliminate it by 2027 (HM Treasury, 2018, pp. 29–34). However, it is not clear, given the political uncertainty at the time of writing, how far the Rough Sleeping Strategy will be implemented.

In comparison to the 1997–2010 period, one issue that was little discussed under the coalition and the Conservatives was anti-social behaviour among homeless people. The Rough Sleeping Strategy considered this issue in carefully neutral language: “Rough sleeping is the most visible form of homelessness and street activity such as begging, street drinking, street based drug use and street based sex work can be more visible again, often causing concern for local communities” (MHCLG, 2018, p. 50).

The only occasion on which there was substantial public discussion of this issue was in the run up to the Royal Wedding at Windsor Castle in May 2018, when Windsor and Maidenhead Borough Council was subjected to sustained criticism for the strategy that it published on Street Dwelling and Anti-Social Behaviour. This strategy advocated “support before enforcement”, and identified a number of measures aimed at meeting the needs of rough sleepers, but was criticised for proposals (later abandoned) to penalise actions such as placing hats or containers in a position to collect money and leaving bedding or belongings unattended in a public area (Royal Borough of Windsor and Maidenhead, 2018).

Housing First

As was noted in Chap. 5, Housing First was an approach that was first developed in New York in the 1990s and was consistent with some of the critiques of supported housing for single homeless people of that time. The first major central government support for this approach in England was announced in May 2018, when Housing Secretary James Brokenshire pledged funding for three Housing First ‘pilots’: £7.7 million for one in Liverpool City Region, £8.0 million for one in Greater Manchester and £9.6 million for one in the West Midlands (Bellis & Wilson, 2018, p. 14). The origins of the Housing First approach will be considered briefly here because it represents a rare example of substantial policy transfer to the United Kingdom in the area of homelessness—for the most part, the unique legislative and policy position appears to prevent ideas from elsewhere from being easily adopted.

Housing First differs from the more traditional ‘staircasing’, ‘treatment first’ or ‘continuum of care’ approach in which a rough sleeper is provided with progressively more independent forms of accommodation according to a judgment as to how far they are ‘housing ready’. It involves rough sleepers being re-housed directly into permanent accommodation and offered support to tackle their broader needs (Bellis & Wilson, 2018, pp. 5–6). The original Pathways Housing First organisation in New York adopted distinctive values such as giving choice to service users, separating the roles of housing and support, adopting a harm reduction approach to addictions, encouraging engagement without coercion and providing support for as long as it is required (Bellis & Wilson, 2018, pp. 9–11). Johnsen & Teixeira, 2012, p. 184) note that the model was replicated with "what could be regarded as 'evangelical' fervour in many parts of North America, Europe and elsewhere".

According to Johnsen and Teixeira, there was a more cautious approach taken to the adoption of Housing First in the United Kingdom for a number of reasons. One was the perception that many of the principles were already being adhered to because some services sought to re-house rough sleepers directly into independent tenancies and many took a harm reduction approach to substance misuse (Johnsen & Teixeira, 2012, pp. 192–194). In addition, some stakeholders had an attachment to a treatment first philosophy and to ensuring that a service user was 'housing ready' before offering them a tenancy; they feared that moving people into independent accommodation too quickly might be setting them up to fail. The relevance of comparisons with the United States was questioned, with agencies suggesting that the United Kingdom had a more effective network of services taking a traditional approach so had less need for Housing First (Johnsen & Teixeira, 2012, pp. 194–197). Similarly, in 2016–2017 the House of Commons Communities and Local Government Select Committee expressed doubts about the transferability of the success that Finland had achieved in re-housing rough sleepers through a Housing First approach (Bellis & Wilson, 2018, p. 13).

However, by 2017, Homeless Link (which represents groups working with homeless people and providing supported housing) were estimating that 19% of accommodation-based services in England were using some form of Housing First model and a further 26% were thinking of using it (Bellis & Wilson, 2018, p. 12). As with most nations that had adopted Housing First, there were some variations from the original New York model, but Homeless Link (2016) were able to identify a number of characteristics that made UK Housing First schemes distinctive from the more traditional methods of providing housing and support to single homeless people. Most notably, other forms of 'floating' (or visiting) support typically involved one worker supporting 20–40 people; the figure was 6–7 for Housing First. In addition, homeless people would usually be offered a self-contained tenancy, unless they expressed a preference for shared housing, and the tenancy offer would not be conditional on the individual accepting support (Homeless Link, 2016, pp. 2–3).

The Ministerial foreword to the government's Rough Sleeping Strategy described Housing First as "a very impressive programme" (MHCLG, 2018, p. 1). The governments of Scotland, Wales and Northern Ireland also expressed support for the extension of Housing First services (Bellis & Wilson, 2018, pp. 14–15). So, at the time of writing, it appears that Housing First is set to become an increasingly common method of seeking to meet the needs of single homeless people, despite the initial resistance.

Statutory Homelessness and the Role of Local Authorities

It was noted above that there were different perspectives on the meaning of localism: the Conservatives presented their approach as empowering local authorities and freeing them from unnecessary data collection, while critics argued that the government was simply trying to pass on the blame for cuts and to avoid the presentation of information highlighting the failure of local services. Consistent with the government's overall approach, and in sharp contrast to the previous period of Labour rule, was the taking of a very limited role in regulating local authority practice in the area of statutory homelessness, despite substantial difficulties and costs arising in this area.

The rise in statutory homelessness from 2010 onwards resulted in increased use of temporary accommodation, with the amount spent on this form of housing increasing 39% in real terms between 2010–2011 and 2016–2017. Of the £1.1 billion spent on homelessness in 2015–2016, over three quarters (£845 million) was spent on temporary accommodation placements, approximately two thirds of them in London (Fitzpatrick et al., 2018, pp. 62–63). Most of the temporary accommodation provided was in self-contained housing, with only 9% of households placed in bed-and-breakfast hotels (Fitzpatrick et al., 2018, p. 64). However, between 2010 and 2014, the number of statutorily homeless households living in bed-and-breakfast accommodation more than doubled to 4700 (Lund, 2016, p. 227). The Local Government Ombudsman's report of 2017 focused on concerns over the use of unsuitable bed-and-breakfast accommodation, in the context of rising private sector rents (Fitzpatrick et al., 2018, p. 28).

Another difficulty associated with the use of temporary accommodation was out of borough placements. At the end of March 2017, 28% of temporary accommodation placements were of this nature—a substantial increase on the 11% recorded in 2010–2011 (Fitzpatrick et al., 2018, p. 64). The NAO (2017, pp. 8–9) noted that 90% of such placements were made by London authorities. In evidence to the House of Commons Communities and Local Government Committee (2016), representatives of both Birmingham and Thurrock Councils reported increasing difficulties with the availability and affordability of housing in their own boroughs arising from the placement of homeless households from elsewhere, usually London.

Questioned about out of borough placements in the Commons in 2014, Housing Minister Kris Hopkins noted that the law required local authorities to take account of factors such as employment and schools when securing temporary accommodation, and also pointed out that the average length of time spent in temporary accommodation had reduced from 20 months to 14 months since the beginning of 2010 (Wilson & Barton, 2018b, pp. 19–22). However, critics suggested that the government's public condemnation of out of borough placements was not reflected in private (Lund, 2016, p. 228). A unanimous Supreme Court ruling in 2015 held that local authorities should place homeless households within their own borough where this was practical (Wilson & Barton, 2018b, p. 21).

One government response to the rise in statutory homelessness was to provide local authorities with the option of discharging their duty through an offer in the private rented sector, regardless of whether the household agreed to this. However, it appears that this change, brought about through the 2011 Localism Act, was motivated as much by historical concerns over fairness as by a desire to relieve pressure on local authorities. The 2010 Consultation Paper *Local Decisions: A Fairer Future for Social Housing* noted that the main homelessness duty was ended by an offer of social rented housing in 70% of cases, compared to acceptance of an offer in the private rented sector on only 7% of occasions (DCLG, 2010b, p. 41). The government's criticism of this situation arose both from the cost of providing temporary accommodation and from familiar fears that the homelessness route was too attractive:

> We believe this encourages some households to apply as homeless in order to secure reasonable preference and an effective guarantee of being offered

social housing. Around 21 per cent of social lets to new tenants are allocated to people owed the main homelessness duty, many of whom will have been provided with expensive temporary accommodation while waiting in the housing queue. (DCLG, 2010b, p. 42)

Under the 2011 Localism Act, the private sector offer with which a local authority could discharge the main homelessness duty had to be a minimum 12 month assured shorthold tenancy. If the applicant became unintentionally homeless within two years of taking the tenancy, they would once again be owed the main homelessness duty, regardless of priority need status (DCLG, 2012). The Act also gave social landlords greater discretion to deny access to applicants on the grounds of their criminal history, rent arrears or lack of connection to the area (Centre for Social Justice, 2018, p. 7). Following the passing of the Act, the government appeared to have concerns over its implementation, with the Homelessness (Suitability of Accommodation) (England) Order 2012 reminding local authorities that they had a power rather than a duty to secure offers in the private sector, that offers should be secured within the authority's boundaries wherever possible, that the accommodation and the landlord should be suitable, and that there must be a written tenancy agreement (Department of Communities and Local Government, 2012).

A series of minor measures sought to persuade local authorities to adopt good practice. Speaking in 2015, Kris Hopkins identified the steps that the government had taken in this area as creating a Gold Standard Programme for homelessness services, investing in a National Homelessness Advice Service for front-line staff and funding Homeless Link to assist local authorities and the voluntary sector to work together (Wilson & Barton, 2018a, pp. 13–14). To achieve the Gold Standard, local authorities were required to take ten steps, some of which were difficult to measure (e.g. "adopt a corporate commitment to prevent homelessness which has buy in across all local authority services"), some of which reproduced longstanding standards of good practice (e.g. "not place any families in Bed and Breakfast accommodation unless in an emergency and then for no longer than 6 weeks"), and some of which reflected the government's own priorities (e.g. "develop a private rented sector offer for all client groups, including advice and support to both clients and landlords") (DCLG, 2012, p. 4).

These measures, together with the new powers in the Localism Act, were widely regarded as inadequate to ensure good practice. The NAO

(2017, pp. 8–10) argued that, despite planning to distribute £800 million to local authorities to tackle homelessness between 2016 and 2020, the government did not have a clear strategy as to how the problem would be reduced. Although there remained a legal obligation for local authorities to publish a homelessness strategy, there was no monitoring by central government of its content or the progress made against it. The government had been slow to put in place measures to assess the effectiveness of the money it spent.

Further criticisms came from the House of Commons Public Accounts Committee (2017, pp. 5–7), which argued that the government had only begun to work closely with local authorities after a substantial rise in homelessness, had failed to collect good enough information and had not taken action to tackle the lack of affordable housing. The House of Commons Communities and Local Government committee noted that another area that the government was failing to monitor effectively was the gatekeeping practices of local authorities. While acknowledging the pressures that local authorities were under, it argued that there was an unacceptable variation in the level of support provided to homeless households and called for a code of practice in this area (House of Commons, 2016, pp. 17–19).

There was evidence of a more co-ordinated and interventionist approach being taken under Theresa May's leadership. Specific pledges were to require local authorities to create an updated homelessness and rough sleeping strategy by the winter of 2019, with annual action plans to monitor progress; to devise new methods of ensuring the accountability of all agencies involved in tackling rough sleeping (MHCLG, 2018, p. 30); and to target government housing programmes on those areas facing the greatest accommodation and affordability pressures (HM Treasury, 2018, p. 32).

Youth Homelessness

As with other areas of policy, the approach taken to young people and homelessness under the post-2010 governments had much in common with previous periods of Conservative rule. There was a focus on the familiar theme of seeking to avoid benefit dependency and encouraging young people to work instead. From April 2017, the government removed the 'automatic' entitlement to help with housing costs for single, childless people aged 18–21. The 2015 Conservative Manifesto (p. 18) explained this measure as part of a co-ordinated approach to discourage dependency:

> [I]t is not fair—on taxpayers, or on young people themselves—that 18–21 year-olds with no work experience should slip straight into a life on benefits without first contributing to their community. So we will introduce tougher Day One Work Requirements for young people claiming out-of-work benefits ... It is also not fair that taxpayers should have to pay for 18–21 year-olds on Jobseeker's Allowance to claim Housing Benefit in order to leave home. So we will ensure that they no longer have an automatic entitlement to Housing Benefit.

However, subsequent DWP figures suggested that 96% of 18–21-year-olds who applied for help with housing costs received it, albeit that 50% of those who were successful were parents (Fitzpatrick et al., 2018, p. 41). Under Theresa May, the policy was abandoned (MHCLG, 2018, p. 10).

Those young people who remained in the family home also faced greater financial pressure if their family was on a low income. Non-dependent deductions, that is, the amount that is deducted from a tenant's benefit on the assumption that a non-dependent (usually an adult child) is contributing to household costs, were frozen between 2001 and 2010. However, George Osborne announced in 2010 that these deductions would be increased over the next three years to the level that they would have been at had they increased with inflation since 2001 (Irving & Spencer, 2014, p. 14).

As with homelessness more generally, initiatives for young homeless people had small amounts of money attached to them. The rhetoric around them often reflected that of the social justice agenda. A £23 million Fair Chance Fund supported projects which were underpinned by social investment and which targeted young people not in employment, education or training. In launching the initiative, the government suggested that young homeless people were "often the victims of difficult and damaging childhoods" (DCLG, 2014, p. 5). Young homeless people, it said "deserved a second chance" and so could be enabled to "play a positive part in their community and live fulfilling lives" (DCLG, 2014, p. 5). Projects supported by the fund were measured against outcomes in accommodation, education and employment (DCLG, 2014, p. 7). Similarly, the Platform for Life programme allocated £25 million for the development of low-rent accommodation for those aged 18–24 who were homeless or at risk of homelessness, with the explicit aim of supporting them to engage in work, education or training (DCLG, 2016).

In line with previous governments, there were extra measures announced to protect care leavers, accompanied by explanations that hinted that they were less blameworthy than other young people who became homeless: "Care leavers will have faced many challenges in their lives and are likely to need much more support than other young people as they make the transition to adulthood" (DCLG, 2017, p. 21). The 2014 Children and Families Act placed a requirement on local authorities to facilitate and support arrangements for young people to stay in care until the age of 21, if this was what they and their foster carers wanted (The Fostering Network, n.d.); £40 million was provided to help local authorities to meet this requirement (DCLG, 2015, p. 8). Other changes included a new fund for care leavers with complex needs (MHCLG, 2018, pp. 9–10), new obligations for local authorities to financially support care leavers who went on to further or higher education (DCLG, 2017, p. 21), and a requirement for Ofsted to assess the accommodation and support provided to care leavers (DCLG, 2015, p. 8).

The Voluntary Sector and Homelessness

It was noted above that £3.3 billion was cut from government support for the voluntary sector between 2010 and 2015–2016; these cuts had an impact on voluntary organisations that were working with homeless people. In terms of direct service provision, a survey undertaken by Homeless Link in 2014 showed that there were 1271 accommodation projects for single homeless people in England providing around 38,500 bedspaces, a decrease of 3% in bedspaces from the previous year, with 33 projects having closed (Homeless Link, 2015a, p. 18). By 2017, the number of accommodation projects had fallen further to 1121 and the number of bedspaces to 34,497 (Homeless Link, 2018, p. 13). (The survey took a slightly different form in the early years of the coalition government, meaning that comparisons were not possible.) The shortfall was not made up by informal action on the part of communities, as envisaged by the rhetoric of the Big Society. The former footballer Gary Neville allowing homeless people to live in his hotel through the winter of 2015–2016 while it awaited refurbishment—at an estimated cost to himself of £150,000 (Taylor, 2016)—was a rare example of philanthropic provision.

Shelter continued to provide substantial levels of housing advice, reporting that it advised 44,134 households over the telephone in 2017–2018 and had 37,216 online conversations. Its impact report of 2017–2018 included case studies where it had challenged both social and private landlords over the manner in which they treated tenants (Shelter, 2018).

The extent to which the voluntary sector was involved in policy issues varied during this period. Jeremy Swain reported more difficulty in communication with central government after 2010, but greater interest once Theresa May became Prime Minister, with both Crisis and Homeless Link being influential in the framing of the Homelessness Reduction Act (discussed further below). In addition, Shelter (2018) noted its own role in campaigning for increases to LHA rates, the removal and replacement of unsafe cladding after the Grenfell Tower fire, a Fitness for Human Habitation Bill and the ending of fees charged in advanced by letting agents. Crisis (2018) claimed credit for £20 million being given to projects to support vulnerable tenants and their landlords in the autumn 2017 budget and launched a high-profile campaign with the title *Everybody in: How to end Homelessness in Great Britain*. So, the sector appeared to enjoy more influence under Theresa May, although there was no restoration of the funding that had been lost.

The Devolved Governments and the 2014 Housing (Wales) Act

It was argued above that Housing First is a rare example of policy transfer to the United Kingdom from overseas and was only adopted with some reservations and modifications. However, one unexpected outcome of the devolution of powers to Scotland, Wales and Northern Ireland was the opportunity to consider whether developments there might be adopted in an English context, as noted by Nick Raynsford:

> I certainly don't think we had any anticipation at all in 1997, 1998, 1999, that there would be significant policy variations. It happened and proved very positive and it's actually great now to be able to quote examples from Scotland and Wales showing how their policies are a long way ahead of England and how there is a need for English policies to catch up.

The most obvious example of policy transfer arose from the 2014 Housing (Wales) Act which, in addition to being an important piece of legislation in its own right, was largely imitated in England through the 2017 Homelessness Reduction Act.

Lund (2016, p. 249) notes that there were few differences between English and Welsh housing policies until 2010. Indeed, the Housing (Wales) Act 2014 was the first piece of housing legislation passed by the Welsh assembly, but it made a significant change in the area of homelessness. The aims of the legislation included reducing homelessness, targeting prevention work more effectively and increasing the help available to non-statutorily homeless households (Wilson & Barton, 2018c, p. 9).

The Act placed responsibilities on local authorities to take preventative action on behalf of anyone who was threatened with homelessness within 56 days. For those who were assessed as already homeless, regardless of whether they were in priority need, there was a duty to help them to secure accommodation—a duty that lasted for 56 days. Individual local authorities were also given discretion as to whether to apply the intentionality clause of the homeless legislation, with a view to eventually abolishing this clause in Wales (Wilson & Barton, 2018c, pp. 9–10). The Act set rights alongside responsibilities—statutory guidance recommended the creation of personal housing plans, identifying steps to be taken by both the local authority and the household (Mackie, Thomas, & Bibbings, 2017, p. 87).

An evaluation of the first year of the legislation showed that the numbers of households in temporary accommodation fell by 18%. However, it should be noted that 17% of those placed in temporary accommodation prior to the Act had been prison leavers, who had been made a priority need group by the Welsh Government, but whose priority status was removed by the Act (Mackie et al., 2017, pp. 91–92). The evaluation noted that both service users and professionals reported more positive engagements since the implementation of the Act. The main actions taken in successful prevention and relief cases were assistance to secure accommodation in the private rented sector (in 39% of cases—almost half with a landlord incentive scheme), assistance to secure accommodation in the social rented sector (in 30% of cases) and assistance to secure supported housing (12%). Only 2% of cases were resolved by other measures such as mediation and conciliation (Mackie et al., 2017, pp. 92–93).

A further development among the devolved governments in this period was Scottish local authorities reaching the target of fully abolishing the priority need test by 2012. This was achieved partly by reducing the number of homeless applications through the Housing Options approach and partly by creating a power for local authorities to discharge their duties with non-permanent accommodation in the private rented sector, provided that the tenancy lasted at least 12 months. In 2013, a new statutory duty came in to effect, requiring local authorities to assess the housing support needs of homeless applicants in some cases (Wilson & Barton, 2018c, p. 13). So, developments in the devolved governments continued to create a range of new responsibilities and powers to support homeless households, but it was the 2014 Housing (Wales) Act that was to be the catalyst for change in England.

The 2017 Homelessness Reduction Act

The idea of a new duty to prevent homelessness in England pre-dated the Welsh legislation: Neil Morland noted that DCLG advisers were discussing the introduction of such a duty prior to the 2010 general election. There was little interest in the idea in England after the election, but it was picked up by the Labour Party in Wales. The Communities and Local Government Committee at Westminster, which included Conservative backbencher Bob Blackman, recommended a piece of legislation similar to that of Wales in its 2016 report. Blackman drew second place in the 2016 Private Members' Bill ballot and introduced the Homelessness Reduction Bill in June 2016 (Wilson & Barton, 2018c, pp. 6–7); it received all party support and was fully implemented in April 2018 (Wilson & Barton, 2018b, p. 4).

The Act re-defined the period in which someone should be treated as threatened with homelessness from 28 to 56 days, clarified the actions that were expected in respect of a person served a notice of intention to seek possession from an assured shorthold tenancy, created new duties to prevent and relieve homelessness for all eligible applicants, and required other public services to inform the local authority when they came into contact with someone they thought might be homeless or threatened with homelessness (Wilson & Barton, 2018a, p. 18). A personalised housing plan was to be created, and kept under review, with each eligible applicant (Fitzpatrick et al., 2018, p. 17) As the Act made its way through parliament, various amendments led to the amount that the DCLG distributed as 'new burdens funding' rising from £48 million to £72.7 million. A revised Homelessness Code of Guidance accompanied the new legislation

(Wilson & Barton, 2018a, pp. 17–18). The Act was very strongly supported by the voluntary sector and largely by local authorities, although it appeared to be more popular in the North of England than the South (Fitzpatrick et al., 2018, pp. 17–18).

There were different opinions about the likely impact of the Act among the people interviewed for this book—there was a consensus that it would not have any damaging effects but considerable variation in expectations as to how much would change. Steve Hilditch exemplified the views of those who were more cautious:

> My feeling is that it will have a marginal beneficial effect. The local authorities will try to implement it, but it's not possible to achieve much in the context of demand and supply and service reductions in London. But I hope it might lead to some better practice, another chance, another opportunity to provide services in a better way.

In contrast, Jeremy Swain thought that it would ensure more consistent good practice among local authorities:

> And I think also it's going with the tide of change anyway, because in the last couple of years all the decent local authorities have recognised that … there's an artificial separation really between statutory and non-statutory homelessness and that they have to do a lot more to prevent homelessness in the first place. And there were figures coming out showing that many of the new people who were turning up on to the street had approached housing options teams and hadn't been given the support they needed.

The timing of the publication of this book does not allow an evaluation of whether either of these expectations was fulfilled as the Act was implemented.

Summary

Reflections on the post-2010 period must centre on the period in which David Cameron was Prime Minister because of the uncertainty at the time of writing as to how long Theresa May will remain in post and how many of her proposed policy developments will be implemented. The Cameron era embodied policies that were consistent with traditional Conservative assumptions of blame on the part of disadvantaged individuals, while using rhetorical devices that discussed such policies in more sympathetic language. Structural explanations of homelessness, based largely on the government's own cuts to social security and local authority spending, were rejected.

Many of the government's initiatives in this period were focused on rough sleeping, with a more co-ordinated approach in this area sought by Theresa May when she became Prime Minister. In the area of statutory homelessness, the key measure was to facilitate the discharge of the main homelessness duty through the private rented sector under the 2011 Localism Act. The government was keen to avoid homelessness becoming an access route for a lifetime spent in the social rented sector, consistent with its view that the sector should only play a temporary role in housing people through a period of urgent need.

Geographical differences in local authority responses appeared to become more distinct during this period, as the increase in statutory homelessness in particular had a disproportionate effect on London authorities. However, it is difficult to establish the extent of differences as the information with which to make comparisons was reduced. One trend that appeared to run across local authority practice was an even greater concern with secondary prevention than had developed under the Labour governments. Consistent with this trend was the passing of the 2017 Homelessness Reduction Act, which was the first major example of policy transfer from the devolved governments.

References

Beatty, C., Foden, M., McCarthy, L., & Reeve, K. (2015). *Benefit sanctions and homelessness: A scoping report*. London, UK: Crisis.

Bellis, A., & Wilson, W. (2018). Housing first: Tackling homelessness for those with complex needs. *House of Commons Briefing Paper Number 08368*, London, UK.

Boughton, J. (2018). *Municipal dreams: The rise and fall of council housing*. London, UK: Verso Books.

Bulley, D., & Sokhi-Bulley, B. (2014). Big society as big government: Cameron's governmentality agenda. *The British Journal of Politics and International Relations, 16*(3), 452–470.

Butler, P. (2015, January 20). Why the 'big society' is now just a hashtag for coalition hypocrisy. *The Guardian*. Retrieved from https://www.theguardian.com/society/2015/jan/20/the-big-society-civil-exchange-audit-shows-coalition-contempt-and-hypocrisy

Butler, P. (2018a, August 8). New 'big society' bid to boost charities' role in public services. *The Guardian*. Retrieved from https://www.theguardian.com/society/2018/aug/08/new-big-society-bid-to-boost-charities-role-in-public-services

Butler, P. (2018b, November 29). Tory-run Northamptonshire county council bailed out by government. *The Guardian*. Retrieved from https://www.theguardian.com/society/2018/nov/29/tory-run-northamptonshire-county-council-bailed-out-by-government

The Centre for Social Justice. (2018). Social housing and employment: Helping social housing be a springboard to a better life. *Housing Commission Interim Report 1*. Centre for Social Justice, London, UK.

Chartered Institute of Housing. (2018). *Rethinking social housing: Final report*. Coventry, UK: Chartered Institute of Housing.

Cornes, M., Whiteford, M., Manthorpe, J., Neale, J., Byng, R., Hewlett, N., et al. (2018). Improving hospital discharge arrangements for people who are homeless: A realist synthesis of the intermediate care literature. *Health and Social Care in the Community, 26*, 345–359.

Crisis. (2018). *Trustees' annual report and accounts for the year ended 30 June 2018*. London, UK: Crisis.

Daly, A. (2018). Embodied austerity: Narratives of early austerity from a homelessness and resettlement service. *Ethics and Social Welfare, 12*(1), 63–77.

Department for Communities and Local Government. (2010a, June 25). *Pickles strips away pointless town hall red tape targets*. Retrieved from https://www.gov.uk/government/news/pickles-strips-away-pointless-town-hall-red-tape-targets

Department for Communities and Local Government. (2010b). *Local decisions: A fairer future for social housing*. London, UK: Department for Communities and Local Government.

Department for Communities and Local Government. (2012). *Making every contact count: A joint approach to preventing homelessness*. London, UK: Department for Communities and Local Government.

Department for Communities and Local Government. (2014). *Fair chance fund: Full bid specification document*. London, UK: Department for Communities and Local Government.

Department for Communities and Local Government. (2015). *Addressing complex needs: Improving services for vulnerable homeless people*. London, UK: Department for Communities and Local Government.

Department for Communities and Local Government. (2016, January 8). *Platform for life: Guidance and allocations*. Retrieved from https://www.gov.uk/government/collections/platform-for-life-guidance-and-allocations

Department for Communities and Local Government. (2017). *Addressing complex needs: Improving services for vulnerable homeless people*. London, UK: Department for Communities and Local Government.

Department for Work and Pensions. (2012). *Social justice: Transforming lives.* London, UK: HM Government.

Edmiston, D., Patrick, R., & Garthwaite, K. (2017). Introduction: Austerity, welfare and citizenship. *Social Policy and Society, 16*(2), 253–259.

Fitzpatrick, S., Pawson, H., Bramley, G., Wilcox, S., Watts, B., & Wood, J. (2018). *The homelessness monitor: England 2018.* London, UK: Crisis and the Joseph Rowntree Foundation.

Fitzpatrick, S., & Watts, B. (2017). Competing visions: Security of tenure and the welfarisation of English social housing. *Housing Studies, 32*(8), 1021–1038.

The Fostering Network. (n.d.). *Staying put.* Retrieved from https://www.thefosteringnetwork.org.uk/policy-practice/practice-information/staying-put

Griggs, S., & Sullivan, H. (2012). Puzzling agency in centre-local relations: Regulatory governance and accounts of change under New Labour. *British Journal of Politics and International Relations, 16*(3), 495–514.

Harding, J., Hugman, C., & Irving, A. (2015). *Benefit sanctions and homelessness.* Newcastle, UK: North East Homelessness Think Tank and the Northern Rock Foundation.

Harley, D., Alston, R. J., & Middleton, R. A. (2007). Infusing social justice into rehabilitation education: Making a case for curricula refinement. *Rehabilitation Education, 21*(1), 41–52.

Hastings, A., Bailey, N., Bramley, G., Gannon, M., & Watkins, D. (2015). *The cost of the cuts: The impact on local government and poorer communities.* York, UK: Joseph Rowntree Foundation.

Hayton, R., & McEnhill, L. (2015). Cameron's Conservative Party, social liberalism and social justice. *British Politics, 10*(2), 131–147.

HM Treasury. (2018). *Treasury minutes: Government responses to the Committee of Public Accounts on the Fourth to the Eleventh Reports from Session 2017–19, Cm 9575.* London, UK: HM Treasury.

Holman, N., & Rydin, Y. (2013). What can social capital tell us about planning under localism? *Local Government Studies, 39*(1), 71–88.

Homeless Link. (2015a). *Support for single homeless people in England 2014.* London, UK: Homeless Link.

Homeless Link. (2015b). *Three years of transition: The Homelessness Transition Fund 34 to 2014, evaluation summary.* London, UK: Homeless Link.

Homeless Link. (2016). *Housing first in England: The principles.* London, UK: Homeless Link.

Homeless Link. (2018). *Support for single homeless people in England 2017.* London, UK: Homeless Link.

House of Commons Committee of Public Accounts. (2017). Homeless households. *House of Commons: Eleventh Report of Session 2017–19*, London, UK.

House of Commons Communities and Local Government Committee. (2016). Homelessness. *House of Commons, Third Report of Session 2016–17, HC 40*, London, UK.

Irving, A., & Spencer, S. (2014). *One year on: Welfare reform and its impacts on single homelessness.* Newcastle, UK: North East Homeless Think Tank and the Northern Rock Foundation.

Johnsen, S., & Teixeira, L. (2012). 'Doing it already?': Stakeholder perceptions of Housing First in the UK. *International Journal of Housing Policy, 12*(2), 183–203.

Kerr, P., & Hayton, R. (2015). Whatever happened to Conservative Party modernisation? *British Politics, 10*(2), 114–130.

Lowndes, V., & Pratchett, L. (2012). Local governance under the Coalition Government: Austerity, localism and the Big Society. *Local Government Studies, 38*(1), 21–40.

Lund, B. (2016). *Housing politics in the United Kingdom.* Bristol, UK: Policy Press.

Mackie, P. K., Thomas, I., & Bibbings, J. (2017). Homelessness prevention: Reflecting on a year of pioneering Welsh legislation in practice. *European Journal of Homelessness, 11*(1), 81–107.

Ministry of Housing, Communities and Local Government. (2018). *Rough sleeping strategy.* London, UK: Ministry of Housing, Communities and Local Government.

Murie, A. (2016). *The right to buy? Selling off public and social housing.* Bristol, UK: Policy Press.

National Audit Office. (2017). *Homelessness.* London, UK: Department for Communities and Local Government.

National Audit Office. (2018). *Rolling out universal credit.* London, UK: Department of Work and Pensions.

Page, R. M. (2015). *Clear blue water?* Bristol, UK: Policy Press.

Pautz, H. (2012). The think tanks behind 'Cameronism'. *British Journal of Politics and International Relations, 15*(3), 362–377.

Pearce, J., & Vine, J. (2014). Quantifying residualisation: The changing nature of social housing in the UK. *Journal of Housing and the Built Environment, 29*(4), 657–695.

Perry, J., Williams, M., Sefton, T., & Haddad, M. (2014). *Emergency use only: Understanding and reducing the use of food banks in the UK.* London, UK: The Child Poverty Action Group, Church of England, Oxfam GB and The Trussell Trust.

Royal Borough of Windsor and Maidenhead. (2018, February 7). *Street dwelling and antisocial behaviour strategy.* Paper presented to the Crime and Disorder Overview and Scrutiny Panel, Maidenhead, UK.

Shaw, K., & Tewdwr-Jones, M. (2017). 'Disorganised devolution': Reshaping Metropolitan governance in England in a period of austerity. *Raumforschung und Raumordnung, 75*(3), 211–224.

Shelter. (2018). *Impact report 2017/18.* London, UK: Shelter.

Smith, M., & Jones, R. (2015). From big society to small state: Conservatism and the privatisation of government. *British Politics, 10*(2), 226–248.

Stephens, M., Perry, J., Wilcox, S., Williams, P., & Young, G. (2018). *UK housing review 2018*. Coventry, UK: Chartered Institute of Housing. Retrieved from https://www.ukhousingreview.org.uk/ukhr18/index.html

Stewart, J. (2014). An era of continuing change: Reflections on local government in England 1974–2014. *Local Government Studies, 40*(6), 835–850.

Taylor, D. (2016, January 28). Gary Neville's hotel for the homeless closes its doors. *The Guardian*. Retrieved from https://www.theguardian.com/uk-news/2016/jan/28/gary-neville-praised-but-homeless-leave-footballers-hotel-for-uncertain-future

Tinson, A., Ayrton, C., & Petrie, I. (2018). *A quiet crisis: Local government spending on disadvantage in England*. London, UK: Lloyds Bank Foundation and New Policy Institute.

Walker, P. (2018, September 19). Housing associations praise May's £2bn plan as 'total step change'. *The Guardian*. Retrieved from https://www.theguardian.com/society/2018/sep/19/housing-associations-praise-mays-2bn-plan-as-total-step-change

Walker, P. (2019, February 11). Universal credit rollout linked to rising food bank use, Rudd admits. *The Guardian*. Retrieved from https://www.theguardian.com/society/2019/feb/11/universal-credit-rollout-linked-to-rising-food-bank-use-amber-rudd-admits

Wilson, W. (2018). Paying for supported housing. *House of Commons Briefing Paper Number 6080*, London, UK.

Wilson, W., & Barton, C. (2018a). Statutory homelessness in England. *House of Commons Library Briefing Paper Number 01164*, London, UK.

Wilson, W., & Barton, C. (2018b). Households in temporary accommodation (England). *House of Commons Briefing Paper Number 02110*, London, UK.

Wilson, W., & Barton, C. (2018c). Comparisons of homeless duties in England, Wales, Scotland and Northern Ireland. *House of Commons Library Briefing Paper Number 7201*, London, UK.

Wintour, P. (2013, September 11). Cameron refuses to endorse Gove's criticism of food bank users. *The Guardian*. Retrieved from https://www.theguardian.com/society/2013/sep/11/david-cameron-michael-gove-food-banks

CHAPTER 8

Reflections on the Post-War Period

It was asserted in Chap. 2 that the post-war history of homelessness policy was best understood using a framework that incorporated five key factors: the explanations for homelessness favoured by policy makers, the different approaches taken to different groups of homeless people, the level of demand for social rented housing, geographical differences and the types of prevention activity that are favoured. This final section will consider the evidence for this assertion in the light of the policy developments discussed in the intervening chapters.

Of the five factors, the explanations for homelessness are the most complex and the one where there has been the most debate. Undoubtedly, the stated explanations are influenced by politics: placing blame on individuals can be a convenient explanation when services are being cut. Similarly, the concept of social exclusion fitted well with New Labour's concern over rights and responsibilities, and with presenting an image that was different from both the Conservatives and 'Old Labour'. However, there has clearly also been genuine debate among policy makers and the public as to why homelessness comes about. The range of factors that can affect this debate was illustrated particularly vividly in the 1960s, when some quite diverse factors appeared to affect public and political opinion, including the full implementation of the 1957 Rent Act, sympathetic press coverage of homeless people, the formation of campaigning charities such as Shelter, and the screening of *Cathy Come Home*.

J. Harding, *Post-War Homelessness Policy in the UK*,
https://doi.org/10.1007/978-3-030-22117-1_8

Individual explanations of homelessness have been the ones that have been most obviously and explicitly linked to policies, manifesting themselves in different ways for different groups of homeless people. Concerns since the passing of the 1948 National Assistance Act that creating a separate system for the housing of homeless families might provide an advantage to the underserving (who lost their home through their own fault) over the deserving (who 'waited their turn' for independent housing) were heightened after the passing of the 1977 Housing (Homeless Persons) Act. These concerns were reflected in measures designed to reduce the access of homeless households to social rented housing that were introduced through the 1996 Housing Act and the 2011 Localism Act.

In the case of single homeless people, concerns have often been expressed to prevent individuals from becoming engulfed in a lifestyle where there are different values to the rest of society. These concerns were reflected in the National Assistance Board's assertion that the creation of a network of Reception Centres might encourage an unsettled way of living and in the efforts under the No Second Night Out initiative to reach new rough sleepers with services before they could become entrenched in a street lifestyle. Young people have been particularly likely to be blamed for their homelessness under Conservative governments, with cuts to their benefits justified by the need to discourage them from leaving the family home unnecessarily.

There have been less examples of specific links being made between structural explanations of homelessness and policy, but there seems little doubt that some measures that strengthened the protection available to homeless households, such as the 2002 Homelessness Act and the 2003 Homelessness etc. Scotland Act, have been partly motivated by such explanations. While the introduction of the intentionally homeless clause into the 1977 legislation was a compromise between those pressing for change and those who wanted to distinguish between the deserving and the undeserving, the moves towards abolishing it in Wales appear to represent a belief that this is an unjustified distinction. The more complex explanation of homelessness that have been adopted in academic circles in the new Millennium have been acknowledged to some extent by policy makers, although usually in the form of lists of possible causes, rather than any suggestion as to how these causes might interact with each other.

Clear policy differences between groups have existed since the 1948 National Assistance Act created separate systems for households with children to those for single homeless people. These different systems did not necessarily prove advantageous to either group: some of the deterrent practices operated by local authorities in their temporary accommodation were almost as harsh as the National Assistance Board's refusal to accommodate single homeless people who had a 'settled' way of life. The greater willingness to accept structural causes of homelessness among families in the 1960s and 1970s was not initially reflected in attitudes to single homeless people; provision for them continued to reflect a belief that their situation arose from deviant behaviour or sickness. Increased public sympathy for one sub-group of single homeless people—rough sleepers—that was expressed in the late 1980s led to forms of provision that emphasised further their distinctive needs, such as the Homeless Mentally Ill Initiative. However, the growth in popularity of the Housing First programme in the United Kingdom, which has much in common with the services provided to statutorily homeless households, may represent a reduction in the gap between responses to homeless households with and without children.

Two perspectives provide the evidence to strongly suggest that levels of demand for social rented housing affect the amount of sympathy that is evident in the response to homeless households. The first is historical: the trend towards the provision of gradually more supportive services to those who are homeless appears to be linked to changes with time to the image of council housing, which was gradually transformed from a tenure of high demand in the immediate post-war years to a less popular and residualised form of provision in the 1980s and 1990s. More specifically, the campaign that eventually led to the passing of the 1977 Act appears to have been successful partly because of the easing of the housing shortage and the beginnings of the process of residualisation. The second relevant perspective is a geographical one: a number of studies have suggested that the local authorities that interpret their obligations to homeless households most liberally tend to be those that face the lowest housing pressures.

The impact of geographical location on policy has increased since the devolution of housing powers in 1999, with the abolition of priority need in Scotland representing a particularly racial step. Even within England, substantially different responses have frequently been observed between regions and local authorities. The diverse environments that local authorities need to respond to was demonstrated most clearly in the 1990s, where continuing high housing pressures in London and the South East contrasted sharply with the experience of low demand and abandonment in former industrial areas of the North and Midlands.

Attempts by governments to ensure more consistent practice between local authorities, regardless of the circumstances affecting their area, were largely limited to persuasion before 1979, with ministerial exhortations and government circulars frequently achieving a very limited response. Indeed, voluntary organisations provided more effective pressure for greater consistency and higher standards among local authorities, particularly with the growth of the housing aid movement and the formation of the Joint Charities Group in the early 1970s. The controls exercised by the Conservative governments of 1979 to 1997 over local authorities were largely financial, although revisions to the Code of Guidance to the homelessness legislation were judged to have had a positive effect. It was under the Labour governments of 1997 to 2010 that the use of a range of measures appeared to have most impact, with the government achieving notable successes in bringing about more consistent practice in relation to the use of bed-and-breakfast hotels and the adoption of a preventative approach. However, even in this period, substantial variations in practice between authorities remained evident, and these differences seem likely to have increased as central government showed less interest after 2010.

The favoured form of prevention is the factor where there is the clearest differentiation between different time periods. From 1945 to the 1970s, there was a very distinct policy focus on the primary prevention measure of building more housing, driven by the war time loss of accommodation, with limited interest in any other measures. The easing of housing shortages and the growing evidence of some poor local authority practice in the 1970s meant that tertiary prevention became the key policy focus. In the period after the passing of the 1977 Act, two contrasting concerns were expressed: one that there was continuing harsh treatment of homeless households by some local authorities and another that an over-generous response was encouraging queue jumping. The decline of both these concerns in the new millennium facilitated a change of focus to secondary prevention, prompted partly by a crisis in the use of bed-and-breakfast hotels. As noted above, this change had a major impact on the services provided by local authorities to homeless households.

The framework for analysis presented here is not, of course, completely comprehensive and cannot fully explain every development in homelessness policy. Indeed, there are some historical developments for which the available evidence offers no clear explanation: for example, the 1972 Local

Government Act reducing local authorities' duties in the area of homelessness to powers, and the change to Conservative Party thinking about statutory homelessness between 1996 and 2001. In addition, there are some elements outside the framework which were influential in one specific time period: for example, the delicate balance of political forces which meant that the path to the passing of the 1977 Act was such a long and complicated one.

The framework does not attempt to allocate weightings to the five factors as their level of influence has varied with time: for example, geographical differences have tended to become particularly important in times of rising statutory homelessness, when difficulty in finding suitable temporary accommodation in London has frequently been a key driver of policy. Nor is it claimed that the framework will be the most appropriate tool with which to analyse policy in the future. Indeed, it is hoped that some of those areas identified as under-developed in Chap. 1—particularly the relationship between homelessness and broad aspects of inequality such as gender and ethnicity—will become major features of research and policy. However, the five factors discussed here are particularly important when seeking to understand the wide range of measures that have been introduced to prevent and tackle homelessness from 1945 to 2019.

Appendix: Key Events in the Post-War Period

There follows a list of the main events in post-war homelessness policy:

1948	National Assistance Act
1961	Full implementation of the 1957 Rent Act
1966	*Cathy Come Home* screened
1972	Local Government Act
1977	Housing (Homeless Persons) Act
1990	Launch of Rough Sleepers' Initiative and Homeless Mentally Ill Initiative
1996	Housing Act
1999	Housing powers devolved to Scotland, Wales and Northern Ireland
2002	Homelessness Act
2003	Supporting People programme launched
2003	Homelessness etc. Scotland Act
2011	Localism Act
2012	Homelessness (Abolition of Priority Needs Test) (Scotland) Order
2014	Housing (Wales) Act
2017	Homelessness Reduction Act

J. Harding, *Post-War Homelessness Policy in the UK*,
https://doi.org/10.1007/978-3-030-22117-1

Index

J. Harding, *Post-War Homelessness Policy in the UK*,
https://doi.org/10.1007/978-3-030-22117-1

The manufacturer's authorised representative in the EU is Springer Nature Customer Service Centre GmbH, Europaplatz 3, 69115 Heidelberg, Germany. If you have any concerns regarding our products, please contact ProductSafety@springernature.com

Printed and bound by CPI Group (UK) Ltd, Croydon, CR0 4YY
05/10/2026
02228125-0004